Implementing Educational Reform

There is constant pressure on governments and policymakers to raise the standard of education and to develop appropriate curriculum and pedagogies for students. It is no easy task. This book presents eight specific case studies of education reform implementation which capture how the design and implementation choices of policymakers are shaped by national and historical contexts. They offer real examples of the choices and constraints faced by policymakers and practitioners. The cases are a mix of nationally and locally mandated reforms with five examples from nations where the state initiated and guided reforms. The concluding synthesis chapter highlights commonalities and differences across the cases and disparate responses to shared concerns. Providing a breadth of real-world research, it will assist policymakers, practitioners and other stakeholders interested in system change.

Colleen McLaughlin is a professor and director of education innovation at the Faculty of Education at the University of Cambridge. She directs the Education Reform and Innovation team, which works internationally and nationally on aspects of education reform and development.

Alan Ruby is a senior fellow in the Graduate School of Education at the University of Pennsylvania. He has worked on education reform projects in over twenty countries.

T0381680

Implementing Educational Reform

Cases and Challenges

Edited by
Colleen McLaughlin
University of Cambridge

Alan Ruby
University of Pennsylvania

CAMBRIDGE
UNIVERSITY PRESS

Shaftesbury Road, Cambridge CB2 8EA, United Kingdom

One Liberty Plaza, 20th Floor, New York, NY 10006, USA

477 Williamstown Road, Port Melbourne, VIC 3207, Australia

314–321, 3rd Floor, Plot 3, Splendor Forum, Jasola District Centre, New Delhi – 110025, India

103 Penang Road, #05–06/07, Visioncrest Commercial, Singapore 238467

Cambridge University Press is part of Cambridge University Press & Assessment, a department of the University of Cambridge.

We share the University's mission to contribute to society through the pursuit of education, learning and research at the highest international levels of excellence.

www.cambridge.org
Information on this title: www.cambridge.org/9781108818988

DOI: 10.1017/9781108864800

First published 2021
First paperback edition 2024

A catalogue record for this publication is available from the British Library

ISBN   978-1-108-83640-1   Hardback
ISBN   978-1-108-81898-8   Paperback

CONTENTS

FIGURES AND TABLES

Figures

Tables

CONTRIBUTORS

Mel Ainscow is Emeritus Professor of education at the University of Glasgow, and Adjunct Professor at Queensland University of Technology. He is internationally recognized as an authority on the promotion of inclusion and equity in education. Mel is a long-term consultant to UNESCO, working on efforts to promote equity and inclusion globally. Examples of his writing can be found in: *Struggles for Equity in Education: The Selected Works of Mel Ainscow* (Routledge World Library of Educationalists series, 2015).

Asmaa Alfadala is the Director of Research and Content Development at the World Innovation Summit for Education (WISE). She is also a visiting fellow at the University of Northwestern in the United States. She has twenty years of professional experience in schools as well as higher education. Asmaa was an associate policy analyst at the RAND-Qatar Policy Institute. Before Qatar Foundation, she worked in the Ministry of Education as a teacher, then as a head of the science department. She is the author of *K-12 Reform in the Gulf Cooperation Council Countries (GCC): Challenges and Policy Recommendations* (WISE, Qatar Foundation, 2017) and co-author of *Developing Agile Leaders of Learning: School Leadership Policy for Dynamic Times* (WISE, Qatar Foundation, 2017). She is a member of the Comparative International Education Society (CIES) and the International Congress for School Effectiveness and Improvement (ICSEI). Asmaa serves as an advisor for the Asia-Pacific Economic Cooperation's education strategy. She is also a board member at Qatar Academy Sidra school in Doha. She has served at Qatar University as an assistant professor of educational sciences at the College of Education. Asmaa holds a PhD and MPhil from the University of Cambridge, UK.

Olena Fimyar is a senior research associate at the Faculty of Education, University of Cambridge, UK, working on the issues of education reform, organizational learning, teacher development and teacher identity in Kazakhstan. Her other research interests include education in emergencies, education policy sociology, governmentality studies and discourse analysis. In 2017–18, Olena coordinated a collaborative research, commissioned by Cara (the Council of At-Risk Academics), on the status of Syrian HE before and after 2011. Olena's PhD thesis (University of Cambridge) explored the issues surrounding education reform, actors and balance of power of educational policymaking in Ukraine. Prior to joining the Education Reform and Innovation team at the Faculty of Education, she led a project on 'Return Academic Migration in Post-Communist Europe' at the Centre for Area Studies, Free University Berlin and, prior to that, a study on the 'Sociology of Post-Communist Intellectuals' at the Collegium Budapest, Hungary. Before embarking on her research and university teaching career, for five years, Olena worked as an English as a foreign language (EFL) teacher in her hometown in Tsyurupynska Gymnasium, Kherson region, Ukraine.

Rachael Fitzpatrick is a researcher at Education Development Trust. Her research interests are in the application of complexity thinking to education policy analysis and parental engagement in education. She has an MA in Social Research Methods from Durham University, and is currently undertaking a part-time PhD in Education at the University of Bath. Her thesis concerns the policy of 'socialisation' of education in Vietnam, with a specific focus on the impact of the policy on parents.

Saravanan S. Gopinathan is an adjunct professor at the Lee Kuan Yew School of Public Policy, National University of Singapore and the Academic Director at the HEAD Foundation, an education think tank in Singapore. In a career spanning close to five decades, Gopinathan, as Dean of Education, was a key contributor to the modernisation of teacher education in Singapore. He was actively involved, as Head of the Centre of Pedagogy and Practice, in laying the foundations for faculty capacity building in conducting rigorous education research. Singapore's growing reputation as a high performing education system led to consultancies with the World and Asian Development Banks. He played a key role in modernising teacher education in Bahrain, Abu Dhabi, Jakarta and Indonesia and is currently involved in a project in Oman. He is internationally recognised as an authority on Singapore's education development. A key selection of his articles is to be found in *Education and the Nation State* (Routledge World Library of Educationalists series, 2013).

Matthew Hartley is a professor of education at the University of Pennsylvania Graduate School of Education. His research focuses on academic governance and the social and democratic purposes of higher education. Dr Hartley is the Associate Dean of Academic Affairs for Penn GSE. He is also the Executive Director of the Alliance for Higher Education and Democracy (AHEAD). Dr Hartley serves on the editorial boards of *Educational Researcher*, *The Review of Higher Education* and the *Journal of Higher Education Outreach and Engagement*. He earned his master's and doctoral degrees from Harvard University's Graduate School of Education. He is currently examining how universities in Kazakhstan are responding to education reforms aimed at promoting greater institutional autonomy and shared governance. He has recently been working with colleagues in India on institutions of eminence and some deregulatory initiatives.

Mary James formally retired as professor and associate director of research from the University of Cambridge Faculty of Education at the end of 2013. She continues to be a fellow commoner of Lucy Cavendish College, Cambridge, and a fellow of the Academy of Social Sciences. She previously held a Chair of Education at the Institute of Education London. She began her career as a teacher in three secondary schools. She is a past president of the British Educational Research Association (2011–13) and was Deputy Director of the ESRC's Teaching and Learning Research Programme (2002–08), within which she directed the 'Learning how to Learn' project (2001–05), which was evaluated as outstanding. She was the founding editor of *The Curriculum Journal* and was a member of the UK Assessment Reform Group from 1992 to 2010. In 2011 she was a member of the Expert Panel to the UK Coalition Government's National Curriculum Review in England. She has been an occasional adviser to the Hong Kong Education Bureau on its educational reforms since 2000, and was the overseas member of the Hong Kong Curriculum Development Council from 2007 to 2009 when it was developing the new senior secondary curriculum and examinations. Since 2013 she has been a member of the International Scientific Advisory Board for NordForsk's 'Education for Tomorrow' programme in the Nordic countries. From 2013 to 2015 she was a non-executive director of Bell Educational Services Ltd. She has published more than 100 books, chapters and articles and, in 2013, her 'selected works' were published by Routledge.

Edmund Lim has wide-ranging experience as a teacher, vice-principal and principal, as well as a teaching fellow in the National Institute of Education (NIE) in Singapore. He was employed by the Ministry of Education (MOE) for more than fifteen years, before engaging in education consultancy and education in the private sector. Since 2004, Edmund has conducted professional development courses for various education professionals in Singapore and overseas, ranging from preschool to tertiary levels. He assisted local and overseas educators, as well as World Bank officials. Edmund has provided education consultancy services to overseas education ministries and authorities in countries such as Tatarstan and South Korea. He was a consultant to the World Bank on a project related to education in Singapore. He also has experience as a group academic director of a cluster of international schools in Thailand and a senior vice president of a listed company involved in education. Edmund has written policy recommendations for education ministries abroad, as well as education-linked opinion editorials for newspapers. The education ministry in Singapore has invited Edmund to share his input on ways to strengthen support for underperforming students. Edmund is a dedicated Singaporean education leader who is also a keen internationalist, striving to contribute significantly to education.

Tony McAleavy is the Research Director for Education Development Trust, a UK-based charity engaged in both education research and support for education reform in many countries. He has worked in the field of school education and education reform for forty years. He is the author or co-author of several publications including: *Lessons from London Schools* (Education Development Trust, 2014), *Interesting Cities: Five Approaches to Urban School Reform* (Education Development Trust, 2015), *Teaching as a Research-Engaged Profession* (Education Development Trust, 2015), *School Improvement in London* (Education Development Trust, 2016), *Rapid School Improvement* (Education Development Trust, 2016), *The Rapid Improvement of Government Schools in England* (Education Development Trust, 2016), *England's Approach to School Performance Data* (Education Development Trust, 2017), *London Schools: Sustaining the Success* (Education Development Trust, 2018), *Technology-Supported Professional Development for Teachers* (Education Development Trust, 2018) and *Promising Practice: Government Schools in Vietnam* (Education Development Trust, 2018).

Colleen McLaughlin is a professor and director of education innovation at the Faculty of Education at the University of Cambridge, where she directs the Education Reform and Innovation team, which works internationally and nationally on aspects of education reform and development. They are working in China, Kazakhstan, Kyrgyzstan, Pakistan and sub-Saharan Africa at the moment. She is currently leading a seven-year research study of the development of the school curriculum, assessment and professional development in Kazakhstani schools. She has significant publishing and editing experience, having edited three journals and many books. She is currently on the editorial board of two journals. Past experience includes leadership in two departments of education, research and publishing on the personal, social and emotional aspects of education, as well as educational reform.

Brian Rowan is the Burke A. Hinsdale Collegiate Professor in Education, a research professor at the Institute for Social Research, and a professor of sociology at the University of Michigan. A sociologist by training (PhD, Stanford University), Rowan's scholarly work has focused on education as an institution, on the organization and management of schools and on issues related to the measurement and improvement of school and teaching quality. A member of the US National Academy of Education, Rowan is also a past recipient of the William J. Davis Award for outstanding scholarship in the field of educational administration. His current work includes a ten-year longitudinal study of changes in teachers' instructional practice before and after widespread adoption of the Common Core State Standards in US education as well as a study of school and instructional quality in the western Chitwan Valley area in Nepal.

Alan Ruby has a long career in government, business, philanthropy and education, ranging from classroom teacher to Australian deputy secretary of education to chair of the OECD education committee. At the University of Pennsylvania, Mr Ruby, a senior fellow in the Alliance for Higher Education and Democracy, focuses on globalization's effects on universities and education around the world. A highly regarded teacher, he leads graduate seminars on 'Globalization and the University'. He earned the School's Excellence in Teaching Award in 2006. Since early 2018 he also served as the initial director of the Global Engagement office at GSE, advising the Dean on ways to increase the school's international impact.

Liz Winter is a senior researcher at the Faculty of Education at the University of Cambridge. Dr Winter holds a PhD from the University of Leicester in Social Psychology examining young people's attitudes towards technology in relation to their gender and career aspirations. Dr Winter has worked extensively in Kazakhstan since 2012 as a Cambridge partner–advisor supporting the establishment and later quality assurance of Nazarbayev University Graduate School of Education (NUGSE). Currently, Dr Winter is the Cambridge project lead for the joint research project of NUGSE and the University of Cambridge, Faculty of Education on school education reform. This collaboration includes evidence-gathering on per capita funding, new pedagogy and the changes in assessment practices. Apart from extensive fieldwork around Kazakhstan in dozens of schools as part of her research role over the last eight years, Dr Winter has provided policy papers to the Ministry of Education and Science in Kazakhstan on topics such as the National Qualifications Framework and the professional development of teachers implementing the renewed content of education.

Stavros N. Yiannouka is the CEO of the World Innovation Summit for Education (WISE), a global think tank of the Qatar Foundation. WISE is dedicated to enabling the future of education through innovation and its activities encompass research, capacity-building programmes and advocacy. Prior to joining WISE, Stavros was the Executive Vice-Dean of the Lee Kuan Yew School of Public Policy (LKY School) at the National University of Singapore, where he spearheaded its ambitious growth strategy. Today, the LKY School is widely recognized as the leading global policy school in Asia. Together with Kishore Mahbubani et al. he is the co-author of *Lee Kuan Yew School of Public Policy: Building a Global Policy School in Asia* (World Scientific, 2012). Before joining the LKY School, Stavros spent five years with McKinsey & Company serving private and public sector clients in Singapore, Indonesia, South Korea and Canada, predominantly in finance, healthcare and education. Prior to joining McKinsey, Stavros practiced corporate law in the City of London with the firms Gouldens and Mayer, Brown & Platt. Stavros holds an MBA (with Distinction) from the London Business School and an LLB (with Honours) from the University of Bristol. He is a member of the Law Society of

England and Wales, a fellow of the Royal Society for the encouragement of Arts, Manufactures and Commerce (RSA), a member of the Board of Trustees of Nazarbayev University in Astana Kazakhstan and a non-executive Director of Blue Diagonal Capital Limited.

Natallia Yakavets is a senior research associate at the Faculty of Education at the University of Cambridge. She holds a PhD in Educational Leadership and Management from the Open University, UK. Her central research interests are leadership in context, school improvement, teacher professional education, educational reform, and inclusive education. Dr Yakavets has been researching extensively the educational context in Kazakhstan since 2012. Recent externally funded projects include an institutional consultancy in collaboration with the United Nations Children's Fund to support the Kazakhstan Ministry of Education and Science in the development and piloting of an early warning system for preventing, identifying and responding to school dropout of children with special educational needs and behavioural difficulties (2018–21). Dr Yakavets has presented the results of her research both at international conferences and at validation meetings with high-level stakeholders (government, international organisations).

Omar Zaki is a senior research associate at the World Innovation Summit for Education (WISE), where he contributes to the organisation's events, research publications and programmes, including the Agile Leaders of Learning Innovation Network (ALL-IN). In his role, he has co-authored a background paper for the MasterCard Foundation titled *Secondary Education Governance in Sub-Saharan Africa*, as part of the foundation's research project: *Secondary Education in Africa: Preparing Youth for the Future of Work*. He also served as one of the editors of the *Education Disrupted, Education Reimagined* (2020), a special edition E-book about responses from education's frontline during the COVID-19 pandemic. Upon completing his master's at the London School of Economics, he interned at the United Nations Economic Commission for Africa (UNECA) in Addis Ababa, where he worked in the Governance and Public Sector Management section of the Macroeconomic Policy Division. He assisted the Chief of Section in conducting research and contributing findings to the Commission's flagship *African Governance Report IV* (2016), the *Illicit Financial Flows on Domestic Resource Mobilization Report*, in addition to writing on public procurement reforms for the study report: *Corruption in Public Procurement: The Case of Infrastructure in Africa* (2017).

PREFACE

Our educational realities seldom conform to our educational intentions. We cannot put our policies into practice. We should not regard this as a failure peculiar to schools and teachers. We have only to look around us to confirm that it is part of the human lot. But ... improvement is possible if we are secure enough to face and study the nature of our failures. The central problem of evidence-informed practice is the gap between our ideas and our aspirations and our attempts to operationalise them.

Lawrence Stenhouse (1975)

We write, upholding Stenhouse's core ideas, that change and particularly implementation are inevitably going to be hard, complex and involve failure; that we can learn a great deal from experiences, especially when the unexpected happens; that we should remain optimistic and keep working on the gap, for it matters; and that this is ultimately a very human process. This book is written in the hope that it will help policymakers and practitioners alike and that it will be a welcome example of detailed human accounts of trying to enact aspirations to improve learning and teaching.

We have chosen to focus on implementation as we think it is often the least discussed and developed. We have chosen to do this through case studies of real attempts at change written by informed participants who are unafraid to offer up failures and successes because we see a need for grounding knowledge in practice.

We have attempted to draw out some truisms and common challenges and link them with research to use when thinking about implementation. We have avoided concluding with simplistic and reductionist checklists but offer threads of learning that we think we see in the tapestry of the cases.

We wish to acknowledge and thank our contributors and all the actors who were responsible for working on the implementation of the ambitious policies in these cases. We hope that you will find them interesting and useful. And we especially thank our partners in life, Julie and Eileen, who heard more of this work in progress than they probably would have liked.

Reference

Stenhouse, L. (1975). *An Introduction to Curriculum Research and Development*. London: Heinemann.

1 Why Focus on Implementation in Education Reform?

Alan Ruby and Colleen McLaughlin

1.1 CURRENT INTERNATIONAL EDUCATIONAL CONTEXT

Around the world there is a constant pressure on governments and policymakers to raise the standard of education and to develop the appropriate curriculum and pedagogies for students which will fit them for the world they will enter post-school. There is also much competition due to the new methods of international comparison, such as PISA and TIMSS, and much writing about change and frameworks for bringing about reform (e.g. Oates 2017; RAND 2018). There is a body of scholarship in the leadership field on change and reform too, which largely focuses on the processes and ways of working (e.g. Fullan et al. 2018). The field is also one where economic and academic organisations mix. Political life cycles are short. With notable exceptions, such as Richard Riley who served all eight years of President Clinton's administration, education 'ministers' last about twenty months. This encourages a culture which proclaims reform and seldom implements it.

1.2 AIMS OF THE TEXT

There has been much discussion of educational reform in the policy and academic world too. Much of this has taken the form of theoretical discussions or critical debates about issues of transnational work, for example, Salhberg (2016) on the global education reform movement. Others have concentrated on school effectiveness or school improvement (see Robinson et al. 2017). Some scholars have explored particular features of or vehicles for reform, such as Peurach's (2016) work on networks. Hargreaves and Goodson (2006) is an example of the examination of perceptions and experiences of educational change.

When we look at reform, we see that the underlying logic model of educational reform is basically four steps:

1. Design

2. Proclaim, sell or promote

3. Implement

4. Evaluate the effect.

There is an abundance of designed reforms (what Elmore (1996) called 'steady work'), some context-specific and some generic. There are plenty of 'effect studies', ranging from gross measures of student knowledge like PISA and TIMSS to national test scores to intervention-specific studies. There is little written about the different rollout measures (step 2) and even less about the process of implementation, exceptions are Pressman and Wildavsky (1973), Odden (1991a, 1991b) and Stringfield's (1995) work on high reliability organisations. There are also syntheses of research studies, e.g. sixteen studies of school reforms by Datnow and Stringfield (2000) and a survey of a sustained programme of school improvement in a high-poverty area in Wales using propositions and practices generated by the principles of high reliability organisations, ones that 'are assigned the very challenging task of operating without critically cascading errors the first time, every time' (Stringfield et al. 2012: 45).

There are also different strategies that have been employed to create innovative approaches to change. These include examples we explore in our text. A highly successful one is the London Challenge model, which operated on collaborative groupings of schools with high external support. Another reform implementation strategy is the practice of creating a 'free space' where existing rules and regulations are put aside to allow for the adoption of new practices. Often these are referred to as Special Economic Zones (SEZs). In an SEZ the 'rules for doing business are different from the rest of the country'. SEZs are different from the surrounding economic environment because they make it easier for companies to get access to reliable infrastructure; offer freedom from or deferral of taxes and customs charges and controls; and provide some fiscal incentives like free movement of capital and subsidies (World Bank 2017: 11–13). In effect they have an 'extraterritorial status which enables them *de facto* immunity from domestic civil laws and government controls' (Jayawardena 1983: 428). The network of Nazarbayev Intellectual Schools and its companion institution, Nazarbayev University, operate under a legal framework exempting them from many regulatory constraints. This is also one of our case studies. Similarly, Qatar's Education City is an enabling environment for a number of branch campuses of foreign universities. The effectiveness of these arrangements in facilitating educational reform is understudied, as is the impact of practices in these zones on the rest of the nation.

There has been some work on teaching standards (by the National Board of Professional Teaching Standards in the United States and by the Department of Education in the United Kingdom); on instructional leadership; on particular initiatives, e.g. literacy in the United Kingdom; and on models of reform and the importance of teacher professional development. In economic terms it is a bit like focusing on inputs and outputs, with no attention to the throughputs. There has also been little study of 'successful' systems, apart from the Finnish miracle, which has also been described as a myth and a folk story (Oates 2017).

This book brings together detailed case studies of implementation over time and mostly written by those who were involved or were close observers. It deliberately represents a range of different models of reform in a range of different cultures and countries; and it includes evidence on the effectiveness, or lack of it, of specific reforms. It uses a grounded approach to study the implementation of reform. In Section 1.3 we outline some of the previous studies of implementation in social programmes and education and the current state of thinking about implementation, and then go on to present the case studies. We then undertake a cross-case analysis exploring aspects already established and those that are not. Some of the themes that we describe come from the literature, like the tension between 'fidelity', the accuracy or rigor with which a particular programme or intervention is applied, and unintended consequences and the professional adaptation of practice to individual student needs and particular contexts or environments. We also look at the 'take-up rate' for reforms that are not mandatory and even for those that are presented as mandatory.

1.3 WHY FOCUS ON IMPLEMENTATION?

This section begins with a synthesis of the literature on implementation in the fields of public policy and education. It then reviews existing thinking and scholarship on reform and implementation. We identify the common under-standings, different approaches and the gaps in the field. We believe this provides a rationale both for the book as a whole and for the choice of case studies.

While evaluations of the US 'War on Poverty' spurred some interest in implementation (Odden 1991a; Weiss et al. 2008) the work of Pressman and Wildavsky on US urban reform programmes launched in the 1960s seems to be the first sustained study of the challenges of implementing social inter-ventions. Initially, Pressman and Wildavsky, in their 1973 edition, thought that it was 'flawed' to separate design and implementation but also acknow-ledged that once implementation began the action of participants shaped the design. This led them to see implementation as part of a complex system of 'reciprocal interactions' (xxv). Six years later, Majone and Wildavsky, in an essay included in Pressman and Wildavsky, third edition (1984), wrote of implementation as evolution. They were rejecting a highly rational, linear, model of implementation; 'implementation as control', because it leaves out the 'lumpy stuff of life' (165) which includes resource constraints and the preferences and actions of individuals. Majone and Wildavsky also find the interactive model of implementation wanting. It 'minimizes the importance of goals and plans' and sees policy as no more than the starting point 'for bargaining among implementers' (166). But they acknowledge that this model has an element worthy of development, the notion that policies evolve as they are implemented. Majone and Wildavsky develop this idea, observing that 'policies are continuously transformed by implementing actions that simul-taneously alter resources and objectives' (170). This leads them to label a model of interactive implementation where the act of implementing the policy changes the policy (177) as an 'evolutionary model'. This is a model that allows for actors to 'learn from experience ... correct errors' and even change 'policy ideas' (177).

This more nuanced and more realistic model of implementation was the backdrop for Browne and Wildavsky's (1983) essay examining the signifi-cance of evaluation in implementation. The essence of their argument is that, while implementation and evaluation are both 'concerned with the relation-ship between resources and objectives' in the evolutionary framework of Majone and Wildavsky where implementation reshapes the desired outcomes, and objectives 'cannot be held constant', evaluation becomes a relative rather than an absolute process (204).

The evolutionary framework evokes the interaction between living organ-isms and the environment, sometimes discussed in terms of adaptation, or in

Browne and Wildavsky's case 'mutual adaption', an idea they borrow from Berman and McLaughlin's (1974) Rand study. McLaughlin adds to the evolutionary metaphor by describing stages of development in implementation studies. She observes that 'Implementation' joined the working vocabulary of policy analysts in the early 1970s when ambitious, sweeping federal reform efforts followed 'prevailing theories of governmental action and organizational behaviour (which) assumed away implementation issues or overlooked them altogether' (McLaughlin 1987: 171). Evaluators of these programmes found that implementers 'did not always do as told', that 'local factors such as size, intra-organizational relations, commitment, capacity, and institutional complexity moulded responses to policy' and that the problems to be addressed also varied by location (172). These lessons were the base for the next generation of social programmes which focused on the linkage 'between policy and practice' because we 'have learned that policy success depends critically on two broad factors: local capacity and will' (172). Training, recruitment and resources might address capacity but motivating local actors was not just shaped by a policy or nicely designed programme. Context matters and many local factors shape the willingness of individuals to act, including 'environmental stability, competing centres of authority, contending priorities or pressures and other aspects of the social-political milieu' (173).

Pointing to a third generation of programme design, McLaughlin observes that 'change ultimately is a problem of the smallest unit. At each point in the policy process, a policy is transformed as individuals interpret and respond to it'. This shifts attention away from institutions and their priorities to 'individuals and individual incentives, beliefs, and capacity' (McLaughlin 1987: 174). Spillane et al. (2002), drawing primarily on US and UK research on education policy implementation, argue that 'implementing agents' interpret a policy message by triangulating their 'including knowledge, beliefs, and attitudes' with their environment or context and 'the policy signals' (388).

In practice this means the differences between actors and between settings produce different problems for implementation, which are addressed through an iterative process of negotiation and adjustment. This leads to a model of implementation that is more nuanced than regarding policy change or a reform programme as an event rather than a process (Hall 1992: 104). It extends implementation past the act of proclamation and the exercise of authority and the distribution of incentives to an explicit acknowledgement that success is likely to depend on some degree of negotiation and adaptation at the site level. Supovitz (2008) draws out this idea; beginning with the proposition that variability is to be expected in implementation as there are many factors which cause 'refraction' and which are beyond the control of designers, policymakers and even supervisors (164). He describes implementation as an interactive process of 'iterative refraction' where 'reforms are adjusted repeatedly as they are introduced into and work their way through school environments' (153). Individual actors adjust their behaviour as they interpret a 'policy signal' using their professional judgement and practice knowledge and taking into account their own circumstances (Spillane et al. 2002: 420). Commenting on curriculum standards in Massachusetts, McDermott (2006: 48) linked successful implementation with instances where 'policies interact with implementers' understandings of their work and day-to-day needs'. We will use these ideas as we review the cases to examine the extent to which stakeholders and practitioners were involved in designing and enacting interventions because, as McDonnell (2004) observes in her study of US student testing and standards reforms, 'involving those who implement a policy develops a sense of ownership' (136) and is likely to increase effectiveness.

This negotiated and adaptive conception of how policies and programmes are implemented often raises questions about the fidelity of implementation. Some argue for flexibility and others for conformity to ensure the right dose. Lytle (2002), drawing on his experience as a US school superintendent, comments that developers of comprehensive school reform models are 'often ... overly concerned about implementation "purity", and not adequately respectful of the need for mutual adaption (and) ... slow to learn from the experience of implementation' (166). They were dismissive of 'practitioner knowledge' and did not consider local conditions. Instead they tended to plan and design centrally and expect schools to act like franchise holders who adhere to 'corporate policies and regulations' (Lytle 2002: 166).

The need for fidelity and consistency in implementation arises when interventions or programmes are scaled up (McLaughlin and Mitra 2001; Bradach 2003) or applied to whole districts or systems. This is sometimes described as organisational replication. School reform efforts in the United States from 1990 onwards were often designed by a single external agency or corporation and enacted by existing schools or by new schools. The emphasis is on schools adopting externally developed programmes rather than developing their own programmes independently or in collaboration with other schools. Peurach and Glaser (2012) identify two assumptions underlying this approach. The first is that innovation, or a change in practice, follows a sequential path of research, design, communication and enactment.

The second is that this type of replication is fast and effective because it delivers proven, ready for use materials or strategies. Both are questionable but provide themes that we will examine from the cases set out here.

An alternative to the apparent uniformity of replication and fidelity is the idea of coherence put forward by Robinson et al. (2017). Prompted by findings about the effectiveness of 'joined up' school improvement initiatives they draw the notions of coherence, coordination and orchestration from organisational literature. They use coherence to refer to instances where the interdependent parts of a system 'are connected in ways that enable' it to produce a desired end or outcome (2–3) and note that there are various forms of connectedness, not just one consistent or logical way to interact or address an issue. A strength of this approach is that coordination sits comfortably with three realities of school life; there is a shared purpose, to educate the next generation, which is a collective endeavour, and while many activities are done independently the process as a whole is based on interdependence. Orchestration is used to describe deliberate leadership acts that aim to align the efforts of actors in the school community. Studying the work of five high schools in a school improvement programme in an environment where school leaders have a lot of discretion, including in decisions to participate in such programmes and in the choice of support services, Robinson et al. found that schools with a high degree of coherence and tight coordination were more likely to realise improved student performance than those schools with lesser degrees of coherence. We will look for these themes in our review of the cases. Similarly we will look for the three characteristics that Hopkins et al. (2014) see to be antecedents of successful school improvement efforts: a 'strategic ... medium term approach', the ready transfer of effective practices across sites, extensive professional support and 'mentoring' (274).

Coherence is often evoked by commentators advocating a systems approach to educational reform and is often linked to the notion of alignment (see for example World Bank 2018: 14). The proposition is that if four elements (learning objectives, assessment, finance and incentives) are all focused on effective teaching or 'towards learning', student outcomes will be improved (World Bank 2018: 174). While this is an appealing notion it overlooks Baker's (2004) caveat that things fall in and out of alignment because the elements are not static. There are people involved, which immediately creates variation. Nonetheless we searched for alignment in the case we present here, be it attempts to harmonise actions or events which foster a sense of purpose. We do so because while 'getting many people to work together on a common problem' is seldom easy, this is the most likely pathway to success (Jochim 2018: 65).

In summary, the rationale for the book is that educational policymakers and reformers need a body of research on the implementation of reform on which to base their decisions and programmes. This is not a new idea. Elmore (1979) observed that there is a 'noble lie' in public administration that policymakers can or should be able to exercise some control over implementation. We know they cannot do so, even in the most autocratic environments, nor do we believe they should be able to dictate professional actions from afar. But we do wish, hope, for policies which are better designed with the realities of implementation in mind. As such we make the case for focusing upon implementation because it is the most significant phase of sustained and sustainable reform and the most ignored. To begin to address this gap we have collected a set of cases of relatively recent reforms and used them to identify some emerging issues in educational reform at a practical and theoretical level.

We have selected cases of reform implementation in a variety of stages, contexts and scales. We present case studies of major and minor reforms and of successes, of failures and of reforms still underway. The cases have been written by knowledgeable participants in the main; they are research-informed and they represent a range of different approaches to reform.

The cases are drawn from different geographies; the United States, the United Kingdom, Singapore, Kazakhstan, Hong Kong, Vietnam and Qatar. This gives us cases in large and small nations, in centralised and locally controlled systems. There are cases in elective democracies, a communist controlled society, in post-colonial and post-soviet states and a monarchy. We have reforms which are mandated and some that are locally adopted. Most cases are in relatively well-resourced systems with reasonably high levels of school completion.

The first case examines a systemic approach to equity. Equity is a major concern within UK education systems and the last ten years have seen efforts to address this issue through a series of 'challenge' programmes, the first of which took place in London. This chapter examines the evidence regarding what has been called the 'London effect', before going on to focus on the work of the Greater Manchester Challenge. This was a follow-up project that involved a partnership between national government, local authorities, schools and other stakeholders, and had a government investment of around £50 million.

The decision to invest such a large budget reflected a concern regarding educational standards, particularly amongst children and young people from disadvantaged backgrounds. The approach adopted In Greater Manchester, which was influenced by the earlier initiative in London, was based on an analysis of local context and used processes of networking and collaboration in order to make better use of available expertise. An independent evaluation concluded that it had been largely successful in achieving its objectives. The evaluators suggested that the strategic factors contributing to its success were the timescale; the focus on specific urban areas; flexibility of approach; use of expert advisers and bespoke solutions; school staff learning from practice in other schools; and the programme ethos of trust, support and encouragement.

Reflecting on the impact and the difficulties involved, plus subsequent efforts to create similar challenge programmes in Wales and Scotland, the chapter draws out lessons that are relevant to other contexts. Mel Ainscow, the author, was involved in these projects as an adviser working on a part-time basis, wherever possible using knowledge of evidence from relevant research to guide decision-making. This involvement provided privileged access to information regarding the way decisions are made within an education system, from the levels of government ministers and senior civil servants, through to that of teachers in the classroom. All of this provided frequent reminders of the cultural, social and political complexities involved when trying to bring about changes in the way that an education system does its business.

The 'city' focus of Ainscow's chapter is echoed to some degree in Mary James's case study of ten years of reform in Hong Kong. In 2002, Hong Kong embarked on a carefully planned and enormously ambitious ten-year reform of its education system of primary, secondary and tertiary education. The central aim of the reform was to promote all-round (whole person) development of students and a disposition towards lifelong learning in order to meet the needs of life and work in the twenty-first century. Changes in curriculum, assessment and pedagogy were thought to be necessary. Far-ranging structural changes were also introduced. Most significant is the introduction of the Hong Kong Diploma in Secondary Education (HKDSE), for all students, awarded at the end of secondary schooling, now at 17, thus replacing the old British system of examinations at 16+ and 18+. The reforms have been successful in increasing access of students to senior secondary studies, whilst maintaining or improving standards of achievement.

These root-and-branch reforms required thorough, on-going coordination, evaluation and renewal. Inevitably this was costly and government expenditure increased. Support for the recruitment and training of teachers and school leaders has been important. There have been worries, particularly about workload for students and teachers, but there is evidence that much has been gained in terms of students' broader knowledge and skills, and enhanced self-confidence.

Hong Kong demonstrates that it is possible to introduce a more broad, balanced and coherent curriculum and assessment system whilst preserving or enhancing excellence. The crucial condition has been the opportunity to plan and implement a long-term, publicly agreed, reform programme protected, thus far, from too much political interference.

In contrast to the Manchester and London challenges, the reforms in Hong Kong were system-wide and this is also true of the case of Kazakhstan, where efforts have been underway for a similar ten-year period. Colleen McLaughlin and colleagues focus on the reform work that began in 2011. It is a large scale, comprehensive reform of the educational system covering the curriculum, assessment, teacher development, language policy, funding mechanisms, leadership, teacher appraisal and teacher working conditions. The authors were partners to the establishment of a group of pilot schools or schools of innovation, which served as models for the later translation to the whole school system that was completed in the 2019/20 school year. The authors have systematically studied this since 2012 and draw on their work and other data to explore this model and examine different perspectives on implementation: the teachers and school leaders, local leaders of education and the national stakeholders and policymakers.

The system-wide theme is taken up by Matt Hartley and Alan Ruby, who document reforms in the governance of higher education institutions in Kazakhstan, focusing on the challenges and opportunities of greater autonomy. One of the predominant strategies many countries have used to foster higher quality higher education systems is granting greater institutional autonomy. The hope is that by moving from centralised systems controlled by Ministries to ones where institutions can pursue their destinies, innovation will inevitably result and performance improves. In reality, moving towards a more autonomous system comes at a cost. Being free to set institutional strategies brings the possibility of making mistakes, something many leaders who have been trained in a compliance-based system find daunting. Further, if leaders have never operated in a more market-based system, their ability to scan the environment to determine and launch new initiatives can be a challenge. Such pressures can result in institutions following practices similar to the old compliance-based model in order to demonstrate to the larger society that they are being responsible and faithful to prior norms of behaviour. Finally, autonomy requires constructing new, alternative systems of accountability (for example, the establishment of boards of trustees). Kazakhstan's higher education reforms offer insights into both the challenges and possibilities of greater institutional autonomy.

A system-wide reform on school autonomy in Qatar is an interesting contrast to the higher education work in the context of Kazakhstan. Asmaa Alfadala, Stavros Yiannouka and Omar Zaki explore the theory and practice on school autonomy reform over almost twenty years. In 2001, Qatar embarked on comprehensive education reform – Education for a New Era – to meet the country's changing needs and aspirations. The reform programme was based on a comprehensive study and recommendations made by the RAND Corporation, which envisaged a K-12 system, modelled in part on the US Charter Schools experience, that would offer autonomy and accountability for schools and variety and choice for parents and students. In its implementation the policy reform effort did not meet the objectives of the original design. Evidence reveals that the failure to meet the objectives can be attributed in part to the fact that important conditions were not present to enable schools to effectively practice autonomy. In particular, school leaders were not equipped to interpret and act on their mandates. As a consequence, the reform policies were partially reversed in 2014–15 and elements of the K-12 system recentralised.

They present evidence and explore in detail the underlying reasons for the lack of success of the initial reform effort and discuss some of the solutions being piloted to address the leadership capacity gap at the school level and promote greater professional autonomy. They ground their observations in the Qatari context, notably the enabling conditions for the exercise of autonomy, what the exercise of autonomy meant in practice, the impact of school autonomy on learning outcomes and student well-being and the strengths and limitations of capacity-building programmes to address leadership gaps in implementation.

Issues of leadership and the impact of system-wide reforms on student learning are also examined in a case study of promising practices in the government schools in Vietnam developed by Tony McAleavy and Rachael Fitzpatrick, who have been observing reform and development in the country very closely. They note that many people were astonished by the performance of Vietnamese students in the OECD-PISA tests administered in 2012 and 2015. Vietnamese students did well relative to students in most other countries, performing well in the science tests, although Vietnam was the poorest participating jurisdiction in terms of per capita income. The significance of the PISA results has been contested, but there are other signs that suggest that Vietnam has an effective school system with good student outcomes in core subjects.

McAleavy and Fitzpatrick outline the way the Vietnamese school system has evolved and works today, drawing upon research undertaken by the Education Development Trust and the Vietnam Institute of Educational Sciences. The case is grounded in an extensive analysis of Vietnamese education policy since the 1990s which has underpinned qualitative fieldwork, involving discussions with a wide range of stakeholders in four contrasting provinces: Ho Chi Minh City, Hanoi, Binh Dinh and Ha Giang. The respondents, unsurprisingly, confirmed that there are powerful cultural forces at work in Vietnamese society which are conducive to good performance in tests. Schools cannot take all the credit for Vietnamese performance in PISA. While recognising the importance of culture, and making no definitive causal claims, the case suggests that particularly 'promising' features of the development of the Vietnamese school system include a high level of consistency of policy priorities over the last three decades. This enabled local middle-tier agencies to play a key role in mediating and implementation of national policies. This was reinforced by a high level of professional accountability through different forms of in-school and external monitoring. This in turn fosters a degree of teacher professionalism and McAleavy and Fitzpatrick discuss the way teachers and others perceive government attempts to change classroom practice in order to encourage more 'student-centred' pedagogical practice. Finally they examine the role of the school principal as the interface between the school community and the external authorities and the unusually high level of parental involvement in the life of Vietnamese schools, with government regulations giving a prominent role to parents in school governance.

Continuing the theme of learning from high-performing systems, Saravanan Gopinathan and Edmund Lim draw implementation lessons from Singapore. They describe Singapore as an improbable success story, not least in education. Small, resource starved, hemmed in by large, occasionally unfriendly neighbours, it had to become a state and a nation, indispensable to first the region, then globally. Today, measured by GDP per capita, it ranks amongst the five richest countries in the world.

Education was central to this transformation. Post-war realities posed major challenges to policy formulation and implementation. How was a school system, segmented by media of instruction, to be unified? How could an academic grammar school curriculum be redesigned to aid rapid and transformative industrialisation? While the school-building programme and enhanced access to education was achieved, a hastily conceived and poorly implemented policy of school bilingualism created major problems in the 1970s.

These problems were overcome by the mid-1980s. Policymakers realised that a hitherto successful education-economy strategy had to give way to emergent globalisation's challenges and opportunities. This in turn unleashed a wave of reform initiatives, at one stage promoting within a strongly nation-oriented system, choice, competition and branding as key drivers. Rapid changes to curricular and pedagogic frameworks, enhanced TVET, re-positioning the universities and upgrading teacher education have completely transformed the system. Singapore ranks highly in all international comparisons of educational quality.

In this case they examine the policies and processes that were responsible for this transformation. But they also caution against a too simplistic reading of the Singapore success story and suggest that a radical rethinking of the aims and purposes of Singapore education is due.

Counterbalancing these system-wide studies, Brian Rowan examines six externally developed 'Instructional Improvement Programmes' in the United States which have been subjects of a sustained programme of inter-vention studies. Over the past fifteen years, Rowan and colleagues have conducted large-scale quasi-experimental and experimental studies of six different, externally designed programmes that seek to change instruction and improve student achievement in US schools. The programmes were developed by not-for-profit and for-profit organisations, sought to change instructional practice in both English Language Arts and mathematics and were adopted by schools both as a result of government incentives and normal 'market' processes. In each of the six studies, they gathered data on how the externally developed programmes were designed and how they worked with school personnel to promote instructional change in schools. In each study, they carefully measured patterns of instructional practice and student achievement in order to assess the extent to which the programmes succeeded in changing teaching and improving student learning. Across the six studies, they found programmes that change teaching and improve student learning (success cases), programmes that change teaching but do not improve student learning and programmes that neither change teaching nor improve student learning. From this, Rowan developed a set of theoret-ical ideas about how to successfully change teaching and improve student learning when change occurs from the 'outside in' in American schools. One key finding is that successful external programmes of instructional improvement have well-specified designs for instruction and provide strong pressures and supports to encourage faithful implementation of these instructional designs in classrooms. But they caution that simply implementing pre-planned instructional designs is not enough to improve student learning. In their work, the central finding is that only when the instructional designs being implemented are different from – and better than – normative practice does improvement occurs in student achievement. Rowan illustrates these points by briefly laying out a theory of externally promoted instructional change and showing how different programmes fit within this theory. He concludes by discussing some of the challenges that governments and markets face in promoting the development of externally designed programmes for instructional improvement in US education. This confirms some of the findings from earlier research on implementation (see Odden 1991b, for example) that good design and thoughtful and sustained support increase effectiveness.

After the cases we offer some closing observations about what we have learned about implementation. We engage in a cross-case analysis of the cases of reform implementation drawing out the cross-cutting themes and lessons learned. We are not looking for consistency or an 'Iron Law of Implementation', but identify some points of commonalities and present the dilemmas and different implementation design options that are presented in the cases. We tie this back where apposite to previous work and sketch out ideas for more work on implementation.

References

Baker, E. L. (2004) *Aligning Curriculum, Standards & Assessments: Fulfilling the Promise of School Reform, CSE Report 645*. Los Angeles: National Centre for Research on Evaluation, Standards & Student Testing, University of California.

Berman, P. and McLaughlin, M. W. (1974). *Federal Programs Supporting Educational Change Vol.1., A Model of Educational Change*. Santa Monica: Rand.

Bradach, J. L. (2003). Going to scale: The challenge of replicating social programs. *Stanford Social Innovation Review*, 1:1, 19–25.

Browne, A. L. and Wildavsky, A. B. (1983). What should evaluation mean to implementation? In Pressman, J. L. and Wildavsky, A. B. (eds.) (1984) *Implementation: How Great Expectations in Washington Are Dashed in Oakland*, 3rd ed. Berkeley: University of California Press, pp. 181–205.

Datnow, A. and Stringfield, S. (2000). Working together for reliable school reform. *Journal of Education for Students Placed at Risk* (JESPAR), 5:1–2, 183–204.

Elmore, R. E. (1979). Backward mapping: Implementation research and policy decisions. *Political Science Quarterly*, 94:4, 601–16. doi:10.2307/2149628

Elmore, R. E. (1996). Getting to scale with good educational practice. *Harvard Educational Review*, 66:1, 1–27.

Fullan, M., Quine, J. and McEachen, J. (2018). *Deep Learning: Engage the World, Change the World*. Thousand Oaks, CA: Corwin.

Hall, G. E. (1992). The local educational change process and policy implementation. *Journal of Research in Science Teaching*, 29:8, 877–904.

Hargreaves, A. and Goodson, I. (2006). Educational change over time? The sustainability and nonsustainability of three decades of secondary school change and continuity. *Educational Administration Quarterly*, 42:1, 3–41.

Hopkins, D., Stringfield, S., Harris, A., Stoll, L. and McKay, T. (2014). School and system improvement: A narrative state-of-the-art review. *School Effectiveness and School Improvement: An International Journal of Research, Policy and Practice*, 25:2, 257–81.

Jayawardena, D. L. U. (1983). Free trade zones. *Journal of World Trade Law*, 17, 427–44.

Jochim, A. (2018). School improvement grants: Failures in design and implementation. In Greene, J. P. and McShane, M. Q. (eds.) *Failure Up Close: What Happens, Why It Happens, and What We Can Learn From It*. Lanham: Rowan and Littlefield, pp. 55–70.

Lytle, J. H. (2002). Whole-school reform from the inside. *Phi Delta Kappan*, 84:2, 164–67.

Majone, G. and Wildavsky, A. B. (1979). Implementation as evolution. In Pressman, J. L. and Wildavsky, A. B. (1984). *Implementation: How Great Expectations in Washington Are Dashed in Oakland*, 3rd ed. Berkeley: University of California Press, pp. 163–80.

McDermott, K. A. (2006). Incentives, capacity, and implementation: Evidence from Massachusetts education reform. *Journal of Public Administration Research and Theory: J-PART*, 16:1, 45–65.

McDonnell, L. (2004). *Politics, Persuasion & Educational Testing*. Cambridge, MA: Harvard University Press.

McLaughlin, M. W. (1987). Learning from experience: Lessons from policy implementation. *Educational Evaluation and Policy Analysis*, 9:2, 171–78.

McLaughlin, M. W. and Mitra, D. (2001). Theory-based change and change-based theory. Going deeper and going broader. *Journal of Educational Change*, 2:4, 301–23.

Oates, T. (2017). *A Cambridge Approach to Improving Education*. Cambridge: Cambridge Assessment.

Odden, A. (1991a). The evolution of education policy implementation. In Odden, A. (ed.) *Education Policy Implementation*. Albany: SUNY Press, pp. 1–12.

Odden, A. (1991b). New patterns of education policy implementation and challenges for the 1990's. In Odden, A. (ed.) *Education Policy Implementation*. Albany: SUNY Press, pp. 297–327.

Peurach, D. J. (2016). Innovating at the nexus of impact and improvement: Leading education improvement networks. *Educational Researcher*, 45:7, 421–29.

Peurach, D. J. and Glaser, J. L. (2012). Reconsidering replication: New perspectives on large scale school improvement. *Journal of Educational Change*, 13:2, 155–90.

Pressman, J. L. and Wildavsky, A. B. (1984). *Implementation: How Great Expectations in Washington Are Dashed in Oakland*, 3rd ed. Berkeley: University of California Press.

RAND Corporation. (2018). *Implementing Education Reforms to Enhance School Performance*. The RAND Blog. Available at: www.rand.org/blog/2015/11/implementing-education-reforms-to-enhance-school-performance.html (accessed 18 January 2019).

Robinson, V., Bendikson, L., McNaughton, S., Wilson, A. and Zhu, T. (2017). Joining the dots: The challenge of creating coherent school improvement. *Teachers College Record* 119: August, 1–44.

Sahlberg, P. (2016). The global educational reform movement and its impact on schooling. In Mundy, K., Green, A., Lingard, B. and Verger, A. (eds.) *Handbook of Global Education Policy*. Chichester: Wiley Blackwell, pp. 128–44.

Spillane, J. P., Reiser, B. J. and Reimer, T. (2002). Policy implementation and cognition: Reframing and refocusing implementation research. *Review of Educational Research*, 72:3, 387–431.

Stringfield, S. (1995). Attempting to enhance students' learning through innovative programs: The case for schools evolving into high reliability organizations, *School Effectiveness and School Improvement*, 6:1, 67–96.

Stringfield, S., Reynolds, D. and Schaffer, E. (2012). Making best practice standard – and lasting. *Phi Delta Kappan* 94:1, 45–50.

Supovitz, J. A. (2008). Implementation as iterative refraction. in Supovitz, J. A. and Weinbaum, E. H. (eds.) *The Implementation Gap: Understanding Reform in High Schools*. New York: Columbia University Press, pp. 151–72.

Weiss, C. H., Murphy-Graham, E., Petrosino, A. and Gandhi, A. G. (2008). The fairy godmother – and her warts: Making the dream of evidence-based policy come true. *American Journal of Evaluation*, 29:1, 29–47.

World Bank. (2017). *Special Economic Zones: An Operational Review of Their Impacts*. Washington, DC: World Bank.

World Bank. (2018). *World Development Report 2018: Learning to Realize Education's Promise*. Washington, DC: World Bank.

2 Promoting Equity in Education through System Change

Lessons from the United Kingdom

Mel Ainscow

Equity is a major concern within the four national education systems of the United Kingdom. The last twenty years have seen efforts to address this issue through a series of 'challenge' programmes, the first of which took place in London. This chapter examines the evidence regarding what has been called the 'London effect', before going on to focus on the work of follow-up initiatives in Greater Manchester and Wales.

My involvement in these projects was as an adviser working on a part-time basis, wherever possible using knowledge from relevant research to guide decision-making. This involvement provided privileged access to information regarding the way decisions are made within an education system, from the levels of government ministers and senior civil servants, through to that of teachers in the classroom. All of this provided frequent reminders of the cultural, social and political complexities involved when trying to bring about changes in the way that an education system does its business.

Reflecting on these experiences leads me to outline a series of propositions that can be used to promote equity within education systems. I also illustrate the sorts of barriers that make it difficult to implement these ideas. These include the current emphasis on the so-called what works approach to educational improvement. First of all, however, I begin by considering international developments in relation to equity in education.

2.1 A GLOBAL CHALLENGE

Recently UNESCO's Institute for Statistics has determined that, globally, some 258 million children and young people are not in school, and that more than 617 million children and adolescents do not achieve minimum proficiency levels in reading and mathematics.[1] It also notes the high rates of student dropout, particularly at the secondary stage, and the challenges experienced by many marginalised groups at the time of transition to higher education.

Whilst this situation is most acute in the developing world, there are similar concerns in many wealthier countries, as noted by the OECD (2012), which reports that, across its member countries, almost one in five students does not reach a basic minimum level of skills to function in today's societies. It is also noted that students from low socio-economic backgrounds are twice as likely to be low performers, implying that personal or social circumstances are obstacles to achieving their educational potential.

In responding to these concerns there is growing interest internationally in the use of strategies that place an emphasis on the power of market forces (Lubienski 2003). In particular, a number of national education policies are encouraging state-funded schools to become autonomous; for example, in parts of Australia, the independent public schools; the academies in England; charter schools in the United States; free schools in Sweden; and in Chile through the voucher reforms. Alongside this emphasis on school autonomy is a focus on parental choice. This usually takes place within education systems where high-stakes testing systems are intended to inform decision-making, whilst at the same time driving improvement efforts (Au 2009). In addition, narrowly-defined measures of effectiveness are used for purposes of accountability (Schildkamp et al. 2012).

Whilst such developments have the potential to open up possibilities to inject new energy into the improvement of education systems, there is growing evidence from a range of countries that they are leading to increased segregation that further disadvantages learners from economically poorer backgrounds (Pickett and Vanderbloemen 2015). So, for example, talking about the development of charter schools in the United States, Kahlenberg and Potter (2014) suggest they have led to increased segregation in school

---

[1] http://uis.unesco.org/sites/default/files/documents/new-methodology-shows-258-million-children-adolescents-and-youth-are-out-school.pdf

systems across the country. Other researchers point to similar patterns in Chile (McEwan and Carnoy 2000) and in Sweden (Wiborg 2010).

There are, however, countries that have made progress by adopting a very different approach, one that combines quality with equity (OECD 2012). In these contexts, the vast majority of students have the opportunity to attain high level skills, regardless of their own personal and socio-economic circumstances. To take an example, in Finland – the country which regularly outperforms most other countries in terms of educational outcomes – success is partly explained by the progress of the lowest performing quintile of students who, in taking the PISA tests, out-perform those in other countries, thus raising the mean scores overall (Sabel et al. 2011). This has involved a much greater emphasis on support for vulnerable students within mainstream schools, as opposed to in segregated provision (Takala et al. 2009).

Reflecting on the success of those national education systems that rank highly on measures of both quality and equity, the OECD (2012: 14) argues:

> The evidence is conclusive: equity in education pays off. The highest performing education systems across OECD countries are those that combine high quality and equity. In such education systems, the vast majority of students can attain high level skills and knowledge that depend on their ability and drive, more than on their socio-economic background.

Further encouragement for this view is provided by the recent 'Report Card' prepared for UNICEF by the Innocenti Centre. This argues that there is no systematic relationship between country income and indicators of equality in education. For example, it is notable that some of the poorest countries in their comparison, such as Latvia and Lithuania, achieve near-universal access to preschool learning and curb inequality in reading performance among both primary and secondary school students more successfully than countries that have far greater resources.

The implication, then, is that it is possible for countries to develop education systems that are both excellent and equitable. The question is: how can this be achieved? In what follows, I draw on experiences in the United Kingdom to suggest some ways forward.

2.2 THE LONDON CHALLENGE

The English education system is a particularly relevant context to consider when thinking about the challenge of equity, as noted in a 2007 OECD study which reported that the impact of socio-economic circumstances on young people's attainment was more marked in the United Kingdom than in any other of the fifty-two countries considered. Summing this up, Benn and Millar (2006: 145) argue that one of the biggest problems the country faces is 'the gap between rich and poor, and the enormous disparity in children's home backgrounds and the social and cultural capital they bring to the educational table'.

London Challenge was introduced during a period of successive Labour Governments (1997–2010) which saw extensive efforts to address these concerns. These developments were part of an intensification of political interest in education, especially regarding standards and the management of the state system (Whitty 2010). This led to a series of highly centralised national strategies to strengthen practices of teaching and leadership. At the same time, competition between schools was seen to be one of the keys to 'driving up standards', whilst further reducing the control of local authorities over provision.[2] All of this was intended to 'liberate' schools from the bureaucracy of local government and establish a form of marketplace. In this way, it was argued, families would have greater choice as to which school their youngsters would attend, informed by school reports from the national inspection agency, Ofsted, and the annual publication of school test and examination results.

During that period, there were also a number of policy efforts to address factors which lie beyond schools. These recognised that children's academic performance cannot be divorced from other aspects of their development and what happens to them outside school – in their families, neighbourhoods and more widely. These initiatives sought to improve and equalise educational outcomes, by aligning schools' core business of teaching and learning with interventions targeting other aspects of children's lives. All of this was part of a Children's Plan which set out a framework for organising child and family services based on the principle that 'Every Child Matters', i.e. that all children should be healthy, stay safe, enjoy and achieve, make a positive contribution and achieve economic wellbeing.

London Challenge was a further element in this reform programme. It began in 2003, concentrating on the improvement of secondary schools. By 2007, the national inspection agency, Ofsted, was reporting that standards in these schools had improved 'dramatically' and that the capital had recorded

---

[2] There are 152 English local authorities. They are democratically accountable for providing a range of services for their local communities, including education.

its best ever examination results, showing London's state school pupils leading the rest of the country for the third year running (Ainscow 2015).

In the light of this success, in 2007 the government took the decision to extend the London programme for a further three years and to include primary schools. At the same time, the creation of a generic City Challenge programme was announced that would include new initiatives in two other regions, the Black Country, in the West Midlands, and Greater Manchester. Meanwhile, there began what is to this day a continuing debate within academic circles to determine what were the key features of what came to be known as the 'London effect'.

As a result of their research into the implementation of the London Challenge, Kidson and Norris (2014) conclude that it was a distinctive example of public service improvement that was practitioner-focused, highly collaborative and applied across a system. They note, too, that, despite other factors at play, all the people they interviewed felt that the initiative had made a major contribution to the exceptional improvement in the capital's schools. This was attributed to: the way credible professionals played a challenge and support role to their peers; the powerful sense of moral purpose and positive framing; and the close working relationships of officials, advisers and ministers, which was focused on a shared, data-led view of where there were strengths and weaknesses in the schools.

There are, however, a range of other views as to what made the difference in London. In a helpful summary of these positions, Lowe (2015) points out that other government interventions that took place around the same time may also have had an impact. He mentions, for example, Teach First, a graduate recruitment scheme launched in 2002 to coax top young graduates into the classroom, which was widely used in London. He also notes the possible impact of the national inspection agency, Ofsted, and the new transparency in relation to school results. In addition, Lowe argues that the role of primary schools cannot be ignored, noting that the national strategies in literacy and numeracy were perhaps taken up far more enthusiastically in London than elsewhere. It is worth noting, too, that there is a view in the field that London schools have benefited from preferential financing.

Simon Burgess, a researcher at the University of Bristol, introduces another perspective, suggesting that the basis for London's progress was the ethnic composition of its school population. In particular, he concludes that a key factor had been the attraction to London of migrants and others aspiring to a better life. This led Burgess to argue:

First, integrated multi-ethnic school systems can be very productive, allowing the ethnic minority pupils to achieve the grades they seek, and (potentially) raising the scores of white British pupils as well. Here is a role for school leadership, in managing a multi-ethnic school system – it could have gone less well. Second, in parts of England where there simply isn't a large community of recent immigrants, a focus on how to encourage pupils' engagement with school, hard work and aspiration may pay strong dividends. (Burgess 2014: 16)

A further worrying factor that cannot be overlooked is regarding the more recent reports suggesting that London schools have seen increases in both temporary and permanent exclusion rates.[3] This reminds me of a comment made by a key figure involved in London Challenge who referred to how they had learnt to 'pull some tricks' in order to improve results. All of which underlines the complexities involved in system change and the problems that exist when trying to establish the nature of the 'local causality' at play within it (Hadfield and Jopling 2018).

2.3 THE GREATER MANCHESTER CHALLENGE

In 2007, I was appointed as the Chief Adviser for the Greater Manchester Challenge, a three-year initiative involving over 1,100 schools in 10 local authorities, with a government investment of around £50 million (see Ainscow 2015, for a detailed account of this initiative). The decision to invest this large amount reflected a concern regarding educational standards in the city region, particularly amongst children and young people from disadvantaged backgrounds. It is important to note at this stage, too, that the London and Greater Manchester Challenge programmes each had the active involvement of a Government Minister. In terms of the impact, the presence of this form of high-status political leadership should not be overlooked.

A detailed analysis of the context led to the conclusion that plenty of good practice existed across Greater Manchester schools. Consequently, it was decided that collaboration and networking between schools of the sort that had occurred in London would form the key strategies for strengthening the overall capacity of the system to reach out to vulnerable groups of learners. More specifically this involved a series of inter-connected activities for

---

[3] www.london.gov.uk/press-releases/assembly/the-link-between-school-exclusions-violent-crime

'moving knowledge around' in order to build a self-improving school system (Ainscow 2012, 2015).

With this in mind, Families of Schools were set up. This approach partnered schools that serve similar populations whilst, at the same time, encouraging partnerships amongst schools that were not in direct competition with one another because they did not serve the same neighbourhoods. Led by head teachers, the Families of Schools proved to be successful in strengthening collaborative processes within the city region, although the impact was varied.

In terms of schools working in the most disadvantaged contexts, more intensive school partnerships were found to be the most powerful means of fostering improvements (Hutchings et al. 2012). Most notably, what was called the Keys to Success programme led to striking improvements in the performance of some 200 Greater Manchester schools facing the most challenging circumstances. A common feature of almost all of these interventions was that progress was achieved through carefully matched pairings (or, sometimes, trios) of schools that, once again, cut across social 'boundaries' of various kinds, including those that separate schools that are in different local authorities (Ainscow 2013). In this way, expertise that was previously trapped in particular contexts was made more widely available.

Whilst increased collaboration of this sort proved to be vital as a strategy for developing more effective ways of working, the experience of Greater Manchester shows that it was not enough. The essential additional ingredient is an engagement with evidence that can bring an element of mutual challenge to such collaborative processes. We found that evidence was particularly essential when partnering schools, since collaboration is at its most powerful where partner schools are carefully matched and know what they are trying to achieve. Evidence also matters in order that schools go beyond cosy relationships that have no impact on outcomes. Consequently, schools need to base their relationships on evidence about each other's strengths and weaknesses, so that they can challenge each other to improve.

Another effective strategy to facilitate the movement of expertise was provided through the creation of various types of hub schools. So, for example, some of the hubs provided support for other schools regarding ways of supporting students with English as an additional language. Similarly, so-called teaching schools[4] providing professional development programmes focused on bringing about improvements in classroom practice.

---

[4] The idea of teaching schools, which act as professional development hubs, has subsequently become part of national policy in England.

It is worth adding that another key factor in the success of both the London and Greater Manchester Challenge programmes was the involvement of teams of expert advisers. Chosen because of a track record of leading successful school improvement, they were given the mandate and resources to intervene in schools, helping them to develop, implement and monitor the impact of their own improvement plans.

An independent evaluation of the City Challenge programme concluded that it had been largely successful in achieving its objectives (Hutchings et al. 2012). Commenting on this, the authors of the report argue:

> Clearly a great many factors contributed to these improvements, including national policies and strategies and the considerable efforts of head teachers and staff. However, these factors apply everywhere in the country. The most plausible explanation for the greater improvement in Challenge areas is that the City Challenge programme was responsible. The vast majority of stakeholders at all levels who contributed to this evaluation attributed the additional improvements that have been made in these areas to the work of City Challenge. (Hutchings et al. 2012: vi)

The evaluators also concluded that the strategic factors contributing to its success were the timescale; the focus on specific urban areas; flexibility of approach; use of expert advisers and bespoke solutions; school staff learning from practice in other schools; and the programme ethos of trust, support and encouragement.

2.4 A NATIONAL INITIATIVE IN WALES

In 2014, I was invited by the Welsh Government to lead Schools Challenge Cymru, a national initiative to promote equity across the country, the design of which was much influenced by what had happened in City Challenge (Ainscow 2016). Wales shares a close political and social history with the rest of Great Britain, and almost everyone speaks English. However, the country has retained a distinct cultural identity and is officially bilingual, with Welsh being spoken by about 20 per cent of the population, mostly in the north and west of the country. Although it is part of the United Kingdom, Wales has a form of self-government created in 1998 following a referendum, and has its own education policies. There are also twenty-two local authorities responsible for a range of public services, including education.

Like many school systems that are seen to be successful (e.g. Alberta, Finland, Singapore), Wales is small, with about 3.1 million inhabitants. Despite its size, however, the performance of the school system has been a cause for concern, particularly in terms of outcomes for learners from low-income families, as noted in a country review conducted by OECD (2014). Most significantly, the review argued that, whilst the pace of reform in recent years has been high, it has lacked a long-term vision, an adequate school improvement infrastructure and a clear implementation strategy that all stakeholders share.

The review noted that the system has many strengths to build on, not least its inclusiveness, before going on to suggest a number of concrete policy options that would strengthen it over the long-term. In particular, it argued for the development a long-term vision, translated into measurable objectives. With this in mind, in 2014 the Welsh government instigated a five-year reform plan for the education of three- to nineteen-year old learners in the document 'Qualified for Life'. This provided a timeline for key activities and identified immediate measures to be taken. One of these was the introduction of Schools Challenge Cymru.

Launched in 2014, the purpose of the initiative was to accelerate progress across the Welsh education system. More specifically, it aimed to bring about rapid improvements in the performance of schools serving the more disadvantaged communities and use lessons from these developments to strengthen the capacity of the education system to improve itself. The budget was approximately twenty million pounds per year.

Building on the earlier experiences in London and Greater Manchester, the Welsh initiative worked with forty secondary schools serving disadvantaged communities (designated as the 'Pathways to Success') and their local primary school partners. Similar to City Challenge, a team of advisers were involved in supporting these schools. In addition, a small group of champions advised on the overall strategic direction of the initiative.

The advisers and champions were directly accountable to the Minister for Education and Skills. As was the case in City Challenge, the Minister was closely associated with the initiative, visiting each of the schools at least twice over the first eighteen months. This provided the political mandate that Claeys et al. (2014) argue is essential to change strategies that mainly emphasise bottom-up action.

In summary, the results over the first two years showed that overall attainment in the GCSE examinations taken by almost all students at the age of sixteen, across the Pathways to Success schools, improved by 7.0

percentage points, with 87 per cent of the schools securing improvements in this measure. This rate of improvement was faster than the overall progress made across Wales over the same period. The attainment of students entitled to free school meals[5] across the schools improved by 8.2 percentage points, with 74 per cent of the schools securing improvements.

In making sense of these trends, it is important to remember that the participating schools were chosen because of the challenges they face and the fact that they had, to varying degrees, performed poorly over many years. Some of them became striking examples of what is possible when the expertise and energy within schools are mobilised. It should be noted, however, that these gains were hard won and remained fragile without continuing support.

Moving beyond the forty schools, there was evidence too that Schools Challenge Cymru began to have a ripple effect across the education system in ways that have raised expectations regarding how rapidly improvements can be achieved (Hadfield and Ainscow 2018). This has particular implications for efforts to improve outcomes for learners from low-income families, where low expectations can be a factor in preventing their progress (Kerr and West 2010).

An independent evaluation of Schools Challenge Cymru (Carr et al. 2017) concluded that the quality of leadership and management had improved in the majority of Pathways to Success schools. In two-fifths of the schools, involvement in the programme were considered to be largely, or wholly, responsible for the changes in pupil engagement. Some schools were optimistic about the sustainability of perceived improvements in pupil attendance, hoping to ensure that good attendance became the norm. The report also concluded that the programme had contributed both to the strengthening of professional development within the schools and, in some cases, extended it.

2.5 DRAWING LESSONS

In thinking about the complexities experienced in the contexts referred to in these accounts, I am occasionally reminded of Karl Weick's argument that educational organisations should be understood as being 'loosely coupled'.

---

[5] An indication of economic disadvantage.

That is to say, they consist of units, processes, actions and individuals that tend to operate in isolation from one another. Weick illustrates this by describing an unconventional soccer match in which the field is round, with several goals scattered haphazardly around. He explains that players enter and leave the game whenever they want, saying 'that's my goal', as many times as they want. He adds that the entire game takes place on a sloped field and is played as if it makes sense (Weick 1985).

Bearing this complexity in mind, my colleagues and I have proposed a way of thinking about system change in order to promote equity (Ainscow et al. 2020). This involves a series of interconnected propositions that point to a need for:

- **A shared understanding of overall purposes.** Many of the difficulties in implementing the initiatives had their origins in a lack of agreement as to what should be the intended outcomes. Given that change requires coordinated efforts across the different levels of an education system, an agreed and clear purpose is an essential condition. Reaching the required degree of clarity is both a cultural and political process in which certain voices might be excluded, whilst others are over-privileged, and in which underpinning assumptions need to be challenged

- **On-going contextual analysis of a system's existing capacity for collaborative improvement.** This must be capable of providing a deeper analysis of the barriers that are limiting progress. At the same time, it should identify areas of promising practice, drawing out key learning and applying this to the development of the necessary human and social capital to support system level improvement efforts. It is important that this analysis continues at different levels of the system.

- **Brokerage that crosses professional and social boundaries, within schools and across networks.** This is in order to increase exposure to various sources of expertise and innovative practice. It requires the orchestration of different forms of individual and organisational networks into integrated sub-systems capable of fostering system level improvements, even in challenging circumstances.

- **The development of capacity for leadership at all levels of a system.** This must be capable of leading collaborative learning within and between schools, and within the wider community. It requires the micro-mobilisation of successful senior staff members to take on system leadership roles, in combination with the macro-mobilisation of a sufficient number of school leaders at all levels to create a professional movement with sufficient momentum to overcome internal and external resistance.

- **The creation and maintenance of a strong political mandate at the national and local levels.** This is necessary in order to create the conditions within the system that are supportive of collaborative local action. It requires new thinking, attitudes and relationships across education systems. It also means that inequalities of power between elements of the system are addressed.

What connects these design principles in a way that makes them coherent is the way they focus attention on the importance of managing and interconnecting individual, organisational and system level learning within complex transitional dynamics. These learning processes help to make the familiar unfamiliar in ways that challenge expectations as to what is possible, whilst, at the same time, drawing attention to examples of different ways of working that can act as the focus of joint practice development. In such contexts, the presence of researchers – acting as critical friends, drawing attention to relevant research evidence from elsewhere and advising about how processes of inquiry can be built into strategies that are trialled – can make significant contributions (Chapman and Ainscow 2019).

Since effective change requires coordinated efforts at all levels of an education system, the use of these propositions has implications for the various key stakeholders within education systems. In particular, it requires teachers, especially those in senior positions, to see themselves as having a wider responsibility for all children and young people, not just those that attend their own schools; it means that those who administer district school systems have to adjust their priorities and ways of working in response to improvement efforts that are led from within schools; and it requires that what schools do must be aligned in a coherent strategy with the efforts of other local players – employers, community groups, universities, public services and so on.

Finally, of course, all of this has significant implications for national policymakers. In order to create the conditions within which this form of research-based change can occur, they need to foster greater flexibility at the local level in order that practitioners, community partners and researchers have the space to work together. This means that policymakers must recognise that the details of policy implementation are not amenable to central regulation. Rather, they have to be dealt with by those who are close to and, therefore, in a better position to understand local contexts.

2.6 BARRIERS TO IMPLEMENTATION

A common feature of the initiatives I have described is the emphasis they placed on bottom-up leadership within a context of top-down political mandate. At the same time, evidence from research was used to inform these developments to a considerable degree. However, we found that the implementation of such thinking was sometimes difficult because of a series of interconnected barriers. Broadly stated, these relate to:

- **Social factors**, including the extent to which relationships exist that encourage the sharing of expertise though mutual support and challenge;

- **Political factors**, due to the impact of the attitudes and preferences of key partners; and

- **Cultural factors**, created by local traditions and the expectations of those involved as to what is possible.

In what follows I reflect on my involvement in the earlier Challenge projects, plus more recent experiences of the Scottish Attainment Challenge and a number of other smaller place-based developments in England, in order to make sense of these barriers (see Ainscow et al. 2020, for accounts of these initiatives).

2.6.1 Social Factors

In reflecting further on these experiences, it does seem that 'size matters'. To give a striking example, I contributed to planning in a small rural district, where there were concerns about poor standards in the schools. To an outsider with lots of urban experience, the closeness of the links between head teachers in this community seemed to be a positive feature in terms of the encouragement of greater collaboration.

In line with the thinking developed in this chapter, I encouraged a restructuring that would enable existing good practices within local schools to be made available to more students and encourage joint practice developments. This was to be achieved through the strengthening of various forms of cooperation between the schools. It required new roles for head teachers, some of whom volunteered to take on the task of leading these developments. With this in mind, I consulted with all the heads within the authority. As a result, a new momentum for change quickly emerged in the primary sector, where a group of five relatively successful head teachers took on responsibility for moving things forward.

In discussing their roles, these heads commented on the social complexities they faced in getting colleagues to cooperate. In particular, they commented on the implications of the fact that amongst schools in a small community 'everybody knows one another'. They explained that relationships were usually warm and cordial, something that I certainly experienced. However, it was also apparent that this closeness between colleagues had the potential to create barriers to genuine collaboration between schools. One headteacher summed this up when she said, 'we don't bare our souls around here'. In other words, if you have a problem in your school, you keep it to yourself. Clearly, such a social climate can make it difficult for colleagues to support one another. It also means that the external researcher – there to support and advise – faces what may well be hidden barriers to an understanding of the dynamics of the local school system.

It follows that the involvement of an 'outsider', acting in the role of adviser, requires constructive relationships with key partners. I have found that maintaining such relationships creates many dilemmas that usually have to be addressed on the spot, as they occur. For example, a meeting was held with senior officers in one local authority where we were concerned about the poor quality of support provided for primary schools. At times the meeting became heated, as authority staff attempted to challenge our analysis and one colleague in particular was clearly distressed. Indeed, at one point he explained that he had never felt so personally humiliated during his long professional career. This particular meeting did not lead to an immediate outcome that could be described as being positive. Nevertheless, I felt that it was necessary to intervene in a context where thinking and practices were limiting opportunities for children. Subsequently, a series of further meetings did lead to agreement as to necessary actions to strengthen the work of this particular local authority in supporting its schools.

In reflecting on incidents such as this one, I am occasionally reminded of Robert Bales' theory of group systems that we had used in earlier research (see Ainscow et al. 1995). As Bales predicts, attempts to get different stakeholders to pull together lead to tensions between the need to establish cohesion amongst groups, whilst, at the same time, taking actions to achieve our goals. Put simply, it is relatively easy to maintain cooperation until the moments when hard decisions have to be made, most particularly regarding the setting of priorities and the allocation of resources.

2.6.2 Political Factors

The most striking evidence of the political nature of large-scale system change projects occurred following two national elections. This led to new ministers being appointed and, as a result, the Challenge projects losing much of their political mandate. The projects did continue, however, although with less power to make things happen. Having said that, in the case of one of the initiatives, we have recent empirical evidence of the continuing impact of its legacy five years later, most strikingly in terms of partnerships and networks (Armstrong and Ainscow 2018).

The programmes emerged during an unprecedented period of change within their education systems, not least in terms of decision-making regarding education policy. The ways in which decisions were made regarding changes varied across the countries. England was in the process of giving schools much greater autonomy, not least regarding the use of financial resources and the appointment of staff members. This was also leading to a much greater role for head teachers as system leaders, working together to coordinate collaborative improvement efforts. In all of the contexts, the role of the local authority in relation to the management of the school system was being questioned and, in the case of England, has massively reduced over the past three decades (Salokangas and Ainscow 2017).

Meanwhile, Wales and Scotland have continued in a much more centralised way, with decisions mainly shared between the national government and local authorities. In both countries there was evidence of continuing tensions between these two levels regarding policies, not least in respect to the determination of priorities and the use of resources.

During the setting up phases of the Challenge programmes, much use was made by government officials of the term 'partnership' in describing what was to happen. I sensed that for some local authority colleagues this was a source of irritation, in that the decisions to introduce the initiatives were largely imposed by national governments in what were clearly seen as processes of intervention in areas perceived to of concern.

One of the factors that was behind these tensions were the differing views as to what needed to happen in order to improve education systems: put bluntly, a difference between those who believe in locally led development and others who continue to adopt a centralising perspective. For example, the latter view was starkly expressed in an email note sent to colleagues within the DfES in London during the City Challenge period, which stated that, as far as improving attainment amongst disadvantaged students was concerned, 'the strategy must be exactly the same, whether it is in Plymouth [in the south west of England], or in Sunderland [in the far north east]'. The implication being, we know what to do: it just needs to be done, irrespective of context.

This instinct to direct from the centre kept surfacing at meetings of the challenge advisers, when civil servant colleagues took opportunities to brief the groups on the latest proposals from central government and the necessity for reporting back to central government through complex reporting mechanisms. In general, the teams found these inputs helpful in the sense that they made them feel ahead of the game regarding policy decisions, while the bureaucratic reporting and accountability systems were perceived to be frustrating and heavy handed. In these cases, my concern was that, too often, they gave the wrong message in respect to the theory of change we had adopted.

A striking example of this, that created a significant distraction, was as a result of the publication of a White Paper about the reform of the English system. The civil servant who led on this initiative as far as primary schools was concerned became particularly dogged in her efforts to impose a centrally determined strategy on the schools. With this in mind, for some months she guided the agenda of the team of primary advisers in a direction that, from my point of view, represented a significant deviation to the rationale we had developed together. During this phase, my own involvement in decision-making was clearly marginalised.

Sustainability was a major concern in all of the initiatives. The history of large-scale, heavily-funded improvement projects is that, even when they are seen to be initially successful, the impact gradually fades once the additional resources are taken away (Ainscow 2015). One way of addressing this problem is to strengthen the so-called middle tier – that is to say, the administrative arrangements that are intended to coordinate the development of education provision within a local area. In Wales, for example, this means the twenty-two local authorities, which are grouped together in four regional consortia that are intended to support school improvement efforts. There are, however, potential barriers to making such regional partnerships work, including the large geographical areas that they sometimes cover, competing philosophies and educational agendas and the struggles they can create regarding decision-making across political boundaries.

Within national systems that continue to emphasise top-down accountability, the responses of local authorities can also, at times, act as a barrier to school-level innovation. For example, one very experienced head teacher in Wales, appointed to improve a school in difficulty, talked about local authority officers frequently commenting negatively regarding the ways he dealt with minor administrative matters.

2.6.3 Cultural Factors

Efforts to inject greater pace into the improvement of schools within the Challenge programmes drew attention to the untapped potential that exists within schools. They also threw light on the factors that had limited the impact of earlier efforts to mobilise this potential. Our monitoring suggests that these barriers mainly relate to existing ways of working, which, although well intended, consume time and resources and delay action in the field. A head teacher echoed the views of many others when he commented that, in his part of the world, school improvement is like trying to drive more quickly down a road with speed bumps every few yards.

The experience of the Challenge programmes suggests that many of the 'bumps' relate to existing ways of working, which reflect taken for granted assumptions as to what is possible. Although well intended, these traditions often consume time and resources and delay action. They include, for example, the overemphasis placed by some local authorities on putting schools, particularly those facing challenging circumstances, under unnecessary pressure. This tends to demoralise those that I see as the key agents of change, i.e. the staff in the schools. It can also lead to considerable time being wasted on debating and disputing plans and targets. My experience is that, whilst plans and target setting can be helpful, without powerful support strategies they are unlikely to lead to sustainable change.

Linked to this are actions by some local authority staff that limit the freedom of school leaders to take responsibility for their own improvement. In particular, we found that there were often what seemed to be multiple reporting arrangements, such that school leaders were spending too much time preparing reports for different audiences, attending various review and scrutiny meetings and being given different (and at times conflicting) advice on the improvements required and how they can be achieved. Despite calls for the empowerment of schools and headteachers this can lead to a sense of dependency on outsiders to lead improvement efforts, rather than those in schools taking responsibility and being accountable for improved outcomes. In such situations, school leaders can feel undermined and disempowered. As a result, they tend to make poor decisions and therefore find it more difficult to prioritise their improvement strategies.

In addressing these barriers, efforts are needed to clarify the roles of local authorities. Specifically, this requires local authority staff to know, trust and support their schools, alongside providing appropriate encouragement to improve. These changes in roles and responsibilities are likely to be particularly challenging during periods of transition, whilst more locally led improvement strategies are developing, but they are a matter of urgency in order that rapid progress can be achieved.

There are also barriers related to the uncertainly that exists within governments regarding the stance that is needed to support the development of locally driven collaborative improvement. In particular, it must be recognised that the use of the power of collaboration as a means of achieving equity in schools requires an approach to national policy implementation that fosters greater flexibility at the local level, in order for practitioners to have the space to analyse their particular circumstances and determine priorities accordingly. This means that policymakers must understand that the details of policy implementation are not amenable to central regulation. Rather, these have to be dealt with by those who are close to and, therefore, better positioned to understand local contexts.

2.7 WHAT WORKS?

The approach I have presented in this chapter involves processes of social learning: the bringing together of different types of expertise to address challenges faced in particular contexts. This often requires structural and cultural changes in order to make it happen. And, as I have explained, there are many barriers that make the use of this approach difficult, not least because the changes that are necessary are likely to challenge the status quo.

There is, however, a very different approach to educational change that is becoming dominant in an increasing number of countries, not least within the United Kingdom. Sometimes referred to as 'what works', the approach is based on very different assumptions regarding how to use research knowledge to inform improvement efforts. In this way of thinking, the task of researchers is to convince practitioners to change their practices in the light of evidence from elsewhere. The implication is that teachers are there to 'deliver' practices that have been designed and evaluated by researchers – this means that practitioners are constructed as users of expert knowledge, not as knowledge creators.

In an earlier era, this approach involved systematic reviews of research findings that were expected to facilitate evidence-based policymaking and practice. Institutional moves were made to increase the production of such reviews; for example, the Evidence for Policy and Practice Information Coordinating Centre established at the Institute for Education, University of London. Commenting on these developments, Hammersley (2001) expresses concerns about the rather instrumental model they present of the relationship between research and practice. He also argues that there are serious questions about whether research can deliver on all of this effectively and about the effects of trying to make it fulfil this function. Specifically, it is not proven that providing solutions to practical problems, or evaluating them, is the most important contribution which research can make to policy-making and practice. Furthermore, he argues, it involves a search for technical solutions to what may well be political or social problems.

My own concern is that the what works movement adopts a view of the role of educational research which can undermine practitioners' expertise because it privileges research evidence. In contrast, we have argued for the use of inquiry-based approaches, which might well incorporate evidence from academic research, to address the technical, cultural and political aspects of change (Ainscow et al. 2020).

More recently, a massive investment has taken place in England using what works thinking through the Education Endowment Foundation (EEF), an independent charity which 'is dedicated to breaking the link between family income and educational achievement, ensuring that children from all backgrounds can fulfil their potential and make the most of their talents'.[6] Most of the studies commissioned by EEF involve randomised controlled trials – meaning that children have to be separated into different groups so that the impact of a specific programme or teaching method can be compared with the progress of their peers who do not experience it. Within the research community, however, there is considerable debate about the appropriateness and effectiveness of such research designs (e.g. Connolly et al. 2018; Siddiqui et al. 2018). They can work well, it is argued, for interventions with a simple causal model and where there is good reason to believe that any improvements can be directly attributed to the intervention – for instance, because it is tightly defined, with easily measured outcomes, specified target groups and implemented in controlled contexts. Such evaluations are, however, ill-suited

---

[6] see https://educationendowmentfoundation.org.uk/

to more complex interventions which seek to address 'wicked problems' (Rittel and Webber 1973). As with the projects described in this chapter, these may involve complex, evolving and iterative causal pathways, requiring multiple partners working together to improve multiple, interrelated outcomes, in open and changing environments, over extended time scales.

None of this is to argue against the value of experimental designs per se – when applied appropriately, they undoubtedly have a role to play in supporting schools to improve student outcomes. However, the worry is that the pervasive and narrowly-formulated understanding of what works is limiting the system's capacity for development, particularly in relation to the challenge of equity.

A related concern is that the challenges involved in promoting equity within unequal societies becomes reduced to a search for more effective technical responses. In this way, it becomes relatively easy to blame schools and teachers for failing their students. In so doing, this distracts attention away from wider community issues that need to be addressed, not least the impact of poverty, as well as the resources that are there within those communities. At the same time, this also overlooks the expertise that is always there within any education system and which must surely be the starting point for professional learning and organisational development.

2.8 FINAL THOUGHTS

Whilst the examples described in this chapter are set in the United Kingdom, I believe that the ideas presented about educational change are relevant to all countries, not least because of the emphasis placed on the importance of contextual analysis. At a time when countries around the world are seeking to address issues related to inclusion and equity raised by the UNESCO Education 2030 Framework for Action, these recommendations seem particularly pertinent. Indeed, they have been incorporated in a recent guidance document that is now being used internationally (UNESCO 2017).

The sorts of barriers that I have described continue to impact on efforts to use research knowledge to guide educational change in both the developed and developing world. The implication is that changes have to be made in the way education systems operate in order to create the organisational conditions within which new thinking based on formal research can be accommodated. Without this, even the most sophisticated ideas and strategies are likely to be ignored or dismissed.

The involvement of university colleagues points to the nature of the conditions that need to be encouraged. In particular, they illustrate the relationships that have to be created amongst practitioners, policymakers and academic researchers. By and large, these are not based on a technical–rational process through which research-based knowledge is presented to practitioners in the hope that this will then be used to guide decision-making and action. Rather, they involve a rather messy social learning process, within which researcher expertise and perspectives are brought together with the knowledge of colleagues in the field. Where this works, it can lead to the development of new, context-specific knowledge that can support change processes.

The implication is that successful change requires the coming together of different perspectives and experiences in a process of social learning and knowledge creation within particular settings. Researchers who get involved in such processes must expect to face many difficulties and dilemmas. Consequently, they have to develop new skills in creating collaborative partnerships that cross borders between actors who have different professional experiences.

The different roles and socio-cultural contexts of policymakers/practitioners and academics create a complex set of power relations, which have to be factored into the process of introducing ideas from research. This reveals how those who work in the field derive their power from being primary actors: they can cause things to happen or to cease to happen in a way that is denied to academics. Meanwhile, researchers derive their power from standing at a distance: they can problematise the actions of practitioners and policymakers.

At their most productive, these power relationships lead to dialogue in which the academics' views are informed by the realities of practice, and practitioners' views change in response to 'outsider' critique. At their least productive, academics mistake their distant position for superiority, and claim moral and intellectual authority over practitioners; while practitioners dismiss academics as being unworldly and resist their critiques. Managing these relationships is crucial to the success of attempts to use research knowledge to guide the improvement of policy and practice in the field.

ACKNOWLEDGEMENTS

Many colleagues have contributed to the work reported in this chapter. Particular thanks go to Chris Chapman and Mark Hadfield, who were closely involved in the analysis of the evidence that I have used.

References

Ainscow, M. (2012). Moving knowledge around: Strategies for fostering equity within educational systems. *Journal of Educational Change*, 13:3, 289–310.

Ainscow, M. (2013). Developing more equitable education systems: Reflections on a three-year improvement initiative. In Farnsworth, V. and Solomon, Y. (eds.) *What Works in Education? Bridging Theory and Practice in Research*. London: Routledge, pp. 77–89.

Ainscow, M. (2015). *Towards Self-improving School Systems: Lessons from a City Challenge*. London: Routledge.

Ainscow, M. (2016). Schools Challenge Cymru: A catalyst for change? *Wales Journal of Education*, 1:1, 6–22.

Ainscow, M., Chapman, C. and Hadfield, M. (2020) *Changing Education Systems: A Research-Based Approach*. London: Routledge.

Ainscow, M., Hargreaves, D. H. and Hopkins, D. (1995). Mapping the process of change in schools: The development of six new research techniques. *Evaluation and Research in Education*, 9:2, 75–89.

Armstrong, P. and Ainscow, M. (2018). School-to-school support within a competitive education system: Views from the inside. *School Effectiveness, School Improvement*, 29:4, 614–33.

Au, W. (2009). *Unequal by Design: High-Stakes Testing and the Standardization of Inequality*. London: Routledge.

Benn, M. and Millar, F. (2006). *A Comprehensive Future: Quality and Equality for All of Our Children*. London: Compass.

Burgess, S. (2014). *Understanding the Success of London's Schools*. Bristol: CMPO Working Paper No.14/333.

Carr, C., Brown, S. and Morris, M. (2017). *Assessing the Contribution of Schools Challenge Cymru to Outcomes Achieved by Pathways to Success Schools*. Cardiff: Welsh Government.

Chapman, C. and Ainscow, M. (2019). Using research to promote equity within education systems: Possibilities and barriers. *British Education Research Journal*, 45:5, 899–917.

Claeys, A., Kempton, J. and Paterson, C. (2014). *Regional Challenges: A Collaborative Approach to Improving Education*. London: Centre Forum.

Connolly, P., Keenan, C. and Urbanska, K. (2018). The trials of evidence-based practice in education: A systematic review of randomised controlled trials in education research 1980–2016. *Educational Research*, 60:3, 272–91.

Hadfield, M. and Ainscow, M. (2018). Inside a self-improving school system: Collaboration, competition and transition. *Journal of Educational Change*, 19:4, 441–62.

Hadfield, M. and Jopling, M. (2018). Case study as a means of evaluating the impact of early years leaders: Steps, paths and routes. *Evaluation and Program Planning*, 67, 167–76.

Hammersley, M. (2001). On 'systematic' reviews of research literatures: A 'narrative' response to Evans & Bene. *British Educational Research Journal*, 27:5, 543–54.

Hutchings, M., Hollingworth, S., Mansaray, A., Rose, R. and Greenwood, C. (2012). *Research Report DFE-RR215: Evaluation of the City Challenge Programme*. London: Department for Education.

Kahlenberg, R. D. and Potter, H. (2014). *A Smarter Charter: Finding What Works for Charter Schools and Public Education*. New York: Teachers College Press.

Kerr, K. and West, M. (eds.) (2010). *Social Inequality: Can Schools Narrow the Gap?* Macclesfield: British Education Research Association, Insight 2.

Kidson, M. and Norris, E. (2014). *Implementing the London Challenge.* London: Joseph Rowntree Foundation.

Lowe, J. (2015). The London schools revolution: Something remarkable has happened in the capital's schools. *Prospect Magazine,* February 2015.

Lubienski, C. (2003). Innovation in education markets: Theory and evidence on the impact of competition and choice in Charter Schools. *American Education Research Journal,* 40:2, 395–443.

McEwan, P. J. and Carnoy, M. (2000). The effectiveness and efficiency of private schools in Chile's voucher system. *Educational Evaluation and Policy Analysis,* 22:3, 213–39.

OECD. (2012). *Equity and Quality in Education: Supporting Disadvantaged Students and Schools.* Paris: OECD.

OECD. (2014). *Improving Schools in Wales: An OECD Perspective.* Paris: OECD Publishing.

Pickett, K. and Vanderbloemen, L. (2015). *Mind the Gap: Tackling Social and Educational Inequality.* York: Cambridge Primary Review Trust.

Rittel, H. J. W. and Webber, M. M. (1973). Dilemmas in a general theory of planning. *Policy Sciences,* 4, 155–69.

Sabel, C., Saxenian, A., Miettinen, R., Kristenson, P. H. and Hautamaki, J. (2011). *Individualized Service Provision in the New Welfare State: Lessons from Special Education in Finland.* Helsinki: SITRA.

Salokangas, M. and Ainscow, M. (2017). *Inside the Autonomous School: Making Sense of a Global Educational Trend.* London: Routledge.

Schildkamp, K., Ehren, M. and Kuin Lai, M. K. (2012). Editorial article for the special issue on data-based decision making around the world: From policy to practice to results. *School Effectiveness and School Improvement,* 23:2, 123–31.

Siddiqui, N., Gorard, S. and See, B. H. (2018). The importance of process evaluation for randomised control trials in education. *Educational Research,* 60:3, 357–70.

Takala, M., Pirttimaa, R. and Tormane, M. (2009). Inclusive special education: The role of special education teachers in Finland. *British Educational Journal of Special Education,* 36:3, 162–72.

UNESCO. (2017). *Ensuring Inclusion and Equity in Education.* Paris: UNESCO.

Weick, K. E. (1985). Sources of order in underorganised systems: Themes in recent organisational theory. In Lincoln, Y. S. (ed.) *Organisational Theory and Inquiry.* Beverley Hills: Sage, pp. 106–37.

Whitty, G. (2010). *Marketization and Post-Marketization in Education.* In Hargreaves, A., Lieberman, A., Fullan, M. and Hopkins, D. (eds.) *Second International Handbook of Educational Change.* Dordrecht: Springer, pp. 405–13.

Wiborg, S. (2010). *Swedish Free Schools: Do They Work?* Centre for Learning and Life Chances in Knowledge Economies and Societies. Available at: www.llakes.org (accessed 12 June 2012).

3 A Decade of Reform in Hong Kong

Mary James

3.1 INTRODUCTION

In 2002 Hong Kong embarked on a bold and radical ten-year programme of pre-primary, primary, secondary and tertiary educational reform, focusing on curriculum, pedagogy and assessment, with profound implications for all aspects of the educational system. The main aims of the reforms were to broaden and deepen students' educational experiences in order to develop their all-round capabilities and dispositions towards lifelong learning in a rapidly changing globalised world and to strengthen their ability to contribute to the continued growth of Hong Kong as a vibrant economy at the interface between East and West. These aims were shaped by personal, social and economic purposes – a familiar trilogy for many educational reform programmes.

3.2 POLICY CONTEXT AND STRUCTURAL CHANGE

Hong Kong is a Special Administrative Region (SAR) of the People's Republic of China (PRC). It has a population of approximately 7.5 million, concentrated in 1,105.7 square kilometres of territory (Greater London's population is about 8.7 million in 1,572 square kilometres). The fertility rate is low and declining (1.20, compared to UK's 1.80) but the population is rising because of inflow of one-way permit holders from Mainland China (42,300 in 2018).

The SAR was established on 1 July 1997 when Hong Kong ceased to be a British colony and was returned to Chinese sovereignty. This was a hugely significant event in the history of Hong Kong's education system, which had been modelled on the British one. The Sino-British Joint Declaration acknowledged that the existing education system would remain essentially unchanged after handover. However, the constitutional document for the HKSAR (the Basic Law), which stipulates a policy of 'One Country, Two Systems', promised a high degree of autonomy in the way Hong Kong would be ruled. Perceiving a need to manage the transition from manufacturing to a knowledge-based service economy based on financial and trading services, the HKSAR Government sought to improve education. One overarching idea was to position Hong Kong as a 'Regional Education Hub' where East meets West and where students are prepared to meet the challenges of a globalised world.

Both before and after handover, the provision of schooling has been diverse based on the steadfast policy to allow some flexibility of choice in schooling and curricula. There are government schools, aided schools run by voluntary bodies (where students do not have to pay), direct subsidised schools (funded by government but where students have to pay) and private schools, some with Government assistance. The first two categories offer free education and deliver the Government's recommended curriculum. Direct subsidy schools can offer non-local curricula, such as iGCSE or the International Baccalaureate, for up to 50 per cent of their students. There are also fifty-one international schools offering non-local curricula, mainly to children of overseas families.

Under the old British system, education was highly selective and elitist. Children were only entitled to nine years of education (to age fourteen) and access to senior secondary education, leading to sixteen+ and eighteen+ qualifications, was limited to one third of the cohort, regardless of their potential to succeeed in Hong Kong's school examination system. Access to the highest of (then) five bands of secondary schools, which allowed progression to senior secondary schooling, was determined by (eleven+) tests at the end of primary schooling. All of these features had been adopted from the pre-1965 British system of selection for grammar schools.

Something had to be done, not only to provide fairer access to senior secondary education but to broaden and deepen the educational experience and achievements of all students in order to meet the challenges of a complex twenty-first-century social and economic environment, locally and globally, and to sustain the development of Hong Kong.

Before handover, the HK Government set up the Education Commission (EC), the most important education advisory body in Hong Kong, made up of representatives of stakeholders. In 2000, after extensive consultation, the EC published a report, *Learning for Life, Learning through Life – Reform Proposals for the Education System in Hong Kong*. This was to set the future direction for radical, root-and-branch reform.[1] For the first time in Hong Kong, it articlated the broader purpose of promoting the all-round (whole person) development of all students, according to their abilities, and to promote their life-long learning. In contrast to the old system, this was premised on the belief that all students can learn and succeed if given appropriate opportunities and that they should be prepared for learning throughout their life as circumstances change. Students were to be encouraged to develop a heightened sense of agency and greater independence in their learning through changes in teaching reducing reliance on rote learning of the content of textbooks and drilling for tests and examinations.

In order to accomplish these goals, major changes in the structure of the education system were needed. The first decision was to create an entitlement to twelve years of free education for all students, from age five to seventeen. This included the introduction from 2009, of a new 3+3+4 academic structure (NAS) for post-primary education. This represents three years of junior secondary education, building on the basic education of six years of primary education. The next three years of senior secondary education was introduced as an entitlement for all students, including those with 'intellectual disabilities'. Previously there had been no senior secondary curriculum provision for students with special educational needs, so their inclusion in the new senior secondary (NSS) curriculum reform programme generated a great deal of debate and successive changes in language and provision. As with all mainstream students, they too would be encouraged to work towards a new, inclusive, Hong Kong Diploma of Secondary Education (HKDSE), to be completed at age seventeen. Four years of higher education would then follow for those accepted for local universities and many universities in other countries, including Mainland China. This was a radical departure from the old 5+2+3 structure which replicated the English model, i.e. five years secondary education, concluding with the Hong Kong Certificate of Education Examination (HKCEE, equivalent to the old GCE O Level in England), followed by two years of education, to eighteen or nineteen years of age, preparing for the HKALE (Hong Kong Advanced Level Examination, equivalent to the GCE A Level in England), followed by a three year degree course which was then the standard in Hong Kong and English universities.

Although part of the motivation for the NAS in Hong Kong was a perceived need to bring the HKSAR into line with academic structures

---

[1] An English Language version can be found at: www.info.gov.hk/archive/consult/2000/Full-Eng.pdf, last accessed March 2021.

elsewhere (other than England and Wales) there were good educational reasons as well. The professional executive branch, the Education Bureau (EDB), tasked with implementing these changes, was well aware of educational debate, proposals and developments elsewhere in the world, including Mike Tomlinson's 2004 proposals for a unified framework for fourteen–nineteen learning in England.[2] Of special concern was the need to create multiple pathways for secondary school graduates because drop-out rates were considered too high under the old system. Not only was there an expectation of better access to higher education (bachelor's degrees, sub-degrees, distance learning) but also access to vocational programmes and the workplace, at home and abroad. A range of one-year diplomas, acting like a foundation year, was introduced to enable students to come back into the university system in the second year of the new four-year courses. One of the greatest successes of the 3+3+4 NAS has been increases in staying-on rates. A survey of students who left secondary education in 2012, the first year of the HKDSE, indicates that around 88 per cent of 59,871 respondents from 432 schools (90.8 per cent of all schools) continued to further studies locally or outside of Hong Kong.[3]

3.3 CHANGES IN CURRICULUM AND ASSESSMENT

Changes in educational goals and academic structures required fundamental changes in curriculum and assessment. These changes began formally in 2001 when the Curriculum Development Council (CDC), the freestanding advisory body to Government on curriculum matters, published a blueprint taking forward the recommendations of the Education Commission in 2000. The CDC document was entitled *Learning to Learn – The Way Forward in Curriculum Development*.[4] 'Learning to Learn' subsequently became the label by which the reforms are known. The current iteration is referred to as *Learning to Learn 2.0*.

In terms of implementation, reforms were introduced progressively, starting in 2002 with changes to basic education in primary and junior secondary. Then, in 2009, the NSS was introduced, with the first 'graduates'

---

[2] This can be downloaded from: www.educationengland.org.uk/documents/pdfs/2004-tomlinson-report.pdf, last accessed March 2021.

[3] http://334.edb.hkedcity.net/doc/eng/FullReport.pdf, last accessed March 2021.

[4] A web edition can be found at: www.edb.gov.hk/en/curriculum-development/cs-curriculum-doc-report/wf-in-cur/, last accessed March 2021.

of the HKDSE emerging in 2012. Those who then went on to four-year university degree programmes graduated, for the first time, in 2016.

3.3.1 Basic Education (Primary 1 to Secondary 3)

The reforms to basic education were premised on five essential learning experiences to promote whole-person development: moral and civic development; intellectual development; community service; physical and aesthetic development; and career-related experiences. The new curriculum framework has eight Key Learning Areas (KLAs): Chinese language; English language; mathematics; personal, social and humanities education; science; technology; arts; and physical education. Running across the KLAs are Generic Skills (communication, critical thinking, creativity, collaboration, ICT, numeracy, self-management and study skills) and Values and Attitudes (perseverance, respect for others, responsibility, national identity and commitment). 'National identity' has been the most controversial element.

Given the scale and reach of the reforms, a whole school approach to curriculum development was encouraged. To this end, an extensive programme of professional development (PD) was implemented for head teachers, curriculum/KLA co-ordinators, moral and civic education co-ordinators, subject leaders (including in primary schools) and new teachers. Foci of PD programmes for 2002 to 2007 included: curriculum leadership in KLAs; managing change; four key tasks (reading to learn, IT for interactive learning, moral and civic education, project learning); generic skills (critical thinking and creativity); assessment for learning; school-based curriculum development; whole school curriculum planning and implementation; catering for learner diversity; and diversified modes of assessment for improving student learning.

PD activity was also supported by a wealth of new materials: a general curriculum guide; exemplars of curriculum development in schools; KLA curriculum guides; subject curriculum guides; and learning and teaching resources (teaching kits, videos, tapes, CD-Roms, booklets, leaflets and reports). The use of 'approved' textbooks had always been a feature of HK schools. This continued but was de-emphasised to encourage school-based development and reduce dependency.

At the time of writing, Hong Kong retains a Territory-wide Assessment (TSA), which tests basic competences in Chinese language, English language and mathematics at the ends of Primary 3, Primary 6 and Secondary 3. The aggregated results at territory-level and school-level are shared with schools for the improvement of learning and teaching and to guide government support to schools. No student's individual results are revealed. However, TSAs have been controversial because of the familiar washback effect on teaching and the pressures on students in a long-established culture of competitive achievement.

Secondary school place allocation at age eleven is not determined by Primary 6 TSA results. These decisions are now settled mainly through neighbourhood catchment areas and parental choice. Three bands of schools still exist. Moving to a fully comprehensive system was a political 'bridge too far' in 2001. However, the worse effects have been mitigated, to some extent, by the fact that the HKDSE is open to all senior secondary students and it is possible for students to achieve highly if their schools provide the appropriate courses and opportunities.

'Assessment for learning' is heavily promoted and prioritised in basic education, although the frequent-testing culture at classroom level is difficult to shift. The quality of teaching and learning is monitored through inspection, although here too developmental purposes are emphasised.

3.3.2 New Senior Secondary (Secondary 4 to 6)

In 2009, having progressed through the new arrangements for basic education, the first students entered the New Senior Secondary (NSS) programme.

The coordinated approach to reform of education in Hong Kong made coherence a key objective: coherence across curriculum, pedagogy and assessment; and coherence across the phases of education. To this end, agreement to a set of common principles and learning goals was essential. In a joint Medium-term Review (MTR) in 2015,[5] the Curriculum Development Council (CDC), the Hong Kong Examinations and Assessment Authority (HKEAA) and the Education Bureau (EDB) reiterated the overarching aim that the reforms should:

> ... provide all students with essential lifelong learning experiences for whole-person development in the domains of ethics, intellect, physical development, social skills and aesthetics, according to individual potential, so that all students can become active, responsible and contributing members of society, the nation and the world. (p. 3)

[5] http://334.edb.hkedcity.net/doc/eng/MTR_Report_e.pdf, last accessed March 2021.

In line with this general aim, the MTR report (p. 4) also re-confirmed seven learning goals. Students should:

- be biliterate (Chinese and English) and trilingual (Cantonese, Putonghua/Mandarin, English) with adequate proficiency;

- acquire a broad knowledge base and be able to understand contemporary issues that may impact on daily life at personal, community, national and global levels;

- be informed and responsible citizens with a sense of global and national identity;

- respect pluralism of cultures and views and be critical, reflective and independent thinkers;

- acquire information technology (IT) and other generic skills as necessary for being lifelong learners;

- understand their own career/academic aspirations and develop positive attitudes towards work and learning; and

- lead a healthy lifestyle with active participation in aesthetic and physical activities.

To these ends, a NSS was constructed comprising core subjects, elective subjects, applied learning, other languages and other learning experiences (OLE).

There are four subjects in the core: Chinese language, English language, mathematics and liberal studies. Mathematics has two parts: a Compulsory Part and an Extended Part. The Extended Part has two options: Module 1 (calculus and statistics) and Module 2 (algebra and calculus). As the labels imply, only the Compulsory Part is considered an essential part of the core and included in outcome measures for this element of the curriculum. The Medium-term Review recommended that, for those students taking the Extended Part, the results should be considered as a separate elective subject. In some respect it is comparable to Further Mathematics in the UK A Level.

Science is not part of the core. This is not unusual in countries where there is an expectation that a second language should be learned alongside the first language and mathematics. One could also argue that in Hong Kong there is no need to make sciences compulsory because they have always been both high status and popular, with high numbers of candidates for examination.

It is worth mentioning the reasons for including Liberal Studies (LS) in the core. In line with the overall aims and goals of the educational reforms, the explicit aim of LS has been to broaden the knowledge base of all students and enhance their social, national and global awareness, as well as developing their ability to examine a wide range of issues from multiple perspectives. Special attention has been paid to developing creative and critical thinking skills, demonstrated primarily through an independent enquiry study (IES).

Elective subjects include twenty more established academic senior secondary (SS) subjects. The knowledge content of established academic subjects does not differ radically from similar courses elsewhere, for example, UK A Levels. What is more radical is the structure of, and access to, the HKDSE as a whole, its overall aims and approach and the attention given to skills, processes, values and attitudes in the curriculum guides for each subject.[6]

Students can also elect to study other languages, and French, German, Hindi, Japanese, Spanish and Urdu are offered. There is also a wide range of Applied Learning (ApL) subjects. ApL subjects aim at enabling students to understand fundamental theories and concepts through application and practice as well as developing their generic skills in an authentic work situation. They have a more vocational orientation. Aviation studies and healthcare practice were the most popular subjects in these categories in 2016 and 2017.

The wide range of NSS subjects available is intended to provide for a broad and balanced curriculum, allowing students to select academic subjects, more vocationally oriented subjects or a combination of both. Thus, any number of combinations is possible, all leading to the common HKDSE. However, schools select from the range of subjects according to their local context and their assessment of their students' needs. Schools in different bands and different contexts offer different subject choices and HKDSE entry levels. Annual surveys by the EDB indicate that schools in general offer ten to twelve electives each. Students are expected to choose two or three electives, in addition to the four core subjects. The Medium-term Review report in 2015 noted that students are now taking fewer electives (usually two) in order to better manage their workload across at least six (but no more than eight) formally assessed subjects. This is roughly the equivalent of six to eight A Levels, against which the core and electives are benchmarked.

Building on the foundation of the learning experiences gained in basic education, Other Learning Experiences (OLE) is considered to be an essential

---

[6] Subject details can be found at: https://cd1.edb.hkedcity.net/cd/cns/sscg_web/html/english/main00.html, last accessed March 2021.

part of the senior secondary curriculum. OLE provides activities in five areas: moral and civic education; career-related experiences; community service; aesthetic development; and physical development. Achievements in these areas are not formally assessed but students are encouraged to develop their own Student Learning Profile (SLP) as a record of, and reflection on, their own learning journey. Achievements in out-of-school competitions and activities may be included in an SLP. The primary purpose is to broaden the scope of learning, personal development and self-evaluation. The SLP should also serve as a reference when applying for admission to post-secondary and university education and employment. This is somewhat reminiscent of the National Record of Achievement that was introduced in schools in England and Wales in 1991 but fell out of use as political priorities changed.

3.4 CURRICULUM GUIDES

As with Basic Education, the framework for the New Senior Secondary curriculum is elaborated in curriculum guides. These set out the aims for each subject area and give details of what should be learned (teaching intentions) and what students should be able to do (learning outcomes). The guides make clear that what is to be learned is more than knowledge and understanding. Skills, processes, values and attitudes are considered to be equally important. For example, the broad aims of the physics curriculum are given as:

- To develop interest in the physical world and maintain a sense of wonder and curiosity about it;

- To construct and apply knowledge of physics, and appreciate the relation-ship between physical science and other disciplines;

- To appreciate and understand the nature of science in physics-related contexts;

- To develop skills for making scientific inquiries;

- To develop the ability to think scientifically, critically and creatively, and to solve problems individually or collaboratively in physics-related contexts;

- To understand the language of science and communicate ideas and views on physics-related issues;

- To make informed decisions and judgements on physics-related issues; and

- To be aware of the social, ethical, economic, environmental and techno-logical implications of physics and develop an attitude of responsible citizenship.[7]

The curriculum guides do not stop at subject aims, content and learning targets. They also provide substantial advice to schools and teachers on: curriculum planning (e.g. suggested learning sequences, adaptations for learner diversity); pedagogy (e.g. scaffolding, flexible grouping); assessment (e.g. formative and summative); and resources (e.g. textbook selection, use of new technologies). What comes over clearly is the extent to which these guides have been informed by the vision, knowledge and experience of professional educators and educational researchers, whilst not ignoring the needs and wishes of the wider community.

3.5 THE HONG KONG DIPLOMA OF SECONDARY EDUCATION (HKDSE)

The HKDSE certificate is, in essence, a profile that records the range of experiences and achievements of students in their senior secondary (SS) schooling. The way in which the various subjects are assessed and reported differs according to the category in which they are placed. There are three such categories: A, B and C.

3.5.1 Category A, Senior Secondary (SS) Subjects, Including the Four Core Subjects and the Twenty Elective Subjects

The HKDSE examination in these subjects adopts a standards-referenced reporting (SRR) system (as do the TSAs mentioned in Section 3.3.2). Student performance is assessed according to a detailed set of prescribed descriptors that define the typical performance of students at each of five levels (Levels 1–5).[8] At the high end of the scale, Level 5 is subdivided into three (5, 5*, 5**).

The HKEAA undertook an extensive international benchmarking exercise in order to set the levels for Category A subjects. This provided evidence for its claim that Level 5 is equivalent to Grade A in UK Advanced Level

---

[7] https://334.edb.hkedcity.net/new/doc/chi/curriculum2015/Phy_CAGuide_e_2015.pdf, section 1.4, last accessed March 2021.

[8] For more detail see: www.hkeaa.edu.hk/en/HKDSE/assessment/the_reporting_system/SRR/#generic, last accessed March 2021.

examinations, and that Level 5* is equivalent to Grade A*. Level 5** exceeds Grade A* but was seen as necessary in order to meet the increasing demands of some elite universities for the highest quality graduates from the school system. There were some suggestions that 5** should be abolished, arguing that this had aggravated the washback effect of the HKDSE Examination on student learning; it had accelerated competition for the highest grades in an already highly competitive environment. However, tertiary institutions supported the use of Level 5** for admissions purposes. So, it was recommended that the current system of grading should be retained, subject to further analysis of results and review.

An important feature of assessment under the NSS framework has been the introduction of moderated school-based assessment (SBA) as a component in the public examination.[9] This involves teachers in assessing certain aspects of students' work (e.g. investigations in science) in their own classrooms using guidelines, assessment criteria and exemplars supplied by the HKEAA. The HKEAA also trains teachers in SBA. Assessed work is then submitted to the HKEAA for moderation. In 2012, the first year of the HKDSE, SBA was implemented in arts and humanities subjects, and to a partial extent in biology, chemistry, physics, combined science and integrated science. SBA is thought to have several advantages: it can reflect the development of individual learning over the whole course; it enables assessment of skills difficult to assess through conventional public examination (e.g. laboratory work); and it enables ongoing feedback for students' subsequent learning (i.e. 'assessment for learning'). As with debates about coursework assessment in the UK and elsewhere, the introduction of SBA presented challenges, mainly in terms of the perceived increase in workload for students and teachers, although there were also concerns about drilling for standard assignments. Interestingly, few concerns were expressed about the dependability of results of the SBA component; the majority of schools implemented appropriate procedures and moderated standards were also found to be generally robust. The Education Bureau appears to remain committed to SBA on educational grounds, although concerns about workload led to recommendations being put in place: cancelling SBA in some subjects and deferring it in others. In 2019, SBA was not implemented in mathematics, Chinese history or in history. In most core and elective subjects, except the arts and technology, SBA contributes 20 per cent of the marks awarded in the HKDSE.

[9] Information on this can be found at: www.hkeaa.edu.hk/DocLibrary/Media/Leaflets/SBA_pamphlet_E_web.pdf, last accessed March 2021.

3.5.2 Category B, Applied Learning (ApL) Subjects

ApL subjects are offered by providers of these courses, who also undertake the assessments of these subjects. These are often located in tertiary institutions in Hong Kong. This represents important collaborations between schools and further education and vocational providers. The assessment results are moderated by the HKEAA to ensure consistency in standards. These results are then recorded on the student's HKDSE certificate. Two levels of performance are recorded: 'Attained' and 'Attained with Distinction'. The latter is deemed to be equivalent to performance at Level 3 in Category A subjects.

3.5.3 Category C, Other Language Subjects

The six Other Language Subjects are examined through the Advanced Subsidiary (AS) Examination of Cambridge International Examinations (CIE) but administered by HKEAA. Marking and grading are conducted by CIE. Results are reported using the current five grades (A–E) used in the United Kingdom.

3.6 UNIVERSITY ADMISSION REQUIREMENTS AND RECOGNITION

The minimum entrance requirement for undergraduate programmes offered in Hong Kong is Level 3 for Chinese Language and English Language and Level 2 for Mathematics Compulsory Part and Liberal Studies. This is known as the '3,3,2,2' profile. Individual institutions, faculties or programmes then determine the attainment level required for one or more elective subjects. Associate Degree (c.f. UK foundation degrees) or Higher Diploma programmes have a slightly lower entrance requirement, accepting Level 2 in five HKDSE subjects, including English and Chinese. A maximum of two ApL subjects at 'Attained' Level can also be accepted.

Securing agreement on admission requirements to universities and post-secondary studies has been crucial for the success of Hong Kong's reform programme. This was achieved only through a lengthy and often difficult process of negotiation.

The HKEAA has also worked closely with international bodies to secure recognition of the HKDSE by non-local and overseas institutions. For example, a study of the HKDSE qualification in 2009 by the Universities and Colleges Admission Service (UCAS) in the United Kingdom set up a tariff points system for HKDSE results. Points have been awarded from Level 3 to Level 5* in all twenty-four core and elective subjects.[10] The HKEAA also worked with the UK National Recognition Information Centre (NARIC) to validate and endorse the HKDSE for general education and employment. The 2010 NARIC report indicates that a wide range of competency is covered in the HKDSE, with Levels 3–5 emphasising sophisticated application of subject knowledge. The NARIC report affirms comparability with standards in the former HK A Level examination.[11] A very important point to note is that HKDSE examinations are taken by students at seventeen, that is one year younger than A Levels taken formerly in Hong Kong and currently in England and Wales.

3.7 TAKE-UP AND PERFORMANCE

There is strong evidence that the reforms in Hong Kong have increased access and opportunity for students to pursue senior secondary studies and to achieve highly. The numbers of students entered and 'graduating' with the HKDSE at seventeen years of age is approximately double the number who graduated with HKALE certificates at eighteen under the old system. For example, there were 59,813 HKDSE candidates in 2015 compared with 31,002 HKALE candidates in 2011, although this had fallen back to 48,305 in 2019. What is just as remarkable is the dramatic increase in the percentage of candidates attaining the highest grades (see Table 3.1 for examples from single science subjects). This trend has continued.

Of course, generalised results tables disguise such things as entry patterns, especially gender differences. The report of the Medium-term Review of the NAS[12] noted that:

> female students, in general do better in language subjects than males, and the gap between females and males in meeting the general requirements for UGC-funded institutions may be due in part to the better performance of females in Chinese and English Languages ... even though males are performing better at Level 5 or more in mathematics and some science subjects. (p. 60)

[10] For detail see: www.hkeaa.edu.hk/DocLibrary/IR/UCAS_Factsheet_Eng.pdf, last accessed March 2021.

[11] See: www.hkeaa.edu.hk/en/recognition/benchmarking/hkdse/naric_2010/, last accessed March 2021.

[12] http://334.edb.hkedcity.net/doc/eng/MTR_Report_e.pdf, last accessed March 2021.

Table 3.1 *Percentage of equivalent high levels attained in single science subjects – final three years of HKALE compared with the first six years of HKDSE*

	HKALE			HKDSE					
	2009	2010	2011	2012	2013	2014	2015	2016	2017
	A/A*	A/A*	A/A*	5/5*/5**	5/5*/5**	5/5*/5**	5/5*/5**	5/5*/5**	5/5*/5**
Biology	2.7	2.5	2.9	15.7	17.2	17.0	18.8	18.9	19.3
Chemistry	3.5	3.3	4.0	21.0	23.3	25.1	26.4	25.6	26.6
Physics	4.0	4.1	4.7	23.8	26.2	27.2	27.1	26.5	28.9

This has been a familiar pattern in other countries and at other times. For example, similar patterns were noted in a review of research on gender and educational performance carried out over twenty years ago by Cambridge University for the UK Office for Standards in Education (Ofsted) (Arnot et al. 1998). This drew attention to evidence of a highly selective female entry for physics, indicating that females who choose subjects such as physics are very able and highly motivated. But there are too few of them. The Ofsted review also noted this 'cross-over pattern' with respect to males who took post-sixteen courses in literature, languages and history. A key issue in Hong Kong, as elsewhere, is how to tackle the continuing problem of gender-stereotyped choices of elective courses in upper secondary education. This is not only a problem for schools but also for the wider community, including universities, employers and the media.

In terms of international comparisons, the OECD's 2012 PISA Study was the first to test fifteen year-old students under the new NAS. The results suggest that with the broader and balanced curriculum, the high levels of student achievement in Hong Kong had been maintained both in terms of country ranking and in mean scores (see Table 3.2). Of the sixty-five participating countries, Hong Kong was positioned third in mathematical literacy, second in scientific literacy and second in reading literacy. It should be noted, however, that since these are tests of fifteen year olds, who would not have experienced the full range of knowledge and skills in the NSS at the time when they were tested, any claims about impact on PISA results needs to be treated with caution.

In PISA 2015, involving seventy-two countries, Hong Kong retained its second place in reading and improved its position to second in mathematics. In PISA 2018, involving seventy-nine jurisdictions, these ranks dropped back to fourth – still well above average. Mean scores have reduced slightly across

Table 3.2 *PISA results: mean scores and rank*

	Reading Literacy		Mathematical Literacy		Scientific Literacy	
	Mean score	Rank	Mean Score	Rank	Mean Score	Rank
2018	524	4	551	4	517	9
2015	527	2	548	2	523	9
2012	545	2	561	3	555	2
2009	533	4	555	3	549	3

the three subject areas. Hong Kong has also dropped to ninth place in science rankings. Several reasons have been advanced for this. The PISA assessment has changed to a computer-based one, which may have put Hong Kong students at a disadvantage because ICTs were not as widespread in Hong Kong schools as elsewhere, for example, Singapore. Another suggestion is that under the new system it is now unusual for students to take all three sciences (only 4.41 per cent do this) whereas under the old system of arts and science streams 40 per cent took three separate sciences. Whatever the reason, this situation is likely to have been a stimulus for the additional resources offered to schools by the HK Government in 2017 to support STEM subjects.

3.8 IMPACT OF SENIOR SECONDARY EDUCATION ON STUDENTS AND STUDENT OUTCOMES MORE GENERALLY

The first students to receive a HKDSE certificate left secondary school in 2012. Those progressing to the new four-year undergraduate courses graduated in 2016. As yet, only limited information about their subsequent pathways is available and it is difficult to assess the full impact of these changes on the labour market and post-graduate trajectories. Probably, the best source of evidence on the impact of the NSS reforms on students is found in the report of the CDC/HKEAA/EDB's Medium-term Review, *Continual Renewal from Strength to Strength*, published in November 2015.[13] This report was the culmination of a wide-ranging review conducted after four cycles of the NSS and HKDSE. It is mostly based on an internal evaluation, but with external advice, involving analysis of national and international outcome data

[13] http://334.edb.hkedcity.net/doc/eng/MTR_Report_e.pdf, last accessed March 2021.

and surveys, interviews and focus groups with a wide range of stakeholders. Chapter 4 of the report focuses specifically on the impact of the reforms on students. It examines the impact on their senior secondary education, further studies and employment.

The report emphasises that achievement of the seven learning goals (see Section 3.3.2) was the major intended outcome of secondary education under the NAS. In an implementation survey, well over 50 per cent of students, teachers, panel heads and school principals agreed that these learning goals had been achieved although they were least positive about students' development of a global perspective and a sense of national identity. This is not entirely surprising because issues around the teaching of national identity created controversy in Hong Kong (Morris and Vickers 2015).

Liberal Studies has attracted similar attention. The Medium-term Review indicates that this core subject has been an important means of developing students' generic skills of critical thinking and independent learning and broadening their perspectives and knowledge. For these reasons it has become highly valued by students and teachers, confirmed by independent studies (Fung and Lui 2016). Although the students and teachers in their study denied it, Fung and Lui refer to claims that Liberal Studies was used as a political instrument to instigate students' participation in the protest movement of 2014. The author of this present case study visited Hong Kong in November 2014, during these protests, known as the Occupy Central or Umbrella Movement. Students were then protesting about the decision by the Standing Committee of the National People's Congress in Beijing to rule out full universal suffrage in Hong Kong. It was clear to the author that some of those opposed to this protest placed some of the blame on the Liberal Studies curriculum and its encouragement of critical thinking around 'issues'. More generally, however, it illustrated the ongoing tensions between pro-China and pro-democracy (or some say 'populist') factions in Hong Kong, which flared up again during the very serious political crisis which began in 2019 and continues at the time of writing. In order to build consensus, designers of the new curriculum had to tread a careful course through this minefield by listening, negotiating, consulting and communicating every step of the way.

As mentioned in Section 3.7, the impact of the NSS on students' results in the HKDSE has been more than satisfactory. For example, in 2015, 2016, 2017, 2018 and 2019 over 40 per cent of day school candidates met the entrance requirements for university admission to undergraduate degree programmes in Hong Kong – something that was simply not possible under the old selective system, which restricted access to SS education to no more than 30 per cent of the population.

In 2012, Hong Kong had the interesting and challenging experience of having two cohorts of students undergoing examination and starting university at the same time. The cohort of eighteen year olds, following the former HKALE, was being examined and leaving school at the same time as the first cohort of seventeen year olds taking the HKDSE under the new NAS. In that year there were 18,302 candidates for the HKALE compared with 26,515 day-school candidates for the HKDSE, an indication of broadening access to SS qualifications – a trend that has continued.

3.9 FURTHER STUDIES AND EMPLOYMENT

Over the three-year period of the Medium-term Review more than 85 per cent of Secondary 6 students progressed to further study. In 2014, 34 per cent of students enrolled in bachelor degree programmes in Hong Kong. Others progressed to university degree courses in other countries. In 2014, 903 students were accepted at UK universities, 1,542 in Taiwan (the most popular destination), 914 in Mainland China, 509 in Australia, 314 in the US, 189 in Canada and 293 elsewhere.

A Graduate Impact Survey carried out for the Medium-term Review provided evidence that two-thirds of respondents were positive about the impact of their SS subjects on their further studies. English Language was judged to have the greatest impact although responses were positive for all core subjects. Most respondents agreed that Liberal Studies enhanced thinking skills. However, some students commented that excessive drilling for the HKDSE examinations had hindered development of their self-directed learning, which they considered crucial for post-secondary study.

Academics and registrars from tertiary institutions gave evidence to the Medium-term Review that students had made successful transitions from secondary education referencing communication skills, a readiness to speak up and to express opinions. Anecdotally, the author of this case study was told, during a visit to Hong Kong University in November 2012, that although the new entry of seventeen year old HKDSE 'graduates' were physically smaller than the eighteen year old HKALE 'graduates', who had entered together that term, it was noticeable that the younger cohort of students were more active, engaged and ready to question.

However, the Medium-term Review reported that some academics and registrars, especially those in the fields of science and engineering, noted some limitations in HKDSE graduates' knowledge base, such as core competences in mathematics and breadth of knowledge in science. In the context of significant increases in the number of students taking science subjects there is a risk of non-negligible decreases in the average academic quality of students. As might be expected, there is a 'trade off' here that needs to be considered. The educational reforms are focused on broadening and deepening all students' all-round experience and achievements. Inevitably this presents challenges to the perceptions of educators who had previously catered to an elite population about the maintenance and growth of academic excellence in a larger more broadly based cohort.

About 8 per cent of the 2014 cohort entered the workforce directly rather than continuing their studies. According to an exploratory survey of 173 employers in 2014, school leavers had met or exceeded their requirements for key skills for the workplace. They were positive about language proficiency, numeracy, generic skills and attitudes, but there were some concerns about problem-solving skills and perseverance. On the whole, however, Secondary 6 school leavers were said to be more pro-active, inquisitive, out-going and adaptable – qualities that have sometimes been regarded as lacking in more passive East Asian students.

3.10 STRESS: AN UNINTENDED CONSEQUENCE?

The Medium-term Review appears not to have explicitly explored unintended consequences of the introduction of the NAS. There is no mention of stress experienced by students. However, a spate of student suicides, in the 2015–16 school year, prompted the EDB to set up a Committee on Prevention of Student Suicides (CPSS), which was tasked to examine the possible causes of recent suicides in Hong Kong and advise on suicide prevention.[14] Suicide of students is not unique to Hong Kong; the mental health of young people is equally a problem in the United Kingdom and elsewhere. Nor is stress necessarily caused by excessive examination pressure. However, records of nine of the thirty-eight 'completed' suicide cases

[14] The final report can be found at: www.edb.gov.hk/attachment/en/student-parents/.109"/>/crisis-management/about-crisis-management/CPSS_final_report_en.pdf, last accessed March 2021.

of primary and secondary school students in Hong Kong in 2015–16 contained evidence of students' anxieties about their academic performance. Five of these students were found to show unsatisfactory academic performance but the rest had average-to-excellent academic attainment. The CPSS also noted gender differences in its analysis. Specifically, among the thirty-eight suicide cases of primary and secondary schools, twenty-four (63%) were males and fourteen (37%) were females. Boys outnumbered girls, particularly in 2015–16, with a ratio of fourteen (74%) boys to five (26%) girls. This is consistent with the global trend of males outnumbering females in completed suicides. The committee concluded that subjective perceptions as to academic performance might be an important risk factor related to suicidal behaviour.

The broad but challenging NSS curriculum in Hong Kong, in which students study six to eight core and elective subjects, each possibly with the cognitive demand of UK A Levels, can impose considerable pressure on students. Inevitably this can become stressful, particularly perhaps for those with the highest expectations of their own performance. This is something to think about both in Hong Kong and in other countries when considering this kind of curriculum and assessment model. Its great strengths have to be set against the high workload and attendant pressures and the potential for perverse unintended consequences.

3.11 IMPLEMENTATION OF THE CURRICULUM MODEL

From 2001, when the Curriculum Development Council first published its recommendations for radical reform, there had been widespread community agreement on purposes and acknowledgement that the implications for the whole system were enormous. Success required very careful preparation, subsequent evaluation and continual renewal. Agreement was secured intially, and throughout, by a great deal of communication and consultation by the Education Bureau using all available means – from 'town hall' meetings to television broadcasts and lots of print materials. This was seen as necessary because implementation would require coordinated reforms from kindergarten through to higher education, and would involve major changes in curriculum, assessment and examinations, pedagogy, student grouping, the allocation of school places, pathways through higher and vocational education, textbook approval, upgrading of plant, equipment and other resources, quality assurance and executive guidance and oversight. Above all there was a need for additional recruitment of teachers and support staff and a huge investment in teacher education and training. For example, every school principal attended a four-day introductory course. Some of this training was carried out by professionals within the EDB but much was in association with tertiary institutions such as the Hong Kong Institute of Education (HKIEd, now the Education University of Hong Kong, EdUHK). Overseas experts were also recruited for short periods as the need arose (Forestier 2011).

None of this could be accomplished without extra money and it is significant that in 2001, when HKSAR initiated its reform programme, expenditure on education, as a percentage of all government expenditure, was 22.4 per cent; in 2009, when the NSS was introduced, it was 23.8 per cent; in 2016, when the first students graduated with HKDSE, it dropped back to 18.1 per cent. For comparison, the UK Government's percentage expenditure on education in the same years was: 12.2 per cent in 2001; 12.6 per cent in 2009; and 13.9 per cent in 2016.[15]

In 2013 the CDC/HKEAA/EDB published a Short-term Review report which addressed issues in the implementation of the change.[16] At school level it highlighted the development of a whole-school approach which differed from the previous emphasis on the subject-level. From being described as examination factories, schools, it claimed, were gradually turning into professional learning communities with participation in curriculum planning, professional sharing and the development of school-based learning and teaching materials, with less dependence on textbooks, direct teaching and rote learning.

The majority of teachers were spending more time developing materials to fit students' needs, abilities and interests. However, there were obvious implications for workload and, for example, secondary schools found it challenging to deliver the NSS curriculum in the recommended time of 2,700 hours over the three years. As a direct result of this review, these hours were modified to allow more time for preparation. In response to pressure from some senior school leaders, hours for Other Learning Experiences (OLE) were decreased to 10–15 per cent of total time but elective subjects retained their allocation of 250 hours each over the three years of NSS.

In order to support the new curriculum, and especially more student-centred learning, resources were made available to alter classrooms, rearrange

---

[15] https://data.worldbank.org/indicator/SE.XPD.TOTL.GB.ZS?locations=GB, last accessed March 2021.

[16] http://334.edb.hkedcity.net/doc/eng/FullReport.pdf, last accessed March 2021.

the use of space, update equipment and enrich libraries, especially with e-resources. Human resources also needed attention and teachers were recruited for new subjects or to facilitate innovations such as split classes or small group teaching. The EDB sponsored more than 2,500 projects to develop and evaluate new practices. Small class teaching in primary schools, involving researchers from Cambridge University, was one of these.[17]

The professional development of teachers was essential to the successful implementation of the reforms and by 2011 virtually all teachers had participated in PD activities, including sharing good practice with peers from other schools. A Seconded Teachers Strategy had also been used to good effect. This network of seconded teachers, acting as curriculum developers, built a crucial bridge between EDB and schools.

By 2011, the Government had invested more than two billion Hong Kong dollars in additional funding to support the implementation of the NSS. Schools had also made good use of the Diversity Learning Grant, the Quality Education Fund and other sources of existing funding and community resources, such as the Hong Kong Jockey Club Life-wide Learning Fund.

When the new NAS reforms worked through to tertiary education, universities and other institutions also received additional resources and support to implement changes. Indeed it was the commitment of funds for new accommodation, equipment and staff that undoubtedly smoothed the transition in 2012–13 when universities had to cope with the double cohort intake.

Agencies at system level also had to change their practices because system-wide implementation required careful coordination within schools and across sectors of education. Effective support of schools, colleges and universities demanded clear communication and coordination across a wide range of agencies: the Education Commission, CDC, EDB, HKEAA, as well as overseas and Mainland agencies. Leadership was distributed through close collaboration, aided by the fact that Hong Kong's relatively small geographic area made it possible for people to meet together relatively easily. However, during the period of the reforms, an effort was made to streamline the various agencies. For example the curriculum and the quality assurance wings of the EDB were brought together in one branch under one Deputy Secretary for Education, Dr Chan. This promoted joined-up thinking between curriculum developers and school inspectors. During one visit, the author of this chapter observed joint sessions when school inspectors, seconded teachers working as

[17] www.edb.gov.hk/attachment/sc/edu-system/primary-secondary/applicable-to-primary/small-class-teaching/study_on_SCT_final_report_(dec2009).pdf, last accessed March 2021.

curriculum developers and EDB staff observed videos of classrooms and harmonised their judgements in subsequent discussions.

It is significant that Dr Chan, an educationalist rather than a bureaucrat, led much of the reform programme from 2000, until her retirement in May 2017, when she moved on to become Professor of Practice at Hong Kong University. This continuity is remarkable and it has contributed enormously to the coherence and consistency of progressive implementation.

3.12 MATTERS TO CONSIDER IN SYSTEMIC REFORM

Despite long being considered a 'high-performing jurisdiction', HKSAR took the bold decision to change just about everything in order to provide a curriculum for its students more suited to the demands of the twenty-first century. This involved not only revising curriculum and examinations but also restructuring the system and promoting a new vision and purpose with greater attention to the needs of diverse learners and a changing society. Most importantly it broadened and balanced the curriculum and promoted changes in pedagogy, placing much more emphasis on generic skills of problem-solving, independent enquiry, critical and creative thinking and team work.

Inevitably this put pressure on teachers and students as the changes were introduced, especially with regard to workload. There was always the risk that things might get worse and that Hong Kong would lose its reputation for excellence. Indeed, newspapers such as the *South China Morning Post* often carried articles and letters from critics of the reforms. However, the EDB stayed steadfastly committed to its goals and students have successfully graduated from the new system with their Hong Kong Diplomas of Secondary Education. Moreover, much is claimed to have been gained in terms of students' broader knowledge, understanding and skills and enhanced self-confidence and sense of agency. Of course, there remains much debate over the difficulty of changing a culture of competitive pressure, and of meeting the needs of children with learning difficulties and much else. These are issues that need further work because education reform involves changing cultures which takes longer than changing structures.

Nevertheless, the experience of implementing systemic reform in Hong Kong may provide encouragement or challenge to other jurisdictions that envision education reform and curriculum change. Clearly there will be substantial differences in history, geography, culture and other aspects of context, but there are likely to be similarities too. So, attention to the following insights, arising from implementation in Hong Kong, may be of benefit.

1. *It is possible to establish a coherent curriculum and assessment system, better suited to educational purposes, without sacrificing excellence.* However, there are risks that must be monitored closely, particularly if standards are to be maintained or raised. This challenge is key because the media, parents, universities, employers and other stakeholders will be watching closely and they will not be supportive if they perceive failure. This is why Hong Kong has kept its eye on international performance measures, engaged in extensive benchmarking of new qualifications and worked strenuously with universities. In the short-term, trade-offs had to be negotiated in the hope that further change might be acceptable once credibility was established. This needs steadfast focus, political will, leadership drive, professional commitment and the injection of substantial financial and human resources.

2. *A long-term educational vision matters.* The fact that Hong Kong first clarified its aims, goals and purposes for the development of the curriculum across all sectors of education, gave the reforms coherence and an essential reference point to keep them on track and focused over a relatively long period of time.

3. *Continual renewal is essential.* Whilst the aims and goals remained unchanged, the Hong Kong EDB recognised that implementation needed to negotiate obstacles and respond to new circumstances. So, by developing strategies for ongoing data gathering, analysis, evaluation and review it was able to adjust and adapt quickly. 'Continual renewal' became the mantra as the new system bedded down.

4. *Curriculum change cannot be isolated from changes in other parts of the system.* Hong Kong recognised that changes in curriculum content and examination syllabuses are, of themselves, not enough. They require accompanying changes in pedagogy and support for students with diverse needs, and these need to be planned and resourced.

5. *Professional development of teachers is crucial.* This needs to be properly supported within schools but also by providing opportunities for sharing across schools and the building of professional learning communities.

6. *Complexity of change at school level has to be reflected in more joined up thinking and collaboration at system level.* This is sometimes difficult in

countries where agencies are numerous and geographically dispersed. But, as Hong Kong attempted, there is a real need for the destruction of administrative silos and better communication and collaboration to ensure coherence across curriculum, assessment, pedagogy and accountability. Securing the agreement and co-operation of the tertiary sector and employers to the changes at school level, for example with regard to admission requirements, was crucial.

7. *Regular communication and consultation with all stakeholders needs to be continuous and genuine.* It was notable that the EDB made consultation with teachers and their unions, parents, employers, politicians, the press and with students themselves an important part of established practice. This was time-consuming and often difficult but vital to making any progress.

8. *Reform needs to be protected from political interference.* Hong Kong is essentially a one party state, so a ten-year reform plan was possible. In countries with more layers of democratic accountability, it might be important to introduce a cross-party, cross-stakeholder, advisory body, rather like Hong Kong's Education Commission (or Finland's Board of Education) to lay out proposals and to monitor implementation of longer term reforms. This would go some way to counter the turbulence that can be created by frequent changes of government. It is worth noting, however, that Hong Kong did not escape political interference, even at the height of reform activity. On 24 June 2017, at a media session, the outgoing Secretary for Education, Mr Eddie Ng Hak-kim, was asked whether he had any regrets after his five years in the post. He replied, 'In terms of regrets, actually I do feel we could have done a lot more. But the problem is political interference. It is a regret that we were not being able to make full move of things we should have done in the area of education.'[18]

3.13 POSTSCRIPT

At the time of writing, in January 2020, Hong Kong is experiencing unprecedented political crisis and civil unrest over demands for greater democracy. Young people, fearful of losing their freedoms, were at the forefront of initially peaceful protests over a badly handled attempt by the Chief

---

[18] www.info.gov.hk/gia/general/201706/24/P2017062400373.htm?fontSize=1, last accessed March 2021.

Executive, Carrie Lam, to introduce an Extradition Bill, which would allow people from Hong Kong to be extradicted to the mainland to stand trial. These weekend protests rapidly turned violent and escalated. There were accounts in the British media of infiltration by criminal elements, including Chinese triads, who may have been paid to cause maximum disorder. One possible reason was to justify crack down by the police and the imposition of 'the Rule of Law' from Beijing. On the other hand, there were local stories of 'radical', 'populist' groups, organised through social media and involving 'foreign forces', whose main objective was to discredit a Government that they regarded as subservient to Beijing.

Until this moment, although there had been adjustments, the implementation of the education reform programme had been relatively unaffected and its successes celebrated. This may not continue. Change was foreshadowed in 2017 when a new Chief Executive of Hong Kong SAR, Carrie Lam, took up the post, and a new Permanent Secretary for Education was appointed, advised by a new Education Commission. According to a leading commentator, Katherine Forestier, Lam's policy addresses on education indicate that Mainland China is the main reference point, rather than international best practices that informed the reforms in the previous fifteen years.[19]

In November 2017, Carrie Lam announced a sweeping review of the education system to be conducted by eight task forces appointed by her. At the time of writing, the indications are that elements of Liberal Studies may be an early casualty of the review of the school curriculum. In June 2019, the task group recommended that the Independent Enquiry Study be dropped,[20] ostensibly because it caused students too much stress. According to Katherine Forestier, and in the more limited experience of this author, opponents of the reforms have held Liberal Studies, in some measure, responsible for the spirit of rebellion among students witnessed in 2014 and 2019. The place of Liberal Studies in the SS core curriculum may therefore be lost, or reduced, which would be a pity considering the very good reasons it was included in the first place.

A new framework for the secondary history curriculum has already been published (in 2019) which focuses on Chinese history, with no dedicated

[19] www.scmp.com/comment/insight-opinion/article/2131727/hong-kong-education-reform-continues-beijings-role-presents, last accessed March 2021.

[20] https://yp.scmp.com/news/hong-kong/article/113470/let-hong-kong-students-drop-liberal-studies-ies-hkdse-says-education, last accessed March 2021.

section on the history of Hong Kong. Significantly also, it makes no mention of the 4 June 1989 events in Tiananmen Square.

Whether further reviews will trigger major changes to the reform programme remains to be seen. It seems unlikely given its substantial achievements. But, in these turbulant political times, across the globe, anything seems possible.

3.13.1 Post postscript

On 1 April 2021 the Education Bureau (EDB) in Hong Kong issued a circular (No: 39/2021) on measures to 'optimise' the four core subjects of the Senior Secondary curriculum, to be enacted from the 2021/2022 school year. In this memorandum Liberal Studies is renamed 'Citizenship and Social Development' and assessment is to be by written public examination graded 'attained' or 'not attained'. The Independent Enquiry Study is removed. The development of critical thinking skills is still promoted but much more emphasis is placed on the acquisition of knowledge and attitudes around national identity, national development, the Constitution, the Basic Law and rule of law. A recommended textbook is to be put in place and students are to be given opportunities to visit the Mainland. The wind was blowing this way for some time; now the influence of Beijing is obvious.

References

Arnot, M., Gray, J., James, M. and Rudduck, J., with Duveen, G. (1998). *Recent Research on Gender and Educational Performance* (OFSTED Reviews of Research series). London: The Stationery Office.

Forestier, K. (2011). *Teacher Education and Education-related Studies in Relation to Hong Kong*. Hong Kong: British Council.

Fung, D. C.-L. and Lui, W.-M. (2016). Is Liberal Studies a political instrument in the secondary school curriculum? Lessons from the Umbrella Movement in post-colonial Hong Kong. *The Curriculum Journal*, 28:2, 158–75.

Morris, P. and Vickers, E. (2015). Schooling, politics and the construction of identity in Hong Kong: the 2012 'Moral and National Education' crisis in historical context. *Comparative Education*, 51:3, 305–26.

4 Reforming a Whole School System

The Case of Kazakhstan

Colleen McLaughlin, Liz Winter, Olena Fimyar and Natallia Yakavets

4.1 INTRODUCTION

Since gaining independence from the Soviet Union in 1991, Kazakhstan has been developing its school system. The reform attempts have been divided into two main eras: 1991–2001 and 2001 to the current day. This case study focuses on the second era, where an ambitious programme was undertaken with the aim of modernising the system. The cornerstone of this programme was new practices and policies established through a network of experimental schools, the Nazarbayev Intellectual Schools (NIS), and the new Nazarbayev University. The authors of this paper have been involved in systematically researching the attitudes and perceptions towards the implementation so as to gain insight into the challenges on the ground and to learn about implementing such a radical transformation in mainstream schools. This chapter focuses upon these matters. The research was conducted with funding from Nazarbayev University.

We would like to acknowledge the full research team who all contributed to this work: L. Abdimanapova, N. Ayubayeva, D. Egea, O. Fimyar, B. Goodman, J. Helmer, D. Hernández-Torrano, Z. Jumakulov, A. Kambatyrova, Z. Khamidulina, K. Kurakbayev, Z. Makhmetova, K. Malone, T. Makoelle, C. McLaughlin, A. Ramazanova, D. Shamatov, M. Somerton, X. Tursunbayeva, M. Tynybayeva, L. Winter, N. Yakavets and Z. Zhontayeva.

4.2 THE REFORM CONTEXT

4.2.1 The Geography, People and Politics of Kazakhstan

There are key features of Kazakhstan that are particularly relevant to educational reform. The first is the geography and scale of the country; it is the ninth largest country in the world, at 2.7 million km², and landlocked between Russia to the north, China to the east, Turkmenistan, Uzbekistan and Kyrgyzstan to the south with the River Volga and the Caspian Sea to the west. The scale makes change from the centre demanding.

The second challenge is the cultural, historical and educational traditions within the country. The two state languages of Kazakh and Russian have Turkic and Slavic origins and great value is placed on these histories, on ethnic differences, on tolerance and on the importance of communication. For the years before independence in 1991, Kazakhstan was part of the Soviet Union and its traditions, educational values and practices are still to be seen in the educational system. Politically Kazakhstan has been stable since independence and the new state has engaged with the common issues of newly independent countries: expenditure, decentralisation and destabilisation, and structural anomalies (Heyneman 1998). Much new policy drew upon European models, suggesting that in developing a new national identity the country was facing both east and west (Cornell and Engvall 2017). While many in Kazakhstan see the nation as a bridge between two continents it has begun to 'identify more clearly as an integral part of the Central Asian region' (Bohr et al. 2019: viii).

4.2.2 Drivers of Change and the Big Plan

The two phases of reform were propelled by different factors. Immediately after independence the two key drivers in education were to preserve the best of the Soviet tradition and to build a new nation (Bridges 2014). There were major challenges: the sudden loss of two million citizens who left the country, limited public funds and resources for schools, coupled with outdated facilities (Yakavets 2014). There was also a desire to reform the school curriculum so that it reflected the nation's cultural and ethnic history and was more connected globally. This entailed looking at language policy, history and cultural emphases. This first phase of reform (1991–2001), while having some far-sighted policy approaches, innovations and ideas, had limited success. The change in the country's financial status, plus a desire to improve on the modest results, led to the second major 'modernisation' period (2011–20). The political drivers, such as the desire to build human capital to fuel economic progress, also influenced educational policy and thinking. These two phases are explored in more detail in Sections 4.2.3 and 4.2.4.

4.2.3 Initial Changes – From 1991 to 2011

The first decade of independence was marked by economic and fiscal crises that had devastating consequences for education: teacher shortages, lower participation rates, rundown facilities and infrastructure became the new norm (Yakavets 2014: 5). To respond to these challenges, the government initiated a major restructuring of key organisations and processes. This included the decentralisation of public spending and, on the advice of the Asian Development Bank (ADB), the closure of 3,667 pre-schools, 590 schools and half of the country's multi-graded schools, leaving 26,900 children out of school (Yakavets 2014: 18). These restructuring initiatives went in parallel with first attempts at curriculum reform, which entailed the move from mainly Russian to Kazakh as the primary language of instruction and introduced the History of Kazakhstan and Geography of Kazakhstan as school subjects.

The economic growth of the 2000s funded investments in education and educational reforms. This coincided with a new emphasis on quality education, which was directly linked to the 'nation's competitiveness'. A proliferation of legislative and policy documents followed, aimed at establishing a foundation for comprehensive reforms with aspirations to 'enter the world arena' and comply with 'world standards'. Proposals included curriculum reform, a move to twelve-year schooling and a new national assessment (the Unified National Test).[1] These last two changes are still controversial.

This first stage of reform was partial, fragmented and uncoordinated (Yakavets 2014: 21; Yakavets and Dzhadrina 2014). And, while it re-oriented the school curriculum towards a new national identity, there was still a lot to be done to modernise the education system. Despite the many proposals and actions, there were still unhelpful aspects of the Soviet legacy; an over-crowded curriculum, mechanistic teaching methods and little connection between schooling and the modern world (Steiner-Khamsi et al. 2006; Silova and Steiner-Khamsi 2008; Yakavets 2014).

---

[1] The Unified National Test (UNT) is a secondary school leaving examination and entrance exam for the higher education institutions in Kazakhstan. The test results of this examination are also considered while awarding the 'Bolashak' scholarship. This exam is held in early June.

4.2.4 Economic Prosperity and Structural Change – From 2011 to 2020

The second reform phase was more coordinated, comprehensive and radical. To respond to increased international competitiveness and growing dissatisfaction of parents and students with educational outcomes, the Kazakhstani government changed its approach. The vision and major changes are in the State Programme of Education Development (SPED) for 2011–20, which clearly articulated strategic and operational objectives for all levels of the education system and the overarching aim to improve the competitiveness of education and develop human capital for sustainable economic growth (NUGSE 2014: 17). The plan proposed a strategy for the development of secondary education, including renewing the content of secondary education and setting some timelines.

4.3 REFORM STRATEGY

To lead the reform strategy, an autonomous educational organisation, NIS and a network of schools were established and worked as beta sites for innovation, testing and the adaptation of approaches in governance, research, pedagogy, curriculum and assessment (Ruby and McLaughlin 2014).[2] It was hoped that this mechanism could bypass some of the bureaucratic hurdles inherent in state-run education reform and bring more flexibility into the system, providing arenas for experimentation and allowing innovative developments to be piloted. The NIS were to develop 'experimental grounds for development, implementation and the piloting of curriculum for kindergartens, pre-school and twelve-year education sectors' (Strategic Plan 2020) (Ministry of Education and Science of the Republic of Kazakhstan, 2010: 18).

Collaborating with a range of international partners, NIS developed a *new secondary*[3] *curriculum* based on a constructivist view of learning, competence-based education, criteria-based assessment, collaboration between teachers and schools, trilingual education, twelve-years of education and a view of the teacher as a reflective practitioner. Teacher development became a focus and a central plank of reform.

[2] Nazarbayev Intellectual Schools (NIS) are a network of schools for high ability students.
[3] Primary school is grades 1–4, secondary is grades 5–9 and high school is grades 10 and 11.

There were two main strategies for wider implementation. First, a teacher development strategy through the establishment of sixteen Centres of Excellence, one in each region, which engaged in teacher professional development. ORLEU, a national training organisation, was also involved.[4] The programmes they offered were connected to a new system of teacher appraisal or attestation which has three tiers of accreditation. The courses became known as 'the three-level training' and the successful completion of a level lead to a significant salary increase of 30 per cent (Level Three), 70 per cent (Level Two) and 100 per cent (Level One). As well as strengthening teacher expertise, the courses and salary increases addressed the issues of low status and the pedagogical qualifications of teachers. The model has been recognised by the OECD as 'ambitious and empirically-based' (OECD 2014: 177) and has been adopted by the whole country.

The second strategy was to have a range of partnerships between NIS and other schools. The first arrangement was to recruit partner schools to apply and develop NIS practice. In 2012–14 the Ministry identified thirty-five partner schools, some large and medium-sized mainstream schools, some selective Daryn schools and some small multi-graded schools.[5] These partner schools were invited to select one aspect of NIS practice, like the mentoring system, criteria-based assessment or trilingual education, and implement it on site. The partner schools were also to share their lessons learned from NIS schools with other schools in the country, initiating a wave of early adaptation of NIS experience to mainstream education. There were also thirty pilot schools which tested the new curriculum rollout a year before the national rollout in other schools.[6] The spread of the schools enabled regional piloting and spreading of practice. Later, other forms of partnership or networks were adopted to support development, such as leading schools (those considered to have the greatest degree of innovative potential).

The 'translation' of NIS experience was supported through complex networks of schools and other organisations, including the National Academy of Education (NAE), ORLEU, local executive authorities (Akimats), sixteen educational-methodological centres, the National Testing

[4] ORLEU is an autonomous organisation of the National Centre for Continuing Education – providing in-service education to teachers, school principals and educational specialists.

[5] Daryn schools are a network of selected schools for gifted and talented children.

[6] The pilot schools were mainstream public schools of different types which were selected as an experimental platform for studying and piloting innovations. Those schools were considered as studying and accepting innovative potential.

Centre, the Centre for Extra-Curricular Education, the Textbook Centre and also nineteen Higher Education Institutes (HEIs) and twenty-five Initial Teacher Education (ITE) colleges. By 2017, there were a total of 7,100 schools that were directly or indirectly adopting NIS experience.

4.3.1 Timelines

The NIS and the NAE developed the 'renewed content of education' and it was piloted in thirty schools starting in September 2015 and then rolled-out following the timeline shown in Table 4.1, where the curriculum for a grade was piloted (P), before being adapted (A) as a result of the pilot and then implemented (I) in all schools. The reforms were introduced incrementally so that learning in prior years could underpin subsequent new content and avoid a complete change in the same year, which might have overwhelmed the schools and exceeded the training capacity of the MoES (Ministry of Education and Science, of the Republic of Kazakhstan). But there were multiple entry points so that the change over to the new curriculum was to be complete in five years.

Table 4.1 *Timeline (as of 2018) of piloting and implementation of the renewed curriculum*

School year	Eleven-year (current) grades											
	Pre-primary	1	2	3	4	5	6	7	8	9	10	11
2014–15		A										
2015–16		P	A									
2016–17		I	P	A		A		A				
2017–18	A	I	I	P	A	I	A	I	A			
2018–19	P	I	I	I	P	I	I	I	I	A	A	A
2019–20	I	I	I	I	I	I	I	I	I	I	I	I
Key												
A	Adaptation by the National Academy of the NIS curriculum to mainstream schools											
P	Piloting of the renewed curriculum by thirty schools											
I	Implementation in mainstream schools											

Source: Winter et al. (2018).

The main aims of piloting were:

- testing of curricular and updated content programmes;
- testing [trial] textbooks and teaching aids;
- testing criteria-based assessment;
- introducing Continuing Professional Development (CPD) for school leaders, teachers and methodologists; and
- ongoing monitoring of the quality of teaching in the piloting mode (MoES and NAE 2015: 214).

4.3.2 What Was the Renewed Content of Education?

The principles of the renewed curriculum in Kazakhstan were:

- Applying spirality in the design of the content of the subject, that is, a gradual increase in knowledge and skills, both vertically and horizontally (the complexity of skills by topic and grade);
- Using Bloom's taxonomy of learning objectives, reconsidering and revising the aims of teaching at all layers of the educational system so that the requirements of the cross-disciplinary and spiral curriculum can be better met and maintained;
- Setting pedagogical goals at the levels of education and throughout the course of training, with the intention of making cross-subject connections where possible;
- The presence of 'cross-cutting themes' between subjects; and
- Matching the content of the curriculum to the modern world so that it is relevant to its time, for example, an emphasis on the formation of social skills.

The renewed curriculum comprised a challenging selection of subjects designed to help children and young people understand the world. A central feature of the renewed curriculum was the integration of knowledge and skills, exemplified by six learning priorities[7]:

[7] These are the key principles of the NIS curriculum – see www.nis.edu.kz/en/programs/AEO %20%E2%80%9CNazarbayev%20Intellectual%20Schools%E2%80%9D%20%E2%80%93% 20NIS-Program/

- Developing functional literacy;

- Problem-solving in maths;

- Observing, measuring and recording in science;

- Handling materials;

- Communicating in languages and literature (Kazakh/Russian/English); and

- Working with others as well as individually.

In the *study of languages* in the renewed curriculum, special emphasis was placed on a communicative approach aimed at developing *four skills*: listening, speaking, reading and writing. Grammar was studied within the framework of the proposed speech themes. A unified recitative mode, which allowed students to expand their vocabulary and to develop communication skills within the framework of integrated speech topics, was introduced in the teaching of all three languages. The subjects were taught according to the Common European Framework for Languages.[8]

The *new model of assessment* included a learning-outcomes approach through criteria-based assessment and reporting back to students and their parents through formative comments called 'rubrics' rather than daily or weekly summative grades. In addition, teachers did 'moderation' – a process of discussing students' work based on summative assessment for the academic term to standardise scoring to ensure objectivity and transparency of assessment (MoES and NAE 2017). The new assessment was a significant shift from the pervasive five-score assessment system that had been in place since the Soviet era.

Teachers' pedagogy clearly had to change to accommodate the constructivist approach and teachers had to learn to use active teaching approaches, like group work, that encourage students to think critically and develop long-term recall and a deeper understanding. These approaches were covered in the training courses at ORLEU and the NIS Centres of Excellence, which were in three-week blocks. There was also in-school training for teachers, new textbooks and teachers' manuals, as well as online resources.

In Section 4.2.4 we described the second 2011–20 wave of modernisation as a radical phase of reform. The detailed account of the new curriculum shows that it was indeed comprehensive and radical, involving the content of the

---

[8] MoES, Guidance letter for the 2015–16 academic year, p. 214.

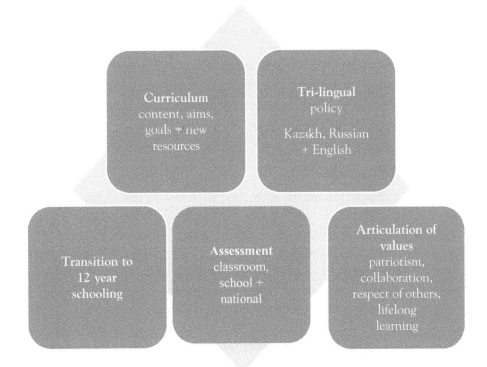

Figure 4.1 Elements of the systemic education reform in Kazakhstan

curriculum, new approaches to pedagogy, the assessment of teaching and learning as well as approaches to the aims of schooling and teaching which were very different from the Soviet model. Figure 4.1 captures the key and equally important elements of the programme of modernisation and transformation.

4.4 STAKEHOLDER RESPONSES: PERCEPTIONS OF PARTICIPANTS

This section focuses upon findings from research undertaken by a team from the University of Cambridge Faculty of Education and Nazarbayev University Graduate School of Education into stakeholder responses to such radical and sweeping reform. There were two major phases of data collection, 2016–17 in the pilot schools and 2018–19 in pilot and mainstream schools. The research projects examined the attitudes and perspectives of school teachers, school principals and other stakeholders towards the implementation of novel features of the primary curriculum and new principles and practice of assessment in pilot schools and latterly in the mainstream schools. The methods used were a survey of 1,157 teachers (2016–18) implementing the new curriculum in their classrooms; focus groups with 316 teachers, principals, vice principals and regional authorities; a task for 92 students requiring comparison of pedagogical approaches; plus 12 interviews with national policymakers and leaders.

4.4.1 General Attitudes to Reform

The need to modernise the education system was widely accepted but seen as challenging, as the renewed content of education required changes in thinking and practices. Whilst many teachers criticised the pace of implementation, those most used to the changes and those who understood the aims of the new curriculum strongly approved of them, sometimes to the point of evangelism. Those in favour specified features such as the spiral curriculum, the new model of assessment, soft skills development and the interdisciplinary nature of the curriculum, as well as active learning. While the spiral principle of the curriculum was understood, there were concerns about too many objectives to fulfil in one lesson. These reactions point to the importance of the professional development programmes undertaken.

The new curriculum, including the self-assessment element, was seen as having improved the learning environment by encouraging creativity and self-reflection and the development of research and interpersonal and communicative skills. It also enhanced the functional literacy of the child by fostering the application of knowledge to real life without dismissing the acquisition of knowledge as an end in itself.

Comments on the rationale behind the new curriculum showed an understanding of the reasons for the reform and suggested some agreement with them. The justifications given ranged from social ones, that is, that the education system and the curriculum had not caught up with modern times, to economic and educational reasons. Many referred to the need to improve Kazakhstan's position economically in the international league tables: 'Our educational system has to improve and achieve the level of developed countries'; preparing graduates for the competitive global labour market is 'very important'; or the 'Low rate of our students' level of education in international research reports'. Others emphasised the educational aims of the changes, 'Kazakhstan wants to contribute to the development of cognitive and creative skills among students, educating an individual, who will be able to think creatively and to make decisions independently in different situations' or 'to form a personality who can think critically, defend his/her opinion and apply his/her knowledge in life'.

Students reported favourably on the new developments and changes in their motivation and learning were noted. Tangible changes were reported by teachers, parents and students themselves. These included that students communicated better, had more developed thinking and social skills, could work independently and had a keener interest in their subjects. The increased student motivation concomitantly increased motivation for teachers. These, mainly positive, comments suggested that these teachers were willing to persist with the reform efforts and there were some unintended outcomes in terms of motivation. Many reported that they had an increased sense of professionalism from the greater autonomy given to them in the choice of materials and methods, for example.

> Motivation appeared. I became interested . . . And self-development . . . I like my job! . . . It is apparent that children are interested. Therefore, I am more interested too . . . (English teacher 1)

In the primary grades, in the main, implementation of the renewed content of education was reported as working well. Rolling out innovation from grade 1 forwards had been a simpler process for children and parents to assimilate than introducing changes part-way through a school career such as for children in grade 5 onwards.

4.4.2 Curriculum and Pedagogy

The qualitative data showed that many teachers and head teachers saw the new curriculum as a steep change or as one head teacher said, 'We have had change before, but this is a paradigm shift' (HT Urban school 1).

The increased autonomy and choice built into the curriculum and pedagogy, albeit limited, was highly prized. Teachers felt empowered and found the content interesting, engaging and complex in some respects. The overall approach was seen to enhance professional identity. Teachers were being asked to do different activities such as preparing their own materials, which sometimes meant finding and paying for resources. But it was also seen as professionally rewarding.

> I have worked in primary school for 30 years . . . we used to get a program, standard; we taught what was written in the textbooks. Students used to retell

what teacher said and get excellent marks. Now it seems worthless. Now teachers speak less, but help students to learn themselves; they direct, suggest and recommend by asking thought provoking questions, such as 'how did you arrive at that?' Students work in groups, cooperate. They learn from each other, especially in the group work, assess each other. (Vice principal 1)

Active learning was reported to help develop teamwork and interpersonal skills and to improve the learning performance as well as the motivation of students and teachers. However, the conditions for active learning in some schools were sometimes limiting, especially when classes were large and time and resources like internet access were limited.

Teachers in Kazakhstan have always relied heavily on textbooks. To augment the renewed curriculum, new textbooks were written and piloted. The piloting led to some important adjustments and there was less criticism of materials for use in the primary grades than in other levels of schooling. Public critiques of errors in the piloted textbooks and opposition to new paradigms in the teaching of Russian had fuelled proposals to reject the renewed content of education completely. The learning from the pilot schools and the subsequent adaptation to more accurate textbooks helped address this issue and encouraged political acceptance (as well as more ready adoption in classrooms).

4.4.3 The Trilingual Policy and English as a Medium of Instruction

An ambitious element of the reform was the introduction of the trilingual approach into the school curriculum. This proved to be the most difficult aspect of the reform. It has had to be modified considerably and is the one area of the plan that has had to be amended. There were real problems with teacher capacity and development. Teachers were not well prepared to deliver four subjects in English. Teachers with good language skills left the profession for higher paid jobs, limiting the capacity of schools to deliver the renewed programme. The support needs in trilingual teaching and learning are high, which, coupled with shortages of skilled teachers, made providing support for every student in a class hugely challenging.

The trilingual approach was also the most politically or culturally controversial aspect of the reforms. The emphasis on the importance of English was troubling for some. Several participants questioned the need for English in the north of the country, which has strong economic links with nearby Russia, and those in the south, 1,200 kilometres or more from the northern border, questioned the need for Russian.

4.4.4 Assessment

Changes in the models of assessment has been one of the most significant shifts in practice and has taken the largest amount of professional development to become assimilated into the understanding and routines of teachers. Participants generally saw the new assessment system as open, reliable and efficient. However, the introduction of criteria-based assessment was a challenging experience for a considerable number of school-teachers. Despite attending courses teachers were still uncomfortable with certain aspects of the new assessment process. Even four years into the reform, many teachers preferred the previous practice of attributing a score from one to five in a daily diary for each lesson for each student to making formative comments with judgements against specific learning objectives less frequently.

Parents were not ready for a new assessment system. Assessment data was regularly communicated to parents in the Soviet system through daily reports of a child's progress on a scale of one to five, so it was highly visible. The shift to formative assessment and the use of electronic portals to share this information was a big step for parents. A lot of explanatory meetings were arranged by schools but there was still a lack of understanding of the system which was so far from the practice that parents and grandparents 'knew' from their own years as school students. Poor planning with the national database and Kundelik[9] were part of the problem and there were big regional variations in the standard of reporting.

4.4.5 Teacher Development

The large-scale three level programme of professional development previously discussed is seen as useful and highly valued in upgrading the qualifications of teachers by participants. It has led to salary increases and teachers who had successfully completed the courses have become highly sought after. It had been undertaken on a large scale. By the end of 2016 the programme had reached around 700 trainers and 120,000 teachers. The extent of the programme is confirmed by 2018 TALIS data (Tremblay 2019), which shows nearly all teachers in Kazakhstan had

---

[9] Kundelik is an e-learning platform, including an e-journal for children, teachers, school administration and parents.

participated in professional development and support each other in implementing new idea.

The Centers of Excellence and ORLEU programme reached large numbers of teachers but our data does not give us feedback on the quality of the depth of the learning about pedagogy. International evidence (Timperley et al. 2007: Cordingley et al. 2020) would suggest that relying on an external model of CPD is a risk and that ideal continuing professional development should be an intrinsic part of a school's organisational culture.

Initial teacher education has lagged behind all other parts of the national school system in re-orienting towards new content and new pedagogy. Many of our participants lamented the current status and quality of teachers and the quality of those entering the profession. Initial teacher education is still following the old Soviet model and there are different routes, some of which are part time and have very low entry levels. Despite being identified by diagnostic reports (NUGSE 2014) and by other agencies as key to the stability of implementation and reform, initial teacher education is still in need of sustained improvement.

4.4.6 Equity and Inclusion

Equity had been an ongoing concern of policymakers in Kazakhstan and was flagged early on as an issue in the reform (NUGSE 2014). The inequity of outcomes and the development of inclusive practices were and continue to be key policy developments. The challenges to equity are related to the policy of urbanisation which has meant that many city schools are over-subscribed due to a faster pace of migration to the cities than anticipated. In addition, the size of the country presents challenges for implementation. There are a large number of rural schools that require much development both in infrastructure and resources. Equity was raised by teachers as an issue and they were referring to the difficulties poorer families and those in rural locations had in accessing digital materials. Some difficulties were financial and some technological, for there is little or no connectivity in remote communities. We were told of cases where students were unable to complete their homework assignments and parents could not access their children's records.

The second area of equity is that of student access to and inclusion in mainstream education. In recent years, the Government of Kazakhstan has undertaken significant efforts to increase the number of students with special needs and disabilities attending mainstream schools aiming to establish that 'children with disabilities can study in their neighbourhood schools'.[10] Two indicators set by the Ministry as measures of progress were that 70 per cent of mainstream secondary schools and 30 per cent of pre-schools would be inclusive by the end of 2019. We do not know if this has been attained. There is still a limited understanding of the concept of inclusion amongst educators (HRW 2019: 25) and our research found that teachers had difficulty differentiating the curriculum to meet student differences and in adopting a more individualised mode of teaching. This is a major challenge requiring changes in pedagogy and much more professional development. The inclusion issues in Kazakhstan are embedded in past Soviet practices and mindsets. There are strong views of fixed ability and ability ranking in past practices and related to all children attending their closest school. Children with disabilities and different needs, such as behavioural and emotional difficulties, had been separately schooled and were viewed as 'deviant'. There are separate schools for orphans, corrective schools for children seen as law breaking and children with 'impairments' are not 'mainstream' and do not currently have access to the new curriculum. These practices increased the likelihood of students being segregated, further limiting their educational opportunities.

4.4.7 Systemic Issues

In this section we explore systemic issues that affected the espoused policy in practice. These issues are often part of the familiar cultural landscape of schools and policy and therefore their role is sometimes underestimated in terms of impact upon the reality of school and classroom practice.

4.4.8 Ways of Working

The renewed content and the new pedagogy made new and different demands on teachers and schools and inevitability past practices were often barriers to development. For example, the new approaches expected teachers to prepare more materials, plan together and liaise with parents in different ways. In Kazakhstan teachers' pay and workload is managed via the '*stavka*', a system that is a Soviet legacy where pay is based on the time spent in face-

---

[10] The Law of the Republic of Kazakhstan, dated 2 July 2018, No. 165-VI 'On Amendments and Additions to Some Legislative Acts of the Republic of Kazakhstan on Social Security Issues'.

to-face classroom contact, with further payments made for specific tasks and extra hours. One of the biggest issues faced by teachers is the increased workload. There is more preparation time needed to plan lessons as teachers are now required to search for and select resources, make materials and design a more creative approach. Paying teachers fairly for the increased workload that includes lesson preparation and working with parents was consistently raised as an issue. In addition, teachers worked six days a week and this was seen as demanding. A five-day week has now been introduced.

Another reason for the increased load was the extensive reporting that the schools had to undertake, and it was not clear how the information gathered was being used. For example, different textbooks were being trialled and one teacher explained the impact of that upon the bureaucratic demands made:

> NIS says that we can pay more attention to particular topics. Almaty kitap strictly follows the plan; hence, we are in two minds. But we fill the school journal (register) attentively. Besides, we have some obstacles with the school journal as well because all topics, goals, chapters should be written there. And now we have 3 journals. For instance, 1st grade teacher has 2 such school journals. The first is filled with lesson's goals, the second one with topics. And with grade also ... (First-Grade Teacher)

The curriculum renewal encouraged teachers and others to talk to each other more about content, assessment of courses and effective practices. Confusion and concerns about changes in practice and policy were mitigated through collective and constructive discussions between stakeholder groups, in some places facilitated by regional authorities. Communication was also strengthened between parents and teachers, between teachers of the same subject across schools and at the oblast level, where there is a better appreciation of the needs and problems within schools. However, in some regions, the role of the district authorities has been unclear and there has not been this increased communication and support.

New ways of working have been established although we have no data as to their efficacy. For example, in a region in the south of Kazakhstan that contains a number of remote schools, the local education authority implemented a system of *clusters* that share resources and information to overcome the difficult terrain and challenging circumstances schools experience in implementing the RCE.[11] Those geographically close to each other in a region

---

[11] RCE (Renewed Content of Education) is an overarching term that includes a new curriculum, assessment and teaching methods in Kazakhstan.

have designated leading and supporting school members so tasks such as adapting the curriculum to overcome poor internet access and downloading materials for sharing from points of access are shared. Additionally, the role of school principals in leading change has been acknowledged and courses bringing groups of principals together have fostered collegiality and collaboration. In many regions, Centres of Modernisation have been established to act as 'supporting' mechanisms to schools with a mission of development of 'high quality' teachers.

4.4.9 Regional and Governance Issues

The system of governance in public administration in Kazakhstan places the power for implementation in the regions or the cities. There is a vital but invisible link between the national governmental directives and implementation of policy at local level. The finance and will to implement policy sit in the regions. There were evident differences in outcomes and in the attitudes within each region. Often there was a relationship between wider challenges and a negative response. Some authorities made excuses; others adopted a 'can do' approach. The stance of the regional leaders was critical as the tone adopted appeared to flow down the administrative chain from oblast to district to school to parents and students, shaping action at the level of school, subject team and classroom.

There was some evidence of cooperation between oblasts, which saved resources, and this is an interesting area of potential development. There was a noticeable lack of professional development for those working at a regional level.

The changes to the curriculum have clearly led to some innovative practices and arrangement in how teachers and regions work and communicate. There is also evidence that some of the sociocultural barriers, such as the *stavka* system and bureaucratic accountability mechanisms, are still acting as blocks to the implementation of new practices.

4.5 CHALLENGES

This section addresses and summarises the major challenges that have emerged from our research up to 2020. Other challenges, such as funding arrangements for schools, have been addressed in depth since we completed our data collection in 2019.

4.5.1 Continuity and Coherence

Kazakhstan joined the European Higher Education Area[12] in 2010, thereby signing up for its higher education system to become compliant with the Dublin Descriptors that underpin the Bologna Process. Embedded in the assumption of compliance is the adoption of a learning-outcomes approach and much of the curriculum design, teaching and learning that takes place in Kazakhstani universities fails to embrace this or even understand what it means (Tamapyeva 2015). With a very well-defined set of learning aims and a learning-outcomes paradigm now becoming established in schools through the reformed curriculum, many ask what will happen when students transfer into higher education. Higher education seems to be lagging in the development of its pedagogies and in fostering faculty members understanding of a learning outcomes-based approach and an appreciation of more sophisticated approaches to assessment. For students aiming to continue into higher education and to prepare for university entrance procedures, there needs to be smooth transitions and alignment in the types of skills, knowledge and competences being developed in schools and higher education. The end of school testing procedures for selection for entry into universities can dominate new content and methods of teaching so these also need to be aligned with RCE. As yet, little news has been forthcoming on the redesign of the selection test and what follows for students graduating in 2022 as they progress into universities and colleges.

4.5.1.1 *A New Emphasis on Leadership* Training for school directors has been introduced by some regions to facilitate implementation of the renewed content and modernisation and to develop different domains of educational leadership. This training seems to have been left to the oblasts to initiate and deliver. There is no national programme. The demands of the new initiatives and the wider portfolio of leadership competences required suggests that leadership development is a key priority.

4.5.1.2 *Teacher Capacity and Skill Shortages in Some Subjects* In addition to the lack of teachers capable of teaching one or more of the four subjects in English, there are skill shortages in some other subjects. These can vary by region, for example there is a shortage of Russian language teachers in the

---

[12] www.ehea.info/page-full_members, last accessed March 2021.

south. Some teachers are unwilling to adapt to the renewed content as they are close to retirement, yet schools retain them as there are no replacements available.

4.6 LESSONS LEARNED AND FURTHER CONSIDERATIONS

The first and most important conclusion is that overall the renewed content has been well-received by those who piloted and applied the reforms. There has been media coverage critical of the reform strategy. The response by the Ministry and NIS was also important. They formed and adopted a media strategy to respond to these political issues. They also realised the need for clear communication to the regions and districts. NIS senior managers, for example, travelled to all the regions and held open meetings with parents and policymakers to explain the aims, processes and content of the reform. 'We went around the regions with the new curriculum from NIS, we had 70–80 meetings, we met with teachers . . .' (NIS manager).

There were of course tangible problems in design and implementation but the positive change in students' attitudes and behaviours in response to the new pedagogy and content was noteworthy and there are suggestions that it is generally improving attainment (Madeev 2019). The second wave of reform has been more effectively communicated and supported and resulted in shifts for our sample of teachers in their perceptions of their role, the curriculum, aims of teaching and assessing, pedagogy and autonomy. All have been welcomed. Teachers valued the small increase in their autonomy and felt their professionalism was enhanced. It has been a huge effort and there is a need to be aware that the Government's push for modernisation and investment in youth as part of its nation-building project has led to much innovation. There is a danger of innovation overload and reform fatigue.

Second, the process of implementation included setting up and using different forms of networks of, and partnerships between, schools to pilot and scale up new complex curriculum and assessment processes. These communication channels informed participants and gave them opportunities for comment and feedback, which helped iron out difficulties in design and delivery, making the change more manageable. Piloting also helped identify and correct mistakes in production that could have been used politically as criticism to thwart adoption of new materials and practices. The role of pilot schools and the teachers within them altered as the modernisation progressed: teachers served as exemplars and mentors and schools became centres and agents of change. Some pilot schools conducted workshops and master classes at the district level and were constantly sharing experience with other sites. They became important participants in disseminating and shaping the new learning that was occurring about the content and the change process. The piloting process, in general, was a worthwhile step as it engendered a growing confidence in, and appreciation of, what the renewed curriculum aimed to achieve. There have been signs of political pressure to speed up the implementation and the final stage of piloting (see Table 4.1) was omitted but this did lead to certain issues being overlooked. Securing the commitment of one group of politicians to the decisions of others is always a difficult issue.

The third learning is that the considerable investment in teacher and leadership development has resulted in teachers and school communities being prepared for change. An important element was the three-level training, which impacted upon teachers' pay and the quality of teaching, thus providing preparation and motivation for change. The OECD 2013 TALIS study found that in all countries, except for Kazakhstan and Italy, more teachers held beliefs in direct transmission, as the preferred mode of teaching and learning, rather than constructivist ones (Wilson 2017: 15). The 2015 Kazakhstan data collected as part of the CoE impact study using the same tool (TALIS 2013 survey) 'show a trend towards a more balanced view of constructivist pedagogy' (Wilson 2017: 15).[13]

During the course of the research we were able to identify some gaps in the implementation process which are discussed here. While the CPD programmes were comprehensive, they did not pay enough attention to inclusive pedagogy. Teachers have found it difficult to confidently adapt their pedagogy to deal with differentiated learning and have tended to have an inflexible approach to lesson-planning and dealing with mixed ability groups. One gap in teacher development is the slow transformation of initial teacher education. Another gap in the preparations for implementation was leadership development for regional stakeholders – especially those overseeing schools in a region. The regional and district education departments are key in the adoption and implementation of the modernisation. For example, district level heads and methodologists play an important role in implementation

---

[13] Centres of Excellence [Nazarbayev Intellectual Schools] (CoE [NIS]) – is an organisation that provides professional development of teachers and school principals; supports development of training programmes and teaching materials; and assists with capacity building of schools.

and change and are somewhat underdeveloped. Training and support to facilitate district education departments to innovate and implement would also make a contribution.

The fourth lesson is that implementation benefited from increased communication between stakeholder groups. Communication between school and home but also between educational authorities, between school leaders, between teachers in school and between schools has been helpful. Some regions have also shared expertise and begun to adopt ways of working that provide easier access to teachers and others to professional development opportunities.

The fifth major issue is that of how to move towards ensuring the *quality of teaching for all students*. There are the issues of rural and urban difference in outcomes which were raised in Section 4.4.6. The inequality related to provision of resources, including the quality of teacher preparation and development, internet access, equipment, furniture and physical infrastructure. How to ensure parity of learning outcomes is a real challenge. There are also matters related to the monitoring of the outcomes and quality. There are few reliable external evaluations of children's learning in a school nor is there much use of data to improve teaching, learning and equity. Kundelik seems a burdensome and unreliable process to gather data on students' learning outcomes, with little moderation of the grades being inserted by the schools, between schools or districts. The National Education Database (NEDB)[14] appears to have few quality control processes and, if it does produce analyses, they are not returned to schools or districts. The use of data for school improvement is limited at the moment in Kazakhstan and is also placing a burden on teacher time. The paradigm of using data only for the accountability of individuals or organisations needs reconsideration. There are also areas of school leadership training which need developing (e.g. managing budgets, the recognition and inclusion of children with special educational needs and attending to teachers' professional development and performance). Existing and future school leaders with greater autonomy will require training and support to be effective and produce the benefits anticipated for all types of students.

The final lesson is that research needs to continue to inform and facilitate implementation. A key policymaker highlighted the importance of a process

---

[14] The NEDB automated the process of data collection for administrative reports, which before were filled in manually and collected in a chain: education institution – education department – education authority – MES RK. It is a sub-system of an e-learning system.

of listening and collecting data on the progress of the implementation, thus enabling policymakers and implementers to act: 'I think you always have to do research. Constant research. And you have to continuously compare and always understand to see if you're going in the right direction. Because otherwise you won't understand what's going on' (D-NEA-pp3). The role of research in helping school and policy leaders to monitor implementation and make adjustments is a key one.

4.7 CONCLUSION

The recent Chatham House report (Bohr et al. 2019) has reminded us of the importance of the educational reform in renewing Kazakh identity. Kazakhstan has an opportunity to 'become a model for other states undergoing or set to undergo complex transition in the post-Soviet region' (xi). There were strong elements of the implementation plan that can be adapted, adopted and learnt from. There is also evidence that neighbours are looking at the model used and are keen to try it. The next major task is to share the learning, create the next generation of implementers and developers, research reform and build our understandings of the complexity of the implementation process.

References

Bohr, A., Bruaer, B., Gould-Davies, N., Kassenova, N., Lillis, J., Mallinson K., Nixey, J. and Satpayev, D. (2019). *Kazakhstan: Tested by Transition*. Chatham House Report. London: Chatham House.

Bridges, D. (ed.) (2014). *Education Reform and Internationalisation: The Case of School Reform in Kazakhstan*. Cambridge: Cambridge University Press.

Cordingley, P., Higgins, S., Greany, T., Crisp, B., Araviaki, E., Coe, R. and Johns, P. (2020). *Developing Great Leadership of CPDL*. CUREE, University of Durham and University of Nottingham.

Cornell, S. E. and Engvall, J. (2017). *Kazakhstan in Europe: Why Not?* A Silk Road Paper published by the Central Asia–Caucasus Institute and Silk Road Studies Program, Stockholm. ISBN: 978-91-88551-02-3. Retrieved 6 February 2020 from https://isdp.eu/content/uploads/2017/10/2017-cornell-engvall-kazakhstan-in-europe-why-not.pdf

Heyneman, S. P. (1998). The transition from party/state to open democracy: The role of education. *Journal of Educational Development*, 10:1, 20–40.

HRW (Human Right Watch) (2019). *'On the Margins': Education for Children with Disabilities in Kazakhstan*. Nur-Sultan: HRW.

Madeev, S. (2019). Presentation on the work of AEO Nazarbayev Intellectual schools and its monitoring of student attainment delivered at the *NIS XI Annual International Research-to-*

Practice Conference Researchers Changing the World of Schooling, Nur-Sultan, 24–25 October 2019.

Ministry of Education and Science of the Republic of Kazakhstan. (2010). State program of education development in the Republic of Kazakhstan for 2011–2020 based on Decree of the President of the Republic of Kazakhstan dated February 1, 2010 No 922 'On Strategic Plan of Development of the Republic of Kazakhstan till 2020' and Decree of the President of the Republic of Kazakhstan dated March 19, 2010 No 957 'On approval of the List of Governmental Programs'. Retrieved 10 March 2021 from https://www.akorda.kz/en/offi cial_documents/strategies_and_programs.

MoES and NAE (2015). (Rus Instruktivno-metodicheskoe pis'mo) About approbation of the educational programmes for primary schools in pilot organisations of secondary education for 2015–2016, Guidance letter, Astana.

MoES and NAE (2017). On the features of organization of educational process in general secondary schools in the Republic of Kazakhstan in academic year 2017–2018 [In Ru. Ob osobennostiakh organizatsii obrazovatelnogo protsessa v obscheobrazovatelnyh shkolakh Respubliki Kazakhstan v 2017–2018 uchebnom godu], Astana.

NUGSE (Nazarbayev University Graduate Schools of Education) (2014). *The Development of Strategic Directions for Education Reforms in Kazakhstan for 2015–2020, Diagnostic Report.* Astana, Kazakhstan: Indigo Print.

OECD (2014). *Review of National Policies for Education: Secondary Education in Kazakhstan.* Paris: OECD Publishing.

Ruby, A. and McLaughlin, C. (2014). Transferability and the Nazarbayev intellectual schools: Exploring models of practice transfer. In Bridges, D. (ed.) *Educational Reform and Internationalisation: The Case of School Reform in Kazakhstan.* Cambridge: Cambridge University Press, pp. 287–300.

Silova, I. and Steiner-Khamsi, G. (2008). *How NGOs React: Globalization and Education Reform in the Caucasus, Central Asia, and Mongolia.* West Hertford, CT: Kumarian Press, Inc.

Steiner-Khamsi, G., Silova, I. and Johnson, E. (2006). Neoliberalism liberally applied: Educational policy borrowing in Central Asia. In D. Coulby, J. Ozga, T. Seddon and T. S. Popkewitz (eds.) *World Yearbook in Education.* London: Routledge, pp. 217–45.

Tampayeva, G. Y. (2015). Importing education: Europeanisation and the Bologna process in Europe's backyard – The case of Kazakhstan. *European Educational Research Journal*, 14:1, 74–85. https://doi.org/10.1177/1474904114565154

Timperley, A., Wilson, H., Barrar, H. and Fung, I. (2007). *Teacher Professional Learning and Development: Best Evidence Synthesis Iteration.* Wellington, New Zealand: Ministry of Education. http://educationcounts.edcentre.govt.nz/goto/BES

Tremblay, K. (2019). Supporting the teaching profession in a changing world: First results and key messages for Kazakhstan in an international perspective. *Key note presentation delivered at the NIS XI Annual International Research-to-Practice Conference Researchers Changing the World of Schooling*, Nur-Sultan, 24–25 October 2019. https://conferences.nis.edu.kz/ wpcontent/uploads/2019/11/%D0%A2%D1%80%D0%B5%D0%BC%D0%B1%D0%BB%D0% B5%D0%B9_2019-10-24-Oct-Kazakhstan-conference-Keynote-KT.pdf

Wilson, E. (2017). *Bringing about Change in Schools: The Case of Nazarbayev Intellectual Schools, Centre of Excellence Teacher and Leadership Programmes.* Cambridge: Faculty of Education, University of Cambridge and Centre of Excellence.

Winter, L., Yakavets, N. and Kurakbayev, K. (2018). Changes in purpose: Examining the radical transition from a longstanding norm-based model of classroom assessment to a new criteria-based system, *European Conference on Educational Research (ECER)*, Bolzano, Italy, 3–7 September 2018. Available at: https://eera-ecer.de/ecer-programmes/conference/23/contribution/43034/

Yakavets, N. (2014). Educational reform in Kazakhstan: The first decade of independence. In Bridges, D. (ed.) *Educational Reform and Internationalisation: The Case of School Reform in Kazakhstan.* Cambridge: Cambridge University Press, pp. 1–27.

Yakavets, N. and Dzhadrina, M. (2014). Educational reform in Kazakhstan: Entering the world arena. In Bridges, D. (ed.) *Educational Reform and Internationalisation: The Case of School Reform in Kazakhstan.* Cambridge: Cambridge University Press, pp. 27–52.

5 The Challenges and Opportunities of Greater Autonomy for Post-Soviet Universities

An Illustration from Kazakhstan

Matthew Hartley and Alan Ruby

5.1 INTRODUCTION

One strategy many countries have used to foster higher quality higher education systems is granting greater institutional autonomy. The hope is that by moving from centralised systems controlled by Ministries to ones where institutions can pursue their own destinies, innovation will inevitably result, and performance improve. However, moving towards a more autonomous system comes at a cost. Being free to set institutional strategies brings the possibility of making mistakes, something many leaders who have been trained in a compliance-based system find daunting. Further, if leaders have never operated in a more market-based system, their ability to scan the environment to determine and launch new initiatives is likely to be undeveloped. It can be simpler and less stressful for institutional leaders to behave as if the old compliance-based model was still the best way to demonstrate to the larger society that they are being responsible and faithful servants. Finally, autonomy requires constructing new, alternative systems of accountability, like boards of trustees. Kazakhstan's higher education reforms over the last fifteen years offer insights into both the challenges and possibilities of greater institutional autonomy.

5.2 CONTEXT

On achieving independence, Kazakhstan was faced with the challenge of taking over a system of public universities and pedagogical institutes that had largely been steered from Moscow. It also experienced a loss of talent as some people opted to move to Russia for economic opportunities and some families returned to their ancestral homelands of Russia or a now-re-unified Germany. Seeking to quickly align the higher education sector with the newly embraced market economy, the Ministry of Education and Science (MoES) allowed the rapid growth of private universities, and many for-profit institutions started up. Some were commercial arms of existing public entities. Others were start-ups seeking to capitalise on a growing appetite for private higher education. In the absence of state regulation, the quality of programmes was at best variable. But as the MoES became more functional it exerted more control. So, by 1996, most of the more than 150 public and private higher education institutions came under the auspices of the national MoES. Its regulatory approach was a direct descendant of the Soviet era. In the words of a former Minister of Education and Science we interviewed the enduring principle was that 'higher education is a strategic area, this is ideology, this is new generations, this is the minds of people so this (needs to be, and) is under (state) control'.

Other Soviet era legacies adopted by MoES included strong central policy control, the institutional separation of research and teaching and the persistence of specialised institutions, including those offering initial teacher education. University rectors were appointed centrally by either the President of the Republic or the Minister of Education and Science and there was national control of university curriculum offerings and an accreditation system requiring institutions to show how they complied with MoES guidelines. The MoES specified the structure and content of over 70 per cent of the undergraduate curriculum and stipulated what were acceptable academic majors.

The prevailing legal framework was described to us by one expert in educational law as one which 'didn't distinguish between the state enterprises that produce something and state enterprises that are providing services, such as education'. The intrusive regulation by the MoES limited programmatic innovation and restricted institutional response to the *needs* of local industry, thereby hindering economic development and constraining growth and diversification of the nation's productive industries that were essential for a stronger connection with the global market.

Along with pursuing greater economic competitiveness, a key priority of the national government was responding to dissatisfaction about the quality of higher education. Simply put, universities were not meeting parental aspirations or serving the expressed needs of employers. This was occurring during a time when there was a marked increase in demand for access to higher education, as people responded to the move to a market economy and an evolving labour market. Tertiary enrolments doubled between 1991 and 2005 and there was a marked growth in the number of higher education institutions, largely through the growth of private entities (see Canning 2017 for a survey of the post-independence era).

To strengthen the human capital base of the new nation and to stimulate economic development, national policymakers adopted two basic strategies. One was to continue to decentralise control with increased institutional autonomy. The other was to establish an exemplar; a high quality internationally oriented university which would serve as a model site for adapting and implementing international best practices and then disseminating them to other institutions nationally and regionally. While we present the two strategies separately, they are inextricably intertwined because the attempts to create an exemplar revealed key barriers to more autonomy and higher quality education.

5.3 STEPS TOWARDS AUTONOMY

In 2001, the government assigned the status of 'national university' to nine prominent institutions. This status allowed them to set their own admissions guidelines and adjust national curricula. Faculty salaries and the value of state scholarships for students were also higher than other public institutions.

These changes did not flow to other universities and institutes. Their institutional autonomy remained limited, with the MoES continuing to control most of their curricula and overseeing institutions' budgets. It remained 'the central body responsible for both the broader management of the sector as well as being the primary body for regulation' (Raza 2009: 30).

Another step towards autonomy was a desire to create an exemplary institution. The most recent example of this effort led to the opening of Nazarbayev University in the national capital in 2009. One of the stated purposes was to create a model of higher education reform featuring shared governance and institutional autonomy, an issue we deal with at greater length in Section 5.5.

Seeing the limited impact of its earlier reforms and aware of its obligations flowing from joining the European Higher Education Area and the Bologna Process in 2010 (Yergebekov and Temirbekova 2012), the national government approved a wider set of reforms proposed by the MoES in the 'State

Program for Education Development 2011–2020'. The State programme's goals included more research capacity and capability and greater emphasis on graduate employability. These and previous reforms were expected to lead to a higher international visibility for the country's leading universities and strengthen the quality of higher education.

Institutional autonomy to foster the attainment of these ends included allowing greater flexibility in programme design by increasing the proportion of the undergraduate curriculum determined by institutions from 30 per cent to 70 per cent. To underscore the reduced oversight role of the MoES, many universities were given boards of trustees which would resemble governing bodies in European and US higher education systems. The aim was to have boards of trustees in all higher education institutions through a staged process; 'national research universities in 2015, national HEIs in 2016 and the rest by 2018' (Ahn et al. 2018: 215).

5.4 IMPLEMENTING REFORMS AND INSTITUTIONAL RESPONSES

Naturally rectors reacted in different ways to these reforms. Some were less enthusiastic, preferring a system of central prescription and institutional compliance. It made understanding what needed to be done and what constituted success easier. Also, leaders had operated in an environment where the penalties for discretionary behaviours that could be construed as corrupt were quite severe. Other rectors, however, welcomed the freedom to respond to local circumstances that they felt could not be understood by a junior ministry official 1,000 kilometres away. Hartley et al. (2016) sought the perspectives of senior leaders at fifteen universities during the first two years of the reform implementation. Their findings underscored a prevailing ambivalence among many rectors and leading academics who doubted that they and their peers had the capacity 'to lead discussions of strategy and institutional policy' without training and support. Moving from a culture where success was measured by piles of papers illustrating diligent compliance to one where leaders would be accountable 'for the results of strategies they formulate and implement with key institutional stakeholders' (Hartley et al. 2016: 286) was almost unimaginable.

Even when boards of trustees were formed to provide oversight, there was considerable variability in how they functioned. Many boards met only twice a year and, even then, meetings were often dominated by administrator's reports and seldom dealt with strategic issues (Hartley et al. 2017). One rector described the board's activities as 'largely formal and symbolic' (53). Some universities did have trustees who were engaged in long-term strategic thinking and brought expertise and knowledge of regional economic directions to the task. In some cases, this was facilitated by the independent status of the entity or by a corporate structure which gives the board of private entities (joint stock companies) more legal authority than the boards of public universities. However, even in these cases there was still a lot to be done before the trustees were as fully engaged as the US and European boards they sought to emulate.

A staged approach to governance reforms allowed the MoES to focus its support on different groups of rectors at different times, but it also meant that progress was 'slower than some would like ... and not immune from error' (Hartley et al. 2017: 63). This did allow for ideas and concepts from other academic cultures to be tested, adapted and adjusted to local circumstances. One site leading that process of customisation and acculturation was Nazarbayev University, which was created in part to serve as a showcase for reform and innovation. However, the presence of a demonstration site does not automatically result in others changing their practice or emulating desired behaviours. Nor is it simply a matter of setting up a model institution.

5.5 DEMONSTRATION SITES AS A CHANGE STRATEGY

The government of Kazakhstan's efforts to create an exemplar institution to serve as a demonstration and innovation site, a beacon of change and reform, was not a one step process. This is not surprising for a new state, nor an unknown circumstance in 'mature' states struggling to design and implement significant change in a complex system.

There were three distinct initiatives aimed at creating a demonstration site before the creation of a research-intensive university with English language instruction, Nazarbayev University. The three precursors are the Kazakh Institute of Management, Economics and Strategic Research (now KIMEP University), Kazakh-British Technical University (KBTU) and the Eurasian National University.

KIMEP was founded in 1992, primarily as a business school, in the old capital city of Almaty, which remained a finance hub for the country. Its initial programmes were master's degrees aimed at preparing people for corporate and financial sector jobs. Instruction was in English and most of the faculty members were foreign nationals. However, it was constrained by the legislative environment and its operating structure. It was set up as a Joint Stock Company and while it had some freedoms it was required to stay with the state standards, which were grounded in practices from the Soviet era. For example, there was a requirement for universities to have a minimum number of books per student, which KIMEP did not meet because it had instead decided to make considerable investments in electronic and digital learning materials rather than printed volumes.

Although it was a joint-stock company, KIMEP had difficulty attracting capital investments, as the majority ownership was vested in the founder, and though it had good facilities it remained tuition-dependent. To increase its revenue, KIMEP established undergraduate courses, even though it was not a recognised provider of initial degrees by the Government. This caused some students and parents to express doubts about the quality of these courses. This, coupled with challenges with faculty retention, raised concerns about the institution. While KIMEP weathered these challenges and today has a strong reputation in the country, it became clear that KIMEP could not alone meet the skill needs of the region nor did it offer a model likely to transform higher education across the country.

While the skills provided by KIMEP had great value, the demand for technical skills related to the oil and gas sector underscored the need for investment in higher education that would support industrial development. The result was the creation in 2001 of Kazakh-British Technical University (KBTU). This too was a joint-stock company and had good facilities in the centre of Almaty. However, it found itself competing with KIMEP for a relatively small population of students able to learn in English. After some initial successes, sustaining a high-quality international faculty proved challenging. KBTU struggled with its dependence on tuition and industry scholarships which were influenced indirectly by volatile oil prices. Eventually the national gas company became a major shareholder with the Public Foundation 'Education Fund of Nursultan Nazarbayev', which helped stabilise KBTU financially.

The impact of KBTU has been confined primarily to the energy sector and, while it has grown by absorbing other institutions, it is still a relatively small narrowly focused university specialising in the extractive industries, chemical engineering and business. And, despite its successes, the institution has remained constrained by the legislative environment. Thus, its efforts have not led to a wider national programme of reform and qualitative improvement in higher education.

The third initiative was linked with the relocation of the nation's capital to the northern Oblast of Akmola. To support the new capital Astana's development, it was decided to establish a comprehensive university, Eurasian National University (ENU). It was created by amalgamating a pedagogical institute with a civil engineering institute and then merging with the Academy of Diplomacy. In 2001 ENU was granted national status and it has since grown to fourteen schools including economics, social sciences and history, as well as physics and technical sciences, energy and transport. With a wider array of programmes, its enrolment grew quickly and now has some 17,000 students.

New buildings and infrastructure were funded by the MoES and more domestic faculty hired to teaching the growing number of students. Unlike the other two projects the language of instruction was principally Russian, although there are courses taught in English at all degree levels. But like its competitors, KIMEP and KBTU, ENU operated in a national regulatory environment that limited its ability to innovate and, therefore, its effectiveness.

The three institutions still exist and serve sectors of the economy and different national priorities. All three struggled in their early years with the same legislative framework and inspection and standards regime. One local education policy expert we interviewed observed that ENU was constrained: 'it was the same system, (same) legal environment, state standard. Old system in new buildings'. These observations applied to all three institutions and they significantly shaped the founding of Nazarbayev University (NU).

The development of NU has been described elsewhere in detail (Ruby 2017). It offers a distinctive example of a national strategy aimed at creating a world class university (Sabzalieva 2017). NU's organisational development (Ruby 2017) and its role in national development (Katsu 2017) have both been described. Here we look more closely at the issues of academic independence and governance and how they shaped a more autonomous institution.

In addition to being mindful of the legislative and regulatory constraints that hindered the first three reform initiatives, the team developing NU were keenly aware of other more relaxed regulatory regimes, sometimes referred to as 'free zones' used to attract leading education institutions to Dubai in the United Arab Emirates and to Education City in Doha, Qatar. They examined the framework of fiscal incentives and legal latitude offered by Singapore and Malaysia to encourage the development of international branch campuses. The free zones – or special economic zones – had also been used by China to attract foreign direct investment and to gain access to manufacturing technology and modern business practices (Zeng 2010).

'Special Economic Zone' (SEZ) is the umbrella term for a geographically delineated space where economic activity, of one or more forms, can take place without abiding by all or some of the laws, norms and practices of the host nation. While 'free ports' date back to the Roman Empire, the free port of Hamburg established in 1888 is probably the modern precursor of SEZs. It was designated as a manufacturing space which could operate freely if all its production was exported (Jayawardena 1983: 427).

In an SEZ the 'rules for doing business are different . . . from the rest of the country'. Conditions in SEZ's are different from the surrounding economic environment because they make it easier for companies to get access to reliable infrastructure; offer freedom from or deferral of taxes and customs charges and controls; and provide some fiscal incentives like free movement of capital and subsidies (World Bank 2017: 11–13). In effect they have 'extra-territorial status which enables them *de facto* immunity from domestic civil laws and government controls' and in some cases have 'constitutional guarantees' inhibiting nationalisation (Jayawardena 1983: 428). This status makes it easier and cheaper to create and move goods, to import or purchase raw materials and to hire, compensate and dismiss workers. They are usually created by government to attract foreign monetary and intellectual capital, to create jobs, to test and lead economic reforms and to experiment with new policies and approaches (Zeng 2015: 2).

This type of arrangement, or at least some legislative equivalent, was important to the potential strategic international partners that the NU start-up team was recruiting. In particular, the partner institutions pressed for clarity about academic freedom and shared governance. Without some assurances on these issues it would be difficult for some globally recognised universities to enter a sustained relationship with a nascent university. Integrity of the admissions processes, freedom in the selection of learning materials, unchecked selection of research topics and priorities and fidelity to international assessment practices were all issues explored as NU was being established (Ruby 2017).

Drawing lessons from its predecessors and from various education free zones and acknowledging the concerns and academic norms of potential international partners, the leaders of the NU start-up team made two tactical choices. One was to signal the national importance of the project by having the sitting Prime Minister oversee the project. The other was to incorporate the University as a 'national company', which would ease some regulatory requirements. These were interim measures until the national parliament passed a 'law granting academic freedom and institutional autonomy in 2011 ... (becoming) the first of the Commonwealth of Independent States to create such a space' (Katsu 2017: 182).

The law passed both houses of parliament and was enacted in 2012. It was drafted with the intent of exempting NU from all oversight by the MoES and from other governmental agencies that regulate commercial activities and service relationships in the nation. In sum, total autonomy. It specified a shared governance model and led to the appointment of a board of trustees, a rector and the creation of an academic council which has faculty and student members in addition to the provost and the heads of schools. All are charged with working collaboratively to manage the university. In addition, an initial endowment of approximately $500 Million (USD) was established to foster longer-term fiscal independence while providing for the receipt of government funds to cover the tuition and living costs of all students admitted. There are some complexities and nuances in the law, such as the provision for a continuing role for the nation's first president, in the oversight of the university but the main achievement of the law was to lay the basic architecture for shared governance and to safeguard NU's academic freedom. This came with the consent of the nation's senior political leaders.

5.6 LEGISLATIVE AUTONOMY AND INTERNAL GOVERNANCE

This autonomy enabled NU to adopt its own merit-based student admissions process instead of using the annual Unified National Test used by public universities. It also ensured that NU could set its own curricula, determine its own degree programmes and adopt and apply its own graduation requirements and create its own faculty personnel policy. NU's first board of trustees was appointed with local and international members and the number of international members has subsequently increased.

While these are important steps to operationalise NU's independence there was also a need to create university wide structures, especially the establishment of a faculty senate that could develop some common academic policies and oversee research approval processes and student assessment practices. This internal regulatory architecture was also a way to encourage the different schools to collaborate and reduce duplication of effort in the creation of processes and procedures. The need for such a structure was reinforced by the profile of the first faculty recruited, who tended to be early in their professional careers and from different academic traditions.

However, by 2012 there was enough common ground to set out a set of core values for the institution. For example, the principle of academic freedom led to the inclusion of 'integrity' and 'transparency and openness' as two of the six core values that are foundations for NU's past and current strategic plans, the latter looking to 2030.

As NU has begun to put in place its operations, it has also been convening higher education leaders from other Kazakhstani universities and regional universities. It has done so through an annual public forum and through invitational meetings. These venues encouraged rectors from other institutions to share their experiences as they moved towards greater autonomy as well as getting a closer appreciation of alternative approaches exemplified by NU. While these and other attempts to share promising practice and establish networks of institutional leaders have been welcome but they also point to one of the inherent challenges in demonstration sites and free zones acting as change agents. NU's role as a change agent is helped and hindered by what Sabzalieva labelled a 'dual-facing role' with 'domestic and international policy objectives'. Domestically it was to lead economic and social development and be a 'figure head' for reforms across the national higher education system. Internationally it was to symbolise the country's commitment to being part of the global academic community and the global market (Sabzalieva 2017: 428). Its role in 'nation building' gives it credibility as an example of the 'Western academic model' but it also encourages its leaders to attend to local priorities and initiatives that extend its footprint past the academic boundaries usually associated with a young institution (Bigozhin 2019: 119). At times the line distinguishing the two roles, domestic and foreign, is blurred; attempts to diversify the local economy through the creation of a pool of skilled graduates also lift the nation's connections with the global market and a wider academic community enhancing an institution's reputation (Koch 2014: 47). But keeping a balance between satisfying local market needs and preparing graduates whose skills and credentials have a wider currency is a challenge for young institutions with close connections to national policymakers.

This is a helpful reminder of the realities of policy transfer or diffusion across nations and cultural and linguistic borders. One of the main principles of comparative education is that ideas and practices change as they move from one enabling environment to another. Policies are interpreted rather than simply transposed because even in hierarchical systems local actors refer to local norms and values to interpret and apply new ideas. For example,

Tanaka's study of the evolution of research universities revealed that the German ideal of the research universities was transferred to the United States by academics who, having experienced directly the benefits of 'freedom of teaching and learning' (Tanaka 2009: 411), embedded it in graduate schools. In contrast, the transfer of the same idea to Japan was led by politicians 'who were trying to build a modern state as soon as possible' (Tanaka 2009: 408) and paid less attention to the fundamentals of academic freedom.

In the case of NU, the domestic champions of the idea of creating an academically autonomous research-intensive university included the nation's president, who had no direct experience of such an institution, and senior political leaders who had studied at US and European universities. Those charged with the managerial task of building the first part of the campus and recruiting international partners also had diverse academic backgrounds. At times this created some tensions, especially around the place of humanities and social sciences in NU's academic programme and in creation of a separate admissions path with a different calendar to the prevailing national secondary school exit exam. In a sense the start-up team and its political overseers were straddling the US and Japanese experiences described by Tanaka; academic freedom mattered to the international partners and defining and symbolising an independent nation-state mattered to local officials and political leaders. These tensions continue as NU evolves and matures as both a research-intensive university and as a force in the growth and diversification of the national economy.

5.7 LESSONS LEARNED

The relative youth of the university limits what lessons we can draw from its first ten years of development and no doubt what we observe will be interpreted differently by others in the future. But we offer a few observations about the processes that led to the creation of NU. The most obvious is that initial reform efforts do not always work and in this case the main reason was that the enabling environment hindered innovation and change. The three earlier models – despite great efforts and significant resources – had too few degrees of freedom to innovate. What was needed was true institutional autonomy and a larger policy environment that began to support and reward institutional autonomy as a practice and an ideal. In this respect, the insights from examining free zones and education cities reinforced the case for legislative protection for the new academic community.

The second lesson is that demonstration sites, as models of good practice, are useful exemplars and can serve as reference points for local institutions but the path to greater academic autonomy for other national universities will be longer and more circuitous. It is easy to find comfort in established practice, especially in hierarchical systems where the central authority is a long way away and dependent on documented compliance. A local board of trustees can offer a welcome connection with community aspirations and regional economic priorities. But it can also skew the institution's interests towards purely local concerns at the expense of national interests. Helping board members and rectors formulate and enact an effective and balanced role takes time and is more successful when the benefits of boards and the appropriate roles of members are clearly communicated through training and concise documentation.

Situating the case in the wider literature on change and control in a post-Soviet environment poses an interesting challenge. State institutions, including schools and universities, had essentially no autonomy in the Soviet era. Twenty years of independence has not negated seventy years of Soviet control which in turn built on the centralised authority of the Tsars. Like Peter the Great who compelled his nobles to cut their beards and taxed those who would not comply, Government officials used force and financial penalties to change behaviour. Both schools and universities had an 'administrative command system run by written directives, instructions, reports and studies' all issued centrally (Kerr 1982: 112; Gregory 2004: 8). Even Gorbachev's goal of overcoming years of stagnation and Stalin's legacy of command and administer had little effect on the highly standardised approach to teaching and learning (Long 1990). One impediment was resistance from the conservative members of institutions like the Academy of Pedagogical Sciences. But there was also limited capacity to act or think independently. 'When you have been told all your life you are a pig, you don't suddenly start thinking for yourself, just because someone told you to do so' (Barnett 1989: 6).

Even though there is a strong and persistent culture of command and some degree of compliance in post-independence Kazakhstan there are some barriers to smooth or seamless adoption of new practices. The very structure that underpins centralised authority creates layers of checks and review that impede the rate of change and often distort priorities and messages as transmission is filtered through different actors; making it difficult to command innovation (Kerr 1982: 113). This is the final lesson we would draw from this case: policy ideas and practices, borrowed ideas, cannot be simply pasted in. To be successful in a new environment they need adjustment and acclimatisation to suit local realities of resources, traditions and capability.

References

Ahn, E., Dixon, J. and Chekmareva, L. (2018). Looking at Kazakhstan's higher education landscape: From transition to transformation between 1920–2015. In Jeroen Huisman, J., Smolentseva, A. and Froumin, I. D. (eds.) *25 Years of Transformations of Higher Education Systems in Post-Soviet Countries: Reform and Continuity.* Palgrave Studies in Global Higher Education. Cham, Switzerland: Palgrave Macmillan, pp. 199–227. www.palgrave.com/de/book/9783319529790.

Barnett, D. (1989). Inside the veil of glasnost. *The Soviet Observer,* 31 March, 6–7.

Bigozhin, U. (2019). 'We love our country in our own way': Youth, gender, & nationalism. In Laruelle, M. (ed.) *The Nazarbayev Generation: Youth in Kazakhstan.* Lanham: Lexington Books, pp. 115–32.

Canning, M. (2017). The context for higher education development in Kazakhstan. In Hartley, M. and Ruby, A. (eds.) *Higher Education Reform and Development: The Case of Kazakhstan.* Cambridge: Cambridge University Press, pp. 65–82.

Gregory, P. R. (2004). *The Political Economy of Stalinism: Evidence from the Soviet Secret Archives.* Cambridge: Cambridge University Press.

Hartley, M., Gopaul, B., Sagintayeva, A. and Apergenova, R, (2016). Learning autonomy: Higher education reform in Kazakhstan. *Higher Education,* 72:3, 277–89.

Hartley, M., Sagintayeva, A., Gopaul, B., Apergenova, R., Zhakypova, F. and Bilyalov, D. (2017). Governance challenges and changes: The evolving role of boards of trustees. In Hartley, M. and Ruby, A. (eds.) *Higher Education Reform and Development: the case of Kazakhstan.* Cambridge: Cambridge University Press, pp. 47–64.

Jayawardena, D. L. U. (1983). Free trade zones. *Journal of World Trade Law,* 17:5, 427–44.

Katsu, S. (2017). Medium and long term challenges. In Hartley, M. and Ruby, A. (eds.) *Higher Education Reform and Development: The Case of Kazakhstan.* Cambridge: Cambridge University Press, pp. 177–92.

Kerr, S. T. (1982). Innovation on command: Instructional development and educational technology in the Soviet Union. *Educational Communication and Technology,* 30:2, 97–116.

Koch, N. (2014). The shifting geopolitics of higher education: Inter/nationalizing elite universities in Kazakhstan, Saudi Arabia, and beyond. *Geoforum,* 56, 46–54.

Long, D. (1990). Continuity and change in Soviet education under Gorbachev. *American Educational Research Journal,* 27:3, 403–23.

Raza, R. (2009). *Examining Autonomy and Accountability in Public and Private Tertiary Institutions.* Washington, DC: World Bank.

Ruby, A. (2017). Kazakhstan's quest for a world-class university: The story so far. In Hartley, M. and Ruby, A. (eds.) *Higher Education Reform and Development: The Case of Kazakhstan.* Cambridge: Cambridge University Press, pp. 29–46.

Sabzalieva, E. (2017). The policy challenges of creating a world-class university outside the global 'core'. *European Journal of Higher Education,* 7:4, 424–39.

Tanaka, M. (2009). The mobility of universities. *Comparative Education,* 45:3, 405–18.

World Bank. (2017). *Special Economic Zones: An Operational Review of Their Impacts*. Washington, DC: World Bank.

Yergebekov, M. and Temirbekova, Z. (2012). The Bologna process and problems in higher education system of Kazakhstan. *Procedia – Social and Behavioural Sciences*, 47, 1473–78.

Zeng, D. Z. (2010). *Building Engines for Growth and Competitiveness in China: Experience with Special Economic Zones and Industrial Clusters. Directions in Development; Countries and Regions*. Washington, DC: World Bank. https://openknowledge.worldbank.org/handle/10986/2501.

Zeng, D. Z. (2015). *Global Experiences with Special Economic Zones: Focus on China and Africa*. Washington, DC: World Bank.

6 School Improvement by Design

Why It's Needed, How It Works and How It Can Be Improved

Brian Rowan

This chapter is about school reform in the United States and, more specifically, about a school reform process that I call 'school improvement by design' (Rowan et al. 2009; see also Cohen et al. 2013). As defined here, school improvement by design occurs when organisations outside of schools create designs (or models) for instructional improvement and then work to get these designs implemented inside of schools.[1] For reasons discussed later in this chapter, school improvement by design is rarely undertaken by government agencies in the United States. Instead, it is mostly undertaken by (free-standing or university-based) not-for-profit organisations or commercial firms (usually in the publishing industry). As this chapter shows, these organisations have developed many different designs for school improvement and pursued a variety of approaches to getting these designs implemented in schools. Despite this diversity, however, the organisations I discuss in this chapter share a common feature. Each organisation takes as its central mission to improve instruction and student achievement in one or more of the core academic subjects of K–12 schooling.

---

[1] This definition signals the focus of this chapter, which is on designs intended to improve *instruction* in schools. The reader should note that school improvement by design can focus on other than instructional improvement in schools. In the United States, for example, many organisations outside of schools often seek to improve students' socio-emotional, health or behavioural outcomes. A large literature base on these kinds of organisations has been developed under the heading of 'prevention science'. For a useful review of that research covering many of the same topics discussed in this chapter, see Dusenbury (2003).

In this chapter, I advance three ideas about school improvement by design. First, I argue that design-based school improvement addresses an inherent problem of education governance in the United States, namely the discretion that schools have to work on instructional improvement. My argument is that school improvement by design not only addresses this governance problem but also can become an essential complement to other school reform strategies (such as standards-based reform or school choice). I then discuss how school improvement by design works. Here, I will present a series of case studies my colleagues and I conducted of design-based assistance to local schools. The intent of the case studies is to illustrate specific conditions under which school improvement by design succeeds (or doesn't) in changing instruction and improving student achievement in schools. Finally, I will discuss the role that markets, governments, and networks can play to make school improvement by design a viable strategy for school reform in the United States, that is, a reform strategy that consistently generates strong designs for instructional improvement that are widely adopted by schools that need them.

6.1 THE PROBLEM

Let's begin with the problem that school improvement by design can address. In the United States, top-down, government-directed reform of schools is difficult. The liberal framers of the US constitution distrusted centralised government and created a national government with strictly enumerated powers. However, since education was *not* one of those powers, authority over public education devolved to states in the US federal system. But, as a practical matter, states ended up consolidating control over K–12 education long after locally-controlled schools were in place and, as a result, local control of schooling became the *de facto* organising principle of American public education. Today, there are more than 13,000 school districts in the United States, most of which are small and exercise very weak control over what is ostensibly their core technology – instruction (Meyer and Rowan 1978). Yet, in the United States, these are precisely the organisations that have primary responsibility for managing instruction and improving student learning in schools.

By the 1980s, many observers had become dissatisfied with this arrangement. Education spending had risen sharply in the post-war years, yet evidence was mounting that student test scores in the United States lagged behind those of peer nations. This led to the emergence of two strategies of school reform. One approach – advanced by those who favoured government intervention into schooling – was 'standards-based' reform. Here, federal and state governments promised to provide sufficient funds to local schools, but in return governments set ambitious student performance goals and held schools accountable for achieving these goals through test-based accountability. A second approach – favoured by those opposed to government intervention – was known as 'school choice'. Here, states worked to create markets for schooling, either by giving vouchers to parents or by authorising charter schools. The assumption was that the creation of markets would spur competition among schools and naturally lead to improved instruction and student learning.

These two reform strategies are now stable features of American education. But forty years after they first appeared, the problem they were meant to address remains. Whether it be regular public schools or schools of choice, local schools in the United States retain considerable discretion over how they organise and manage instruction and, as a result, school performance remains quite variable, with a substantial percentage of schools neither meeting government performance standards nor having the capacity to improve student performance on their own. In the US context, local constituencies have little appetite for closing down these low-performing schools and governments have little appetite (or capacity) for intervening directly into their operations. This raises the central question of this chapter: when local schools lack the capacity to improve student achievement on their own, when local consumers won't close them down and when direct government intervention is effectively checked by American-style education governance, is there anything organisations *outside* of government can do to promote instructional improvement in America's low-performing schools?

6.2 EMERGENCE OF SCHOOL IMPROVEMENT BY DESIGN

As it turns out, US policymakers asked this same question fifty years ago. At the time, policymakers were disappointed by the limited impact new federal education funding was having on early childhood and K–12 student outcomes. This led to questions about how schools might make better use of the new federal funds they were receiving. One idea that surfaced was to provide schools with incentives to adopt 'innovative' projects. In early childhood education, this led to a policy of planned variation in the federal government's Follow Through programme – a policy in which schools using Follow Through funds were required to implement a particular model of schooling to be chosen from among a set of predetermined models approved by the government. Importantly, these preapproved models were not developed locally but rather by various university-based or other not-for-profit organisations (Kennedy 1978; Watkins 1997). A similar move occurred in K–12 education. Here, new federal funding under Titles III and VII of the Elementary and Secondary Education Act (ESEA) went to local schools willing to undertake what the ESEA legislation called 'innovative projects'. In this programme, some projects were developed locally by schools, but many others were developed by organisations *outside* schools.

These 1970s initiatives mark the beginnings of school improvement by design in the United States. However, the results of these initiatives were mixed. On one hand, evaluations of the Follow Through and ESEA initiatives showed that many externally-developed models had little impact on school operations or outcomes and were quickly disbanded. On the other hand, some other models produced real change and improvement in schools (Berman and McLaughlin 1975; Kennedy 1978). As a result, the federal government created the National Diffusion Network (NDN) in the 1970s to identify, call to public attention and help disseminate these effective models (or projects or programmes) of school improvement.

Although funding for these efforts lapsed in the 1980s, that was not the end of the school improvement by design. Indeed, the idea resurfaced in the 1990s in a somewhat different form. The chief proponent this time was George H. W. Bush, whose administration intended to rely on a 'thousand points of light' (not just government) to promote the public good in American society. In K–12 education, the practical manifestation of this idea was the New American Schools Development Corporation (NASDAC), a not-for-profit organisation run by business interests with the strong endorsement of President Bush. In 1991, NASDAC held a design competition in which organisations from across the field of education were asked to bring forward 'break the mould' designs for school improvement (Bodilly 1996). Ultimately, NASDAC selected eleven such designs and, with great fanfare, funded the developers to begin implementing their designs in schools. By 1998, this work had captured the imagination of the US Congress, which passed the Comprehensive School Reform (CSR) Demonstration Act, which was later folded into the 2002 reauthorisation of ESEA (commonly known as No Child Left Behind). That programme gave Title I schools $50,000 to adopt and implement a CSR model. As a result of this initiative, more than 600 different

CSR models were developed and implemented in about 7,000 schools across the United States (Orland et al. 2010). Thus, for a brief time during the early 2000s, there were as many schools in the United States using a CSR design as there were charter schools.

The widespread adoption of CSR programmes brought about a new wave of programme evaluations, the best of which were summarised in a meta-analysis by Borman et al. (2003). Their analysis of data on twenty-nine (widely-adopted and externally-operated) CSR programmes once again showed that programme effects on student achievement were varied. About half the programmes included in the meta-analysis had positive effects on student achievement, with many showing effects in the range of Cohen's $d_{sd} = .3$ (Borman et al. 2003). However, the other half of the programmes did not have positive effects (with hardly any showing negative effects on student achievement).

Federal funding for the CSR programme also lapsed. But federal support for school improvement by design reignited yet again in 2009 as part of the American Recovery and Reinvestment Act. This act created the Investing in Innovation (i3) programme which allocated \$1.4 billion in competitive grants funding to three kinds of organisations – those seeking to develop new programme designs, those with already-developed designs that wanted funds to conduct rigorous evaluations and those operating programmes that had been evaluated already, had strong evidence of effectiveness and wanted to implement their designs in larger numbers of schools. As of 2019, this programme was still in operation (in much reduced form) as the Education Innovation and Research (EIR) programme in the US Department Education.

Importantly, the i3 programme required all grant recipients to conduct rigorous programme evaluations, producing yet another wave of evaluation research. In 2018, Abt Associates was commissioned by the US Department of Education to summarise these evaluations (Boulay et al. 2018). As in previous analyses of evaluation research, the Abt study showed a great deal of variability in programme effectiveness. In the i3 case, about 25 per cent (of sixty-seven) i3-funded programmes had positive impacts on student achievement, while 75 per cent showed virtually no effect on student achievement outcomes.

6.3 HOW DESIGN-BASED IMPROVEMENT WORKS

The variable success of school improvement by design brings me to the second issue I want to discuss in this chapter. If only some externally developed designs for school improvement succeed, what features of school improvement by design distinguish successful from unsuccessful efforts?

One answer – particularly important for the theme of this edited volume – is that design-based school improvement succeeds only if a programme's design is implemented in schools. In this chapter, however, I will argue that implementation is only one part of the explanation for why school improvement by design succeeds or fails. Indeed, the Abt Associates report on i3 programmes (Boulay et al. 2018) found that 75 per cent of i3 designs were well implemented in schools, yet only 25 per cent actually succeeded in improving student achievement. So, something besides good implementation is needed to make school improvement by design work. What, then, is this missing ingredient?

In this chapter, I will show that design-based school improvement consists of *two* essential features: a design for instruction and a design for implementation. A programme's design for instruction is a blueprint for what the programme wants students to know and be able to do along with associated guidance about the instructional activities that teachers and students need to undertake as students learn to do these things. Then, to get this instructional design put into place in schools, design-based improvement requires a second design component – a design for implementation. An implementation design is a blueprint for how school personnel should manage the programme's new instructional design *in situ*, including what local personnel need to learn to enact any new practices embedded in the programme's instructional design, the kinds of materials local personnel need to purchase and use to mount the new instructional design and any administrative and structural supports needed to enact the instructional design in schools.

Over the next several pages, I am going to present a set of cases showing how these two design components explain the success (or failure) of school improvement by design. These cases will show that design-based school improvement succeeds only when externally-developed programmes: (1) have an instructional design that is different from and better than the one replaced in local schools and (2) have an implementation design that assures this new instructional design is put into place. Table 6.1 presents this idea in tabular form. In the upper left-hand cell of the table are success cases, that is, organisations with effective instructional designs and successful strategies for putting those designs in place in schools. The other three cells are failure cases. One kind of failure occurs in the lower left-hand cell of the table. These are programmes with good instructional designs but weak implementation

Table 6.1 *Four patterns of school improvement by design*

Effective Design for Implementation?	Effective Design for Instruction?	
	Yes	No
Yes	Design leads to changes in instruction and improved student achievement	Design leads to changes in instruction but no improvement in student achievement
No	Design leads to no changes in instruction or student achievement	Design leads to no changes in instruction or student achievement

designs. Another kind of failure (shown in the upper right-hand corner of the table) is cases with good implementation designs but instructional designs that are no better than what they replace. The final case appears in the lower right-hand cell, where programmes are built around instructional designs no better than what they aim to replace and that lack a sound strategy to get these designs in place.

6.4 SUCCESSFUL CASES

6.4.1 Success for All

Let's begin with a successful case of school improvement by design called Success for All (SFA). This programme evolved out of systematic programme of research and development conducted by Robert Slavin and Nancy Madden at Johns Hopkins University in the 1980s. When my colleagues and I studied this programme (at the peak of the CSR movement), it was operating in 1,100 schools in the United States, and it remains one of America's most widely implemented and widely researched designs for school improvement.

The hallmark of the SFA programme is that its highly specified instructional design is coupled to an implementation design that constrains teacher discretion and enforces compliance. SFA's instructional design is a 'skill-based' reading programme built around a well-defined, sequentially-organised reading curriculum meant to be delivered through fast-paced, teacher-directed instruction and cooperative group activities (Correnti and Rowan 2007). The SFA design includes: (a) a carefully sequenced set of five-day instructional cycles that cover targeted reading comprehension strategies; (b) specific instructional routines that teachers are expected to use during every lesson in these five-day cycles (including direct teaching routines and cooperative learning routines); (c) specific reading assignments students are asked to complete each day (such as answering brief questions orally, completing multiple-choice and/or fill-in-the-blanks comprehension worksheets, writing brief answers to comprehension questions, discussing text with peers); and (d) a set of formative assessments that determine which lesson cycles students are assigned to during the school year. Thus, SFA has an explicit instructional design describing the content of instruction, the instructional routines to be used in lessons, the instructional assignments students should complete and formative assessments that determine how students matriculate through the curriculum.

To get this instructional design in place, SFA developed an implementation design that works to assure these instructional practices are used in schools. The design calls for three days of initial training and eight days of follow-up training for teachers. More importantly, it has teachers use 'scripts' during every ninety-minute lesson in the sequenced curriculum. At grades K–2, instruction is further standardised by use of programme-developed curricular materials. SFA supplements these stringent controls on classroom instruction by also reorganising school management structures and processes (Camburn et al. 2003; Rowan and Miller 2007). In particular, SFA schools are expected to appoint a full-time literacy coordinator who is given responsibility for school-wide coordination of the reading programme and SFA's implementation design calls for school leaders to enforce implementation of SFA instructional routines, including use of lessons scripts. As a result, levels of instructional supervision are high in SFA schools (Camburn et al. 2003).

Evaluation research shows that SFA is a successful case of school improvement by design on two counts. First, it leads to changes in instructional practice that are consistent with its instructional design. For example, in a large quasi-experiment, Correnti and Rowan (2007) found that teachers in SFA schools were more likely than comparison teachers to use practices embedded in its instructional design, including more teaching of reading comprehension strategies, more use of teacher-directed instruction, more checking of students' comprehension by eliciting brief answers from students and (because of extensive use of cooperative grouping arrangements) more small group discussion of text. In the same quasi-experiment, Rowan and Miller (2007) found that about 70 per cent of teachers in SFA schools implemented SFA-specific teaching routines with high fidelity.

Second, SFA has been found to improve student achievement (Borman et al. 2003, 2005, 2007; Rowan et al. 2009). In the quasi-experiment my colleagues and I conducted (Rowan et al. 2009), the programme had positive effects on students' reading achievement of $d_{sd} = .2$, or about two additional months of achievement per year. However, these effects were only evident for students at grades K–2, with no positive effects for students in grades 3–5 – even though the programme was well-implemented at these grades. Thus, my colleagues and I concluded that SFA's skill-based reading programmes was not effective at all grades – even if it was well-implemented. Rather, the SFA instructional design works best in the early grades of schooling.

6.4.2 America's Choice

A second case of successful design-based school improvement is America's Choice (AC). This programme was developed at the National Centre for Education and the Economy (NCEE), a not-for-profit, Washington, DC-based think tank. This programme was never as widely-adopted as SFA, nor did it survive the demise of CSR funding. In 2001 – when my colleagues and I studied the programme – it was operating in 145 elementary schools, and in 2010 it was sold to Pearson, LLC, which ultimately took it off the market as the Common Core State Standards were adopted widely in states. Like SFA, the AC programme was built around a well-specified instructional design coupled to an effective approach to implementation. But as we shall see, it differed in many respects from the SFA programme.

To begin, when we studied AC, the programme focused on improving a school's writing programme. The AC design for writing instruction called for teachers to spend more minutes per day teaching writing and for teachers to change the way writing was taught. In the design, teachers were asked to move away from teaching writing mechanics and to focus on having students produce more written text. Teachers were also expected to use specific instructional practices, including a writers' workshop routine in which students went through various steps of the writing process (i.e. generating ideas, drafting, reviewing/revising and publishing and evaluating written products). The programme further called for an important shift in the kinds of writing assignments students worked on, shifting away from personal narratives and toward writing about the texts being used in reading comprehension lessons. This particular feature led us to label the AC design as a form of 'literature-based' reading instruction.

AC coupled this well-specified instructional design to a robust design for implementation. In the AC design, schools were expected to create two new leadership positions at the school: a design coach and a literacy coordinator. The design coaches helped mount and supervise programme implementation, while the literacy coordinator worked directly with classroom teachers to design core writing assignments and common scoring rubrics for these assignments. Teachers' instructional practices were thus closely monitored in AC schools, although monitoring was built around coaching, not supervision for compliance. Thus, AC schools showed high levels of instructional leadership (Camburn et al. 2003).

The AC programme has not been studied as often as the SFA programme. However, the research my colleagues and I did suggests that AC is another successful case of school improvement by design. Correnti and Rowan (2007), for example, found large differences in literacy instruction in AC vs. comparison schools in a large quasi-experiment. Consistent with the AC instructional design, AC teachers spent more time teaching writing and, when writing was taught, AC teachers were more likely to teach the writing process explicitly, to provide instruction on literary techniques or different writing genres, to have students revise and share their writing, to have students write multiple connected paragraphs and to combine instruction in reading comprehension with lessons on writing. Overall, Rowan and Miller (2007) estimated that about 62 per cent of AC teachers in the large quasi-experiment implemented the AC teaching regime with high fidelity.

In the same quasi-experiment, my colleagues and I found evidence that AC had positive effects on students' reading comprehension outcomes – although, as with SFA, these positive effects were only present at certain grades. In grades 3–5, students in AC schools experienced significantly greater gains in reading comprehension than students in comparison schools, with an effect size of about $d_{sd} = .2$, or about two additional months of achievement per year. However, the data also showed that AC's instructional design was *not* effective in grades K–2, despite being well implemented at those grades. At those grade levels, students in AC schools made the same learning gains as students in comparison schools (Correnti 2009; Rowan et al. 2009).

6.4.3 How School Improvement by Design Fails

The SFA and AC programmes illustrate how school improvement by design succeeds. Although SFA and AC had different designs, both designs had common features. Both designs were very explicit about the curriculum content to be taught and both designs had explicit ideas about the instructional routines to be used when teaching that content, including specific ideas about teaching practices, student interactions and student assignments. In addition, both programmes had very strong implementation designs. Both programmes reorganised schools to increase instructional leadership, although SFA relied on lesson scripting and close supervision to assure that scripts were in use in lessons, whereas AC relied on intensive coaching to get its instructional routines in use. Finally, both programmes were instructionally effective, although only at certain grades.

With those findings as background, I will now describe some cases where school improvement by design *failed*. As Table 6.1 shows, failure results from a variety of design shortcomings. In what follows, I will describe one programme (BURST: Reading) that had a very explicit and potentially effective instructional design but failed to develop an effective implementation design. Then I will describe a programme (the Accelerated Schools Project) with a very explicit design for implementation that lacked an effective instructional design. Finally, I will discuss the case of a programme (Agile Mind) that lacked important components of instructional design and implementation design.

6.4.3.1 BURST: Reading The first case of failed improvement by design is BURST: Reading, a model of school improvement that had a potentially effective instructional design but an incomplete implementation design. BURST was developed by Amplify, Inc., a Brooklyn-based education service provider, and was intended to work as a supplementary instructional programme that identified and provided targeted instruction to struggling readers in grades K–5. Amplify launched BURST in 2007 and by 2016 it was in use in 651 schools across the United States. My discussion of this programme is based on a randomised field trial my colleagues and I conducted over a four-year period beginning in September 2013. In this study, twenty-seven schools were randomly assigned to the BURST treatment and twenty-five to a control condition (Rowan et al. 2019).

BURST's instructional design is very similar to SFA's. It consists of a well specified, skill-based reading programme that has a solid basis in empirical research. The instructional design includes a well-specified sequence of lessons through which students proceed, 'scripted' lesson plans for each lesson in that sequence, a set of materials for use in these lessons and a set of assessments that determine students' movement through these lessons. BURST differs from SFA in implementation design. It offers a one-day introductory training session and (at additional cost) several more days of on-site consulting by BURST professional staff. Importantly, BURST does *not* rely on local staff to support programme implementation to the same extent as SFA. Whereas SFA appoints a school leader to facilitate programme operations, BURST handles many programme functions through remote, computerised interactions. For example, schools submit standardised data to Amplify and Amplify uses a data algorithm to assign students to lessons. Apart from this algorithm schools are given considerable leeway in programme implementation, including discretion over how frequently they offer BURST instruction, which staff offer BURST instruction and how many students are served by BURST.

Data from our randomised field trial showed that the most routinised aspects of BURST were faithfully implemented in study schools. Teachers regularly submitted student data for lesson assignments, teachers almost always used BURST materials in lessons and teachers regularly followed BURST lesson scripts. In areas where implementation guidance was weak or lacking, however, there was much more variation in implementation, including variation in the frequency with which schools delivered BURST instruction and the percentage of 'struggling readers' who were served. This variability conditioned the effects of BURST on students reading achievement. BURST programme developers recommended that struggling readers got about 150 hours of BURST instruction (roughly 45 minutes a day in a 180-day school year). Yet most schools in the study offered BURST instruction two-to-three times a week, and many students received BURST instruction for only half a year. Thus, most schools offered far less than the recommended 'dose' of BURST, and that had important consequences for programme effectiveness. In the randomised field trial, programme effects on students' reading achievement were near zero at typical dosage levels and increased steadily as students received more hours of BURST instruction. In that sense, BURST appears to be a design-based intervention with a *potentially* effective instructional design (i.e. a programme that works at recommended dosage) coupled to a design for implementation that typically fails to get the instructional programme implemented with sufficient intensity in schools.

6.4.3.2 *Accelerated Schools Project* The Accelerated Schools Project (ASP) presents a different case of failed school improvement – a failure arising from a weak design for instruction coupled to a strong design for implementation. ASP was founded by Henry Levin at Stanford University in the 1980s and has worked with about 1,700 schools across the United States. Most evaluations of

ASP have examined cases where the programme was reputedly successful. But from 2000 to 2004, my colleagues and I studied ASP as part of a large, quasi-experiment involving different CSR designs (Rowan et al. 2009).

My colleagues and I have characterised ASP's instructional design as a form of what Ouchi (1980) called cultural control. Essentially, ASP sought to orient the instructional work of teachers to a cultural ideal: a norm of 'powerful learning' for all children. From the outset, however, ASP was never very specific about what this ideal looked like in practice. The programme made no attempt to define specific curriculum objectives or performance standards. Instead, its goals for instructional change were generic in form – aiming at broad changes across the board rather than targeting specific areas of the curriculum for change. Moreover, the kinds of changes teachers were supposed to make to achieve powerful learning were not clearly specified. Instead, each school (and each teacher within a school) was asked to 'discover' the most appropriate means of producing powerful learning within their particular context. Thus, teachers were given a great deal of autonomy in the ASP system and, as a result, there was little specificity in the instructional design.

However, ASP did have a highly specified design for implementation. Each ASP school was expected to hire a local employee or outside consultant to serve as a coach. The coach then received training and support from ASP staff and worked a day a week with the school during the first year of implementation. During that year, the main implementation task was to create an ASP-style governance structure within a school involving creation of various types of committees in a school. Members of these various committees were then taught a specific set of management routines to build a common culture, take stock of their current situation, set priorities for change and form problem-solving task groups. These task groups were then taught to use well-specified inquiry routines to develop reform ideas, pilot these ideas and evaluate them.

Our quasi-experiment suggested that the management routines central to the ASP design were well implemented in schools (Rowan and Miller 2007; Rowan et al. 2009). Data from the study showed that ASP schools had a strong press for innovation, a strong emphasis on making improvement decisions consistent with school culture and high levels of staff collaboration and trust. However, given the lack of specificity in instructional design, teachers in ASP schools also reported very low press for standardisation, very low levels of instructional guidance and low levels of instructional leadership and monitoring.

The quasi-experiment also showed that, in the end, these successful efforts to get schools to adopt ASP-style governance ended up producing little change in instructional practice or student achievement. In the quasi-experiment, teaching practices in ASP schools were no different from teaching practices in control schools (Correnti and Rowan 2007). It is therefore not surprising that ASP schools also showed no better reading achievement than schools in the control group (Correnti 2009; Rowan et al. 2009; cf. Bloom et al. 2001). For this reason, ASP can be seen as a failed case of school improvement by design, one in which a strong design for implementation was coupled to a weak design for instruction.

6.4.3.3 *Agile Mind (Algebra 1)* The next case describes Agile Mind (AM) – a small (but thriving) software company that develops on-line courseware for use in schools. My colleagues and I worked with this company in 2007, when the company was relatively new and was producing courseware for high school mathematics courses. Since that time, the company has expanded its courseware offerings and changed how it works with schools. In what follows, we describe a three-year study of Agile Mind's Algebra 1 courseware as it was used in Texas high schools during the school years 2003–2006 (Correnti et al. 2008). The main finding from this work is that Agile Mind had an incompletely specified instructional design coupled to a weak design for implementation.

At the time our study, Agile Mind defined itself as being in the 'curriculum as service' business. In this model, AM delivered its Algebra I curriculum services via the internet. These internet-delivered services were built around lesson resources for the teaching of specific areas of the Algebra I curriculum coupled to a number of on-line planning tools and teaching tips that teachers could use to customise their lesson plans. Agile Mind also had a set of student assignments and formative assessments that were tied to specific lessons and that could be scored in real time, allowing students to get rapid feedback and teachers to engage in responsive lesson planning. Finally, Agile Mind had online professional development integrated with the planning tools in the service, which also could be delivered in real time.

As a design for school improvement, Agile Mind's 'courseware' model was built around an incomplete instructional design and a weak design for implementation. The courseware itself was the main instructional design. To be sure, the courseware had many essential elements of a strong instructional design – a clear set of curriculum objectives, a set of lesson materials (featuring attractive, engaging and instructionally sound animations) and a set of curriculum-aligned formative assessments for use by students and teachers. But the courseware did not contain clear guidance about specific instructional routines that teachers and students were expected to use during lessons. Moreover, the company's design for implementation was missing critical ingredients. The company viewed the courseware as its main product and it encouraged teachers to use this courseware at their own discretion. The main support for implementation was a teacher guidebook distributed with the courseware (which resembled the teacher guidebooks distributed by publishers of print textbooks). On-site professional development (prior to implementation) and on-site visits from company-trained mentors were available, but optional and offered at additional cost.

Our study of Agile Mind's Algebra 1 courseware and its effects on students' tested achievement produced several discouraging findings. To begin, there was a great deal of teacher-to-teacher variation in the use of AM's courseware and a general decline in use of the courseware over time. The decline occurred, in part, because teachers were often assigned to teach Algebra I on a yearly basis, and there was a great deal of course re-assignment in years after initial adoption. This churn in teacher assignments interacted with the programme's incompletely specified instructional design and *laissez faire* approach to implementation to condition use in schools. As time wore one, the percentage of teachers using AM's Algebra 1 courseware declined, with fewer and fewer (and sometimes no) trained teachers remaining in a school to use the service a few years after adoption. This was unfortunate, since our research showed that teachers who used the courseware across successive years and received support from company-trained mentors also used the courseware more fully and changed their patterns of use over time in directions that AM's developers intended.

Given AM's incompletely specified instructional design and *laissez faire* approach to implementation, it should not be surprising that use of AM courseware had no effects on students' mathematics achievement – either on average or at heightened levels of use. Importantly, when we reported these findings to Agile Mind leadership, they took aggressive steps to improve their designs for instruction and implementation. Indeed, after the study, the company appointed a vice-president of professional services with extensive experience managing school improvement programming, expanded its professional development staff and offerings and more fully elaborated the teaching routines it recommended for use with the courseware.

6.5 IMPROVING THE VIABILITY AND QUALITY OF SCHOOL IMPROVEMENT DESIGNS

The cases just presented demonstrate the good and bad news about school improvement by design. The good news is that researchers know a great deal about how school improvement by design works, that is, what it takes to change instruction and improve student achievement in schools. Successful school improvement by design has two central features: good designs for instruction and good designs for implementation. Good designs for instruction consist of well-specified blueprints for the content to be taught to students (in a particular subject, at a particular grade, with a particular learning trajectory), clear routines for teaching that content, clear routines for what students should do as they learn that content and clear routines for the use of curriculum-based assessments to plan instruction. Good designs for implementation are also well-specified and multifaceted. Good implementation designs provide extensive training for those who will mount an instructional design, provide strong written guidance, scripts or coaching so that instructional routines are implemented with fidelity, and reorganise schools to monitor and promote implementation fidelity. All of this is well-known, both in the older literature on planned educational change (see, for example, Emrick et al. 1977; Louis et al. 1981; Crandall and Loucks 1983) and in the emerging, multidisciplinary field of 'implementation science' (Moir 2018).

The bad news is that effective designs for school improvement are scarce. Indeed, if America's experience with the Investing in Innovation (i3) program is used to estimate a base rate for success, we can speculate that only about 25 per cent of designs for school improvement succeed (Boulay et al. 2018). That finding brings me to the final question I want to discuss in this chapter: If school improvement by design only works sometimes, what can be done to make this process a more viable – and more reliable – approach to school reform? To answer this question, I now want to describe the role that markets, governments and networks play in making school improvement by design a viable and reliable approach to school reform.

6.6 MARKETS

At its heart, school improvement by design involves a market exchange between organisations that provide designs for school improvement and schools that contract for their services. A fundamental problem, however, is that this market transaction is fraught with uncertainty. Uncertainty exists because designs for school improvement are in many ways what economists call a 'credence' good (for definitions, see Balafoutas and Kerschbamer 2020). A credence good is a product or service with attributes that are difficult to ascertain, both at the time of purchase and after use. In the case of school improvement by design, for example, school personnel might not be able to ascertain the precise kind of design they need or want and, once the design is put into use, they might find it difficult to ascertain if it is having the desired effects.

Much has been written about how these uncertainties affect the producers of credence goods. One prominent theme is that markets for credence goods drive out high quality producers, since buyers are unwilling to pay a higher price for products about which they have no information. This creates what Akerlof (1978) called a market for 'lemons', that is, a marketplace in which only low cost producers can make a profit. Another prominent idea is that the marketplace for credence goods can disappear altogether if buyers, facing uncertain payoffs from a purchase that can be neither warrantied nor enforced through liability claims, simply choose to pursue school improvement on their own (Williamson 1981).

In fact, there is good reason to think the market for design-based school improvement has exactly these features. For example, only a fraction of design-based programmes appear to have positive impacts on teaching or learning in schools, yet none are warrantied. Moreover, there appear to be relatively few buyers of designs. For example, even when the market for design-based improvement was at its peak during the height of the CSR movement, only about 5 per cent of public and private schools worked with a CSR provider. The rest of the schools went about improving instruction and student achievement in other ways.

6.7 GOVERNMENTS

Importantly, governments can improve this situation. One way to stave off a collapse in markets for credence goods is to lessen the costs of participation. In the market for design-based improvement, for example, ESEA funding for innovative projects and CSR funding provided cash incentives for schools to work with design providers and, with incentive payments, more schools were willing to purchase design services despite uncertainties. This prevented a total collapse of the design market. Governments can also give incentives to producers and thereby offset some of the costs of developing higher quality products. This approach was taken in the Investing in Innovation (i3) programme, which gave grants to design providers to develop and scale up high quality interventions; it is also the approach taken in the US Department of Education's Small Business Innovation Research programme. The history of both types of programmes suggests that government investments can stimulate a market for design-based improvement, although, at the end of the day, the marketplace for design-based improvement still seems have a disproportionate percentage of 'lemons' and remains small.

In this light, additional government actions might be needed. Rather than stimulate supply and demand, governments can take actions to fundamentally alter the information dynamics in a market for credence goods. The basic idea is to change credence goods into search goods (i.e. goods about which consumers have advance information). This can be done through product labelling and certification. The US federal government has taken promising actions like these in education, dating from the National Diffusion Network and currently with the What Works Clearinghouse. Both efforts label and certify designs for improvement. However, as currently configured, these efforts do not apply to all designs available in the marketplace, nor have they led to the kind of well-understood and widely embraced grading and labelling systems that exist in other markets (such as USDA meat and poultry grading systems or USDA organic food certification).

6.8 NETWORKS

All of this brings me to yet another way to alter the market for design-based school improvement – the use of social and inter-organisational networks. Here, for example, consumer and producer networks can replace government agencies as the chief architects of labelling and certification systems. Such networks are common in many markets. The formation of the Consumers Union (now Consumer Reports) in 1936 represents one model of how civil society can provide product certification. A similar model has appeared in education, where EdReports.org rates textbook quality. Producer networks also engage in certification, for example, Fairtrade International, which provides 'fair trade' labelling of coffee, tea, honey, sugar and other products. In education, a good example of this kind of producer network is the Collaborative for Academic, Social and Emotional Learning (CASEL), which developed SELect Certification to label and certify programmes in the area of socio-emotional learning.

Still, efforts to subsidise producers and consumers or label and certify products might not be enough to build strong markets for school improvement by design absent a strong national commitment to using this approach to improve schools. Thus, yet another kind of network might be needed – a policy network (Rhodes 2006) composed of central actors and agencies that can influence public opinion and government actors to support design-based improvement. The use of inter-organisational networks to spread new practices through a field are especially evident in healthcare, where quality improvement (QI) campaigns have been successful (Schneider et al. 2017), and in education, an example of a policy network spreading an innovation is the policy network that orchestrated the rise and spread of the Common Core State Standards in US education (Hartong 2016).

Note, however, that it makes little sense to stimulate markets for credence goods if the goods themselves are no better than the status quo. Thus, a final way to improve school improvement by design is through innovation networks. Inter-organisational networks that create and refine products exist in many industries (Malerba and Vonortas 2009) and are increasingly being used to spread and improve evidence-based practices in the healthcare industry (Clancy et al. 2013). Such networks have also been described in education, where they are used both to create, evaluate and spread effective designs for school improvement (Bryk et al. 2011) and to replicate and improve existing designs (Peurach and Glazer 2012).

6.9 SUMMARY

In this chapter, I argued that school improvement by design could be an important supplement to standards-based reform and school choice as a means for improving instruction and student achievement in America's highly decentralised education system. I also argued that we know the conditions under which design-based improvement succeeds (and fails) in this task. But I also argued that the market for school improvement by design is fraught with uncertainties about quality that have led schools to shy away from using this process. I therefore discussed some ways to shore up and improve this marketplace. Governments (and perhaps venture philanthropists) can stimulate supply and demand by investing in innovation; producers and consumers can form innovation networks that create, refine and spread designs; and governments and/or producers can label and certify effective designs for broader dissemination in the markets for school improvement. None of this will happen, however, without a strong, national commitment to the process of school improvement by design and such a commitment is unlikely absent strong action by one or more well-placed policy networks in the field.

References

Akerlof, G. A. (1978). The market for 'lemons': Quality uncertainty and the market mechanism. In *Uncertainty in Economics*. Cambridge, MA: Academic Press, pp. 235–51.

Balafoutas, L. and Kerschbamer, R. (2020). Credence goods in the literature: What the past fifteen years have taught us about fraud, incentives, and the role of institutions. *Journal of Behavioral and Experimental Finance*, 26, 100285.

Berman, P. and McLaughlin, M. W. (1975). *Federal Programs Supporting Educational Change, Vol. 4: The Findings in Review*. Santa Monica: RAND.

Bloom, H. S., Ham, S., Melton, L. and O'Brien, J. (2001). *Evaluating the Accelerated Schools Approach: A Look at Early Implementation and Impacts on Student Achievement in Eight Elementary Schools*. Washington, DC: MDRC.

Bodilly, S. (1996). *Lessons from New American Schools Development Corporation's Demonstration Phase*. Santa Monica: RAND.

Borman, G. D., Hewes, G. M., Overman, L. T. and Brown, S. (2003). Comprehensive school reform and achievement: A meta-analysis. *Review of Educational Research*, 73:2, 125–230.

Borman, G. D., Slavin, R. E., Cheung, A. C., Chamberlain, A. M., Madden, N. A. and Chambers, B. (2005). The national randomized field trial of Success for All: Second-year outcomes. *American Educational Research Journal*, 42:4, 673–96.

Borman, G. D., Slavin, R. E., Cheung, A. C., Chamberlain, A. M., Madden, N. A. and Chambers, B. (2007). Final reading outcomes of the national randomized field trial of Success for All. *American Educational Research Journal*, 44:3, 701–31.

Boulay, B., Goodson, B., Olsen, R., McCormick, R., Darrow, C., Frye, M., Gan, K., Harvill, H. and Sarna, M. (2018). *The Investing in Innovation Fund: Summary of 67 Evaluations: Final Report (NCEE 2018-4013)*. Washington, DC: National Center for Education Evaluation and Regional Assistance, Institute of Education Sciences, US Department of Education.

Bryk, A. S., Gomez, L. M. and Grunow, A. (2011). Getting ideas into action: Building networked improvement communities in education. In Hallinan, M. (ed.) *Frontiers in Sociology of Education. Frontiers in Sociology and Social Research*, vol 1. Dordrecht: Springer, pp. 127–62.

Camburn, E., Rowan, B. and Taylor, J. E. (2003). Distributed leadership in schools: The case of elementary schools adopting comprehensive school reform models. *Educational Evaluation and Policy Analysis*, 25:4, 347–73.

Clancy, C. M., Margolis, P. A. and Miller, M. (2013). Collaborative networks for both improvement and research. *Pediatrics*, 131(Suppl 4), S210–14.

Cohen, D. K., Peurach, D. J., Glazer, J. L., Gates, K. E. and Goldin, S. (2013). *Improvement by Design: The Promise of Better Schools*. Chicago: University of Chicago Press.

Correnti, R. (2009). Examining CSR program effects on student achievement: Causal explanation through examination of implementation rates and student mobility. *Paper Presented at the Conference of Society for Research on Educational Effectiveness*, Washington, DC, March.

Correnti, R. and Rowan, B. (2007). Opening up the black box: Literacy instruction in schools participating in three comprehensive school reform programs. *American Educational Research Journal*, 44:2, 298–339.

Correnti, R., Hansen, B. B. and Rowan, B. (2008). *Early Implementation and Student Achievement Outcomes in Texas Schools using Agile Mind Algebra 1 Services*. Ann Arbor, MI: Institute for Social Research, University of Michigan.

Crandall, D. P. and Loucks, S. F. (1983). *A Roadmap for School Improvement. Executive Summary of the Study of Dissemination Efforts Supporting School Improvement. People, Policies, and Practices: Examining the Chain of School Improvement, Volume X*. ERIC Number: ED240722. Andover, MA: Network of Innovative Schools, Inc.

Dusenbury, L. (2003). A review of research on fidelity of implementation: Implications for drug abuse prevention in school settings. *Health Education Research*, 18:2, 237–56.

Emrick, J. A., Peterson, S. M. and Agarwala-Rogers, R. (1977). *Evaluation of the National Diffusion Network: Volume 1, Findings and Recommendations*. Menlo Park, CA: Stanford Research Institute.

Hartong, S. (2016). New structures of power and regulation within 'distributed' education policy – the example of the US Common Core State Standards Initiative. *Journal of Education Policy*, 31:2, 213–25.

Kennedy, M. M. (1978). Findings from the Follow Through planned variation study. *Educational Researcher*, 7:6, 3–11.

Louis, K. S., Rosenblum, S. and Molitor, J. A. (1981). *Strategies for Knowledge Use and School Improvement*. Washington, DC: US Department of Education, Office of Educational Research and Improvement.

Malerba, F. and Vonortas, N. S. (eds.) (2009). *Innovation Networks in Industries*. Cheltenham, UK: Edward Elgar Publishing.

Meyer, J. W. and Rowan, B. (1978). The structure of educational organizations. In Ballantine, J. H. and Spade, J. Z. (eds.) *Schools and Society: A Sociological Approach to Education*. Thousand Oaks, CA: Pine Forge Press, pp. 217–25.

Moir, T. (2018). Why is implementation science important for intervention design and evaluation within educational settings? *Frontiers in Education*, 3, Article 61.

Orland, M., Hoffman, A. and Vaughn, S. E. (2010) *Evaluation of the Comprehensive School Reform Program Implementation and Outcomes: Fifth-Year Report*. Washington, DC: US Department of Education, Office of Planning, Evaluation and Policy Development, Policy and Program Studies Service.

Ouchi, W. G. (1980). Markets, bureaucracies, and clans. *Administrative Science Quarterly*, 25:1, 129–41.

Peurach, D. J. and Glazer, J. L. (2012). Reconsidering replication: New perspectives on large-scale school improvement. *Journal of Educational Change*, 13:2, 155–90.

Rhodes, R. A. W. (2006). Policy network analysis. In Goodin, R. E., Moran, M. and Rein, M. (eds.) *The Oxford Handbook of Public Policy*, Vol. 6. Oxford: Oxford University Press, pp. 425–47.

Rowan, B. and Miller, R. J. (2007). Organizational strategies for promoting instructional change: Implementation dynamics in schools working with comprehensive school reform providers. *American Educational Research Journal*, 44:2, 252–97.

Rowan, B., Hansen, B. B., White, M., Lycurgus, T., and Scott, L. J. (2019). *A Summary of the BURST: Reading Efficacy Trial (Carried Out Under IES Award # R305A120811)*. Ann Arbor, MI: Institute for Social Research, University of Michigan.

Rowan, B., Miller, R., and Camburn, E. (2009). *School Improvement by Design: Lessons from a Study of Comprehensive School Reform Programs*. Philadelphia: Consortium for Policy Research in Education.

Schneider, E. C., Sorbero, M. E., Haas, A., Ridgely, M. S., Khodyakov, D., Setodji, C. M. and Goldmann, D. (2017). Does a quality improvement campaign accelerate take-up of new evidence? A ten-state cluster-randomized controlled trial of the IHI's Project JOINTS. *Implementation Science*, 12:1, 51.

Watkins, C. L. (1997). *Project Follow Through*. Cambridge, MA: Cambridge Center for Behavioral Studies.

Williamson, O. E. (1981). The economics of organization: The transaction cost approach. *American Journal of Sociology*, 87:3, 548–77.

7 Promising Practice in Government Schools in Vietnam

Tony McAleavy and Rachael Fitzpatrick

There is mounting evidence that Vietnam has an effective basic education system as measured by cognitive outcomes in core subjects. Vietnamese students did well in the 2012 and 2015 PISA tests (OECD, 2013, 2016a). The significance of PISA data is contested but encouraging data has also emerged from the Oxford University Young Lives study, which has tracked the academic performance of a sample of children in Ethiopia, India, Peru and Vietnam since 2002. In 2013, Young Lives Director Jo Boyden described the performance by Vietnamese Grade 5 students during the school year 2011–12 as 'truly exceptional':

> Pupil performance in Vietnam (where per capita GDP [gross domestic product] is broadly similar to that of India) is truly exceptional. Around 19 out of every 20 ten year-olds can add four-digit numbers; 85% can subtract fractions and 81% are able to find X in a simple equation. The education system in Vietnam is relatively equitable and this means that poorer children can expect a decent quality of schooling. Our data show children from disadvantaged as well as average or better-off backgrounds make good progress in classes taught by motivated and well-trained teachers ... (Boyden 2013)

Of course, there will be many factors beyond school effectiveness that contribute to the academic achievement levels of Vietnamese students. To explore why some Vietnamese students do well in tests and to identify those aspects of the Vietnamese government school system that appeared promising we explore, in a holistic way, the relationships between key components of the system.

7.1 METHODOLOGY

Our research was undertaken in partnership with the Vietnam Institute for Education Sciences, Hanoi (VNIES). We were also assisted by the Vietnam office of the market research company, Ipsos. Data collection was iterative and took place over three years, building on data collected for a previous study in Ho Chi Minh City (Elwick and McAleavy 2015). The primary data collection approach was interviews and focus groups, in addition to a policy analysis and a survey across the four regions. Purposeful sampling was used to identify stakeholders who could offer different perspectives about the functioning of the system.

The first phase of data collection took place in 2015 in Ho Chi Minh City, with additional data collected in 2017–18 in Hanoi, Ha Giang and Binh Dinh. The provinces were selected to gain insight from different settings in Vietnam: rural and mountainous, with a large population of ethnic minority students (Ha Giang); large metropolitan cities, with a predominantly ethnic majority Kinh population (Hanoi and Ho Chi Minh City); and a semi-rural, semi-industrial coastal province (Binh Dinh) (General Statistics Office of Viet Nam 2016).

Interviews and focus groups were conducted with a variety of stakeholders in the education system. In all provinces stakeholders were selected to get a range of different perspectives from different levels of the system, from policymakers to school leaders and teachers. Interviews and focus groups ranged in length from sixty minutes to four hours. Interviews and focus groups were co-facilitated between VNIES and the Education Development Trust research team, with the assistance of an interpreter providing simultaneous translation. In certain instances where the presence of non-Vietnamese researchers was deemed inappropriate, VNIES conducted the interviews and focus groups. All interview and focus group data were transcribed and translated into English.

A survey was conducted in the four provinces with 350 parents, 50 local business owners and 40 teacher trainers from pedagogical colleges. The survey was designed to fill knowledge gaps from the first phase of qualitative fieldwork and to shape the second phase of qualitative fieldwork in Hanoi and Ha Giang. The three groups were identified as important survey participants for the following reasons:

- *Parents*: Throughout the first phase of data collection the role of parents in the system became increasingly apparent. Questions were designed to understand the role parents play in their children's education and the extent to which they pay for additional lessons.

- *Local business owners*: 'Socialisation' was identified as a key policy during the first phase of data collection. This policy, in part, involves collecting money for schools from the local community, particularly from parents and local business owners. Survey questions centred on local community involvement in schools including volunteering and financial support.

- *Pedagogical college teacher trainers*: To elicit more information on policies about teacher pre- and in-service professional development.

7.2 OUR FINDINGS

We have identified five interesting features of the Vietnamese school system. While the five factors are analysed separately, they are clearly interrelated. National policy created the framework for the development of the accountability regime and mandated measures intended to improve teaching, school leadership and parental partnership. The three most important groups of 'agents' at school level – teachers, principals and parents – interact at local level and, according to regulations, all three are involved in the accountability system.

The five distinctive features of the Vietnamese school system elements highlighted by our research are: policy, accountability, teaching, leadership and school community partnership. We consider each one in turn.

7.2.1 Purposeful Policy

7.2.1.1 *School Education: A Top Policy Priority for Many Years* The government of Vietnam has consistently stated, over many years, that school education is a national priority. Official statistics indicate that spending on education has been relatively high compared with other forms of public expenditure during the past two decades and there has been a longstanding commitment to devote at least 20 per cent of all public spending to education (VUFO 2015). Since the 1990s, government spending has also been supplemented by contributions in cash and in kind by parents and businesses under the policy of 'socialisation'.

The motive to make education a priority was economic. The government believed, and believes, that the scale and quality of the education system will determine economic success and secure Vietnam's transition from a low-income, largely agrarian, country to a much wealthier country with a thriving diverse economy. Remarkable growth in the size of the Vietnamese economy since the 1990s has increased government tax revenues and the value of the commitment to 20 per cent of all public spending going to education.

7.2.1.2 *The Government's Theory of Action* The government of Vietnam has been consistent in identifying education spending as a priority and in the way the money has been spent. Since 2000, there has been a twin-track approach, addressing access to school and the quality of learning in schools.

Enrolment rates have improved. In 1992, 86 per cent of eligible children were enrolled in primary schools; by 2014 this proportion had reached 98 per cent (Dang and Glewwe 2017: 41). There has been a larger increase in lower secondary enrolment, from 72 per cent to 95 per cent during the period 1992–2014. Challenges remain. Many students are taught only for a half-day shift and, while enrolment in upper secondary schools has increased, many children still do not have access to a high school education.

Increased enrolment required increased amounts of school places and school buildings and know that school buildings and equipment have changed for the better in recent years.

Importantly the improved facilities were combined with other improvement strategies to encourage greater impact. There was a deliberate twin-track approach, expanding and improving facilities was combined with attempts to improve key factors likely to influence school quality, such as the school readiness of five-year olds, the pre-service qualification level of teachers and the quality of teaching. For example, since 2000 the government has invested in public kindergartens so that now almost all children have spent a year in kindergarten before beginning primary school. There has been a consistent emphasis on encouraging teachers to use more engaging pedagogical techniques in the classroom to develop students' higher-order thinking, although the impact of this policy is contested. The government has also raised the pre-service training requirements for teachers at all levels of the pre-school and school system. Across many interventions, the government has repeatedly emphasised the importance of closing the opportunities–outcomes gap between the Kinh majority and Vietnamese people from other ethnic minority groups.

Improvements in infrastructure were mentioned by teachers and school principals in Ha Giang province who had previously taught in informal bamboo structures.[1]

> Now I no longer see classrooms built from bamboo as was the case many years ago, I go to other places and see changes as well. (Ha Giang primary school teacher)

> The facilities and equipment in our school have been upgraded greatly. (Ha Giang secondary school teacher)

> [our school] is in a mountainous region with fewer than 150 students, but students are ethnic minorities, who mostly learn Vietnamese [as a second language], yet the school receives very big investments which include multipurpose facilities. (Binh Dinh secondary school teacher)

7.2.1.3 *Policy Implementation and the Role of 'the Middle Tier'* All governments face a policy delivery challenge. Sarason pointed out many years ago, when describing the failure of much educational reform in the United States, that schools are often 'intractable to change and the attainment of goals set by reformers' (Sarason 1990: xiii). Simply issuing edicts or ordering change is not enough. There is a need for a policy delivery system and a functioning middle tier that mediates between central policymakers and frontline professionals.

Vietnam's government education system appears to have an effective middle tier. Primary schools and lower secondary schools are supported and monitored by a district-level Bureau of Education, whereas government high schools are supervised in a similar way by a provincial-level Department of Education. These officials are expected to explain policy to schools and provide both support and monitoring to ensure fidelity of implementation.

There is a two-way process of engagement between schools and the middle tier. The interaction between schools and the local representatives of the state were often described to us as 'the logical system', which operated simultaneously; both 'top down' and 'bottom up'. Mandated policies are cascaded down from the national government to schools via district and provincial officials. Our interviewees describe a feedback loop that involves the rapid

---

[1] All interview and focus group participants in Ha Giang province commented on improvements in infrastructure in the past fifteen years. This was also raised by participants in Binh Dinh from the pedagogical college and the province-level department of education and by secondary school principals.

reporting of frontline views on implementation problems through the middle tier to the national ministry.

> In the logical system of education, information is two-way, bottom up and top down, very tightly connected. Officials at higher levels are aware of things happening at lower levels, and those at the lower level report well. (Binh Dinh primary school principal)

> I think our system is logical ... each unit has its own responsibility and function within the system, so I don't see which is strong or weak. I think balance and collaboration is important, from the ministry to the district, down to the individual schools. (Binh Dinh secondary school vice principal)

The school principal has a pivotal role as the interface between the school community and the external state authorities and is highly accountable for local management of any mandated changes. Principals are expected to work closely with either district or province officials to ensure policies are implemented 'correctly'. They are also expected to provide officials with honest feedback on implementation problems.

7.2.1.4 *A Lively Professional and Public Debate on Education* There is respect for hierarchy in much of Vietnamese society and the education system has many hierarchical features. At the same time there is a lively professional and public discourse relating to education. As we discovered, teachers and parents are not afraid to speak openly about their concerns with teachers and school principals identifying problems they faced implementing policy. This suggests that there is a professional culture in which teachers and principals are fundamentally conscientious and compliant but not afraid to tell their superiors about practical difficulties.

In some ways the government encourages professional and public debate. For many years the central government has campaigned, for example, against 'achievement disease'; the widespread perception that an emphasis on good grades can foster undesirable practices, including different forms of gaming and cheating on assessments and examinations.

In summary, Vietnam appears to have benefitted from policy consistency over many years. The broad thrust of policy has not altered since the beginning of the century. We did not get any sense of disquiet about multiple 'initiatives' and frequent changes of direction. The execution of policy appears to benefit from the existence of an effective 'middle tier' which mediates policy and can provide valuable feedback to the central ministry on frontline views about any implementation difficulties.

7.2.2 High Levels of Accountability

7.2.2.1 *The Accountability of Teachers Begins with Self-Review and Peer Assessment* Vietnamese teachers are highly accountable. Regulations require participation in a continuous cycle of professional review based on in-school monitoring systems which are collaborative. The classroom performance of every teacher is formally graded on a regular basis through self- and peer review, including lesson observation, and teachers are required to analyse their own personal strengths and weaknesses.

It was clear from many of our interviews with teachers that the 'subject group' was significant in the way that accountability operates at school level. Each teacher is a member of a subject group. Teachers within each group, working collectively, check and moderate self-review grades. The results are reported upwards to the school principal.

Every subject group has a designated leader known as the 'subject lead' who is central to the system of peer review. The subject leads often combined an accountability function with a strong orientation towards professional development. Subject leads observe lesson observations and conduct feedback sessions in conjunction with other members of the subject group, so that all teachers participate in the peer review process.

7.2.2.2 *The Principal as an In-School Inspector* The school principal plays an important role in the accountability process. We heard that principals received regular reports about each individual teacher from the subject lead. If a teacher receives 'excellent' or 'poor', the top and bottom grades on a four-point scale of quality, in the peer review, the school principal must verify this. In addition, school principals play a direct role in monitoring the quality of teaching through classroom observations.

Teachers reported that principals made planned visits and occasional 'unannounced' visits, describing the monitoring of classroom quality as an essential task for school principals. Classroom observation was seen as both a form of monitoring and a source of professional learning. Principals, as with subject leads, were expected to grade performance and provide advice on ways of improving professional practice.

One subject lead explained that the subject team peer review system was fundamentally the responsibility of the principal. The principal valued the data and judgements of the subject group but also personally gathered evidence and verified the peer judgements. All school principals interviewed in fieldwork in Ha Giang, Binh Dinh and Hanoi supported this interpretation.

The head of each subject reports to the principal. The subject group assesses individual teachers' lesson plans and reports, but at the highest level the principal oversees everything. She visits the classes to evaluate teacher's teaching quality, utilises experienced teachers and provides more training for less experienced ones. (Binh Dinh subject lead and secondary school teacher)

Data from the PISA 2015 survey of principals in Vietnam confirms the central role of school principals in monitoring of teacher quality. The percentage of Vietnamese principals reporting the use of classroom observation by principals or senior staff for the purposes of monitoring teaching quality was one of the highest in the world, and some way above the average for the richer OECD countries (OECD 2016b: 149).

7.2.2.3 Parents Are Encouraged by the Government to Hold Schools to Account The World Bank's 2004 World Development Report articulated the idea that 'the short route of accountability' was potentially a powerful mechanism for improving public services (World Bank 2003: 154). The 'short route' requires service users – such as the parents of schoolchildren – to have a 'voice' within local accountability systems. At least in theory, parents in Vietnamese government schools have such a voice.

Government regulations state that each government school should have a Parent Board which meets at least three times a year. The ministry regulates the constitution of these Parent Boards. There should be a Parent Committee at every class level and representatives of these should sit on the schoolwide Parent Board. The Parent Board is legally responsible for providing feedback on educational quality to the professionals in the school and for organising extra-curricular enrichment activities. The teachers and principal we interviewed described their experiences of the 'hands-on' approach of some Parent Boards, including monitoring teaching quality and checking on the quality of school lunches.

Parent Boards are described in some detail in ministry regulations. For example, *The Parents Committee Charter*[2] stipulates the following for all government schools – from kindergarten to upper secondary:

Article 3.1 Class Parents Committee

a. Each class has a parents committee comprising from three to five members, including a chair and a deputy chair.

---

[2] Circular No. 55/2011/BGDDT, Article 3.1.

b. Members of the class parents committee are enthusiastic persons, responsible for coordinating with the homeroom teacher, subject teachers and school and representing the parents of students in the class, [together] implementing educational activities for students.

One distinctive aspect of the Vietnamese regulations for government schools is the way they describe a two-way form of parental accountability: the power parents should have in holding professionals accountable and the power of a school's expectations of parental support. Just as the regulations set out the role parents have in holding schools to account, they also stipulate that parents should ensure their children's good behaviour and hard work in school. The parents are entitled to ask difficult questions of the work of the professionals but are also personally responsible 'for their children's mistakes and faults'.

Experts we interviewed offered a note of caution in the interpretation of government regulations regarding Parent Boards. They suggested that the 'theory' of the regulations was not always fully reflected in practice.

7.2.2.4 *A Robust Regime of External Accountability* A secondary school principal from Ha Giang province observed that 'My work is monitored by many parties'. This is no exaggeration. As well as internal monitoring, the functioning of government schools is subject to close, external scrutiny. Depending on the age of their students, schools are supervised closely by either province-level or district-level officials. Schools are also answerable to local representatives of the Communist Party.

The principals we interviewed described frequent meetings to report on progress to 'middle tier' officials and within each school there is a political Board that monitors its work. Membership includes representatives of the local Communist Party and the teachers' Trade Union. These Boards have, by law, wide-ranging monitoring powers. In addition, schools are formally inspected at least once every five years, with more frequent inspections for schools causing concern.

To sum up, Vietnamese schools are highly accountable. The work of teachers is monitored and challenged by many different parties from both within and without the school. Although teachers were prepared to criticise many aspects of school life, those that we interviewed did not express a general sense of unhappiness about the level of professional scrutiny to which they were subjected.

7.2.3 The Quality of Teaching and Teachers

7.2.3.1 *Teachers Are Members of a Highly Respected Profession but They Consider Themselves to Be Badly Paid and Many Supplement Their Income by Working as Private Tutors* In Vietnamese society teaching is highly respected. Many teachers we interviewed were proud to belong to an important profession. When describing the characteristics of a good teacher they emphasised ethical dimensions and the importance of idealism, before mentioning the desirable technical pedagogical skills of a highly effective teacher. But they consistently stated that they were badly paid, although recognising that pay had improved in recent years. Some were disillusioned and said they were both highly accountable and underpaid. Teachers receive an incremental pay rise based on years of service, which means the most experienced teachers can be paid over three times more than new teachers. Bonuses are available for teachers whose performance is graded as 'excellent' but many teachers comment that these are not significant.

Many teachers supplement their income by working after school as private tutors. Private tutoring is discouraged officially but is widespread.[3] Of 350 parents we surveyed, three quarters of them were paying private tutors and almost all these private tutors were 'by day' government teachers. Our sample of parents was overall more economically advantaged than the general population so the results may overstate the use of private tutors, but the high response rate suggests that private tutoring is common. Despite official disapproval of these 'extra classes', low wages and parental demand encourages the practice. It is possible that without the income from private tuition many teachers would leave the profession.

7.2.3.2 *The Teacher Workforce Is Better Qualified Than Before and Well Regarded by Many Parents* Many of our respondents felt that the quality and qualification level of the workforce had improved in recent years. After 2000, the government systematically sought to raise the qualification level of new teachers. It also provided a 'catch-up' series of summer institutes for

---

[3] Decree No. 242/Prime Minister, 1993 prohibits compulsory and mass-scale extra classes at schools, and Circular No. 16/Prime Minister-Interministerial, 1993 stipulates the range of extra-classes that are considered legal. In addition, Circular No. 15/MOET, 2001 provides further prohibitive measures on extra classes. The latest regulation in 2012 (Circular No. 17, Regulations on Supplementary Education) stipulates teachers cannot teach extra classes to their own students, unless they gain official permission to do so by their supervisors. Should they be found in violation of this law teachers can face prosecution.

existing teachers. Minimum standards for teacher training were established for each phase of the education system. Teaching today is more 'professionalised', with many teachers qualified at graduate or post-graduate level or engaged in post-graduate study.

Evidence from PISA 2015 suggests that some Vietnamese teachers have a good level of subject-related knowledge. The PISA survey of school principals found that in science lessons students in Vietnam were more likely than students in OECD countries to be taught by a teacher with a degree and major in science. In Vietnamese secondary schools, 92.4 per cent of science teachers possessed a university degree and a major in science, well above the OECD average of 73.8 per cent (OECD 2016b: 279).

Parental perceptions of teacher quality reflected these findings. We asked parents to compare schools today with the schools they had attended as children. They were strongly of the view that the quality of the teaching workforce had improved. Nearly 90 per cent stated that their children's teachers were more experienced than those who had educated them.

7.2.3.3 The 'Subject Group' Is an Important Mechanism Providing Informal In-School Professional Learning

Teachers in Vietnam are required to take personal responsibility for their professional development. Circular 32,[4] for example, states that teachers must act to improve their capacity and the quality of their teaching. Teachers are expected to design and implement an annual personal professional development plan based on feedback from the performance management system. The school principal monitors the plan and must ensure teachers are engaging in development programmes.

The teachers and principals we interviewed described how informal professional learning took place regularly through the work of the subject group. As described in Section 7.2.1.1 the subject group provides a forum for professional development based on classroom-level peer monitoring and coaching. Visits from other members of the in-school subject team as part of the accountability regime also have a coaching and improvement function.

Our witnesses suggested the in-school subject lead was an important 'middle management' role within the Vietnamese government school combining an accountability function with a strong orientation towards professional development. Subject leads do not act alone; they review individual teacher quality in conjunction with other members of the subject group.

---

[4] Circular No. 32/2011/TT-BGDĐT.

We were told repeatedly about the significance of the subject group within the professional life of the school:

> I am the head of the subject group. Every month we visit classes, assess the teaching quality and report the results for each teacher to the principal and vice-principals. (Ha Giang primary school teacher)

> We form an evaluation group of two or three people to observe each teacher's lesson and make an evaluation. This approach is applied to all teachers of all subjects at the school. (Binh Dinh primary school teacher)

Subject teachers observe each other, grade each other's teaching and provide diagnostic feedback. This is all coordinated by the subject lead. A subject lead from Binh Dinh province emphasised the 'nurturing' and 'problem-solving' dimensions of the dialogue:

> I have gained a lot of experience throughout the years of teaching, for example in teaching methods, solving different situations that arise during a lesson and nurturing the talents [of teachers]. (Binh Dinh upper secondary school subject lead)

Other teachers made a similar point. While visits from the subject team are part of the accountability regime there is a collegiate quality to the best of the accountability conversations:

> Lesson reviews among teachers are very helpful, the teacher can choose a topic or a lesson that they feel not confident about, then after this period everyone can help solve the problem. (Binh Dinh secondary school teacher).

> We learn a lot from class visits ... the feedback is very honest and helpful and not superficial. (Ha Giang secondary school teacher)

The PISA 2015 data also points to the prevalence of in-school mentoring of teachers; almost all Vietnamese teachers in the sample were involved in mentoring relationships – a much higher rate than the OECD average (OECD (2016b: 149).

7.2.3.4 *Teachers Used a Mix of Traditional and More Modern Pedagogical Methods* Teaching methods have been subject to extensive review during the past twenty years. During this time, the government, encouraged by international agencies, has consistently promoted practices which give students opportunities to work collaboratively and apply knowledge to unfamiliar problems.

We heard different accounts about classroom practice today. Some officials stated that students were now far more active as learners. Some experts disagreed and suggested that changes had been largely superficial. Many of the teachers and principals we interviewed suggested that the official push for new student-centred practices had in practice been negotiated and modified by teachers, who had created their own mixed-methods approach drawing on what they saw as the best of both traditional and modern methods. The ministry has not explicitly approved this hybrid model but tolerates it, as long as the outcomes meet the required standard.

> Currently, in my school, both the traditional approach and the new teaching approaches are combined to teach students. In doing so, we have drawn the best of both approaches combined together. Specifically, when it comes to the traditional approach, teacher play an active role. (Ho Chi Minh City teacher)

> The ministry has proposed many teaching methods to teachers, so they can combine or integrate these methods, find one they think most suitable, with the ultimate goal to convey the knowledge to students most effectively. Teachers should be allowed to use various teaching methods, and even assessment methods, but of course still based on some regulation, not just entirely on their own. (Binh Dinh district official)

The emergence of a *de facto* mixed-method pedagogy is possible because teaching methods are not centrally prescribed. Various 'student-centred' practices have been promoted but in the end schools and teachers decide what teaching methods they adopt in the classroom.

While in many ways Vietnamese schools are not autonomous compared with international norms, it is clear that in terms of pedagogy teachers have a large measure of day-to-day decision-making power, which allows them to use a mixed approach.

> The school decides what methods to apply; this is the policy of the school … No method is universal, teachers must be flexible in organising their lessons to fit students. As a Grade 1 teacher, I need to use Grade 1-specific methods. We need to be flexible when it comes to methods of teaching. (Ha Giang primary school teacher)

> Teachers can make decisions 100% of the time as long as they achieve high learning outcomes. Each class is different so the teachers need to pick the most suitable ones. (Binh Dinh primary school principal)

There is some evidence from PISA that the learning experience in a Vietnamese government school is engaging and enjoyable. As part of the 2015 PISA survey, students were asked whether they enjoyed learning science. The Vietnamese responses were the highest of any country: 89 per cent of Vietnamese students agreed with the statement 'I generally have fun when I am learning science topics' and 88 per cent agreed that 'I am happy working on science topics' (OECD 2016a: 122).

PISA data also suggests that another promising aspect of the Vietnamese system is the way teachers use diagnostic feedback in the classroom. The 2015 PISA student survey found that Vietnamese students were less likely than students from any other participating country in the world to agree that 'The teacher never or almost never tells me how I can improve my performance'. Only 5 per cent of Vietnamese students agreed with this statement (OECD 2016b: 290). This is particularly impressive as the average class size in a Vietnamese school is much higher than OECD norms, making individual-level feedback in the classroom more challenging.

The idea that emerged from our interviews with school staff about the common use of a mixed-method pedagogy appears to be consistent with PISA data. The PISA 2015 student survey asked questions intended to ascertain whether teaching included 'teacher-directed' characteristics. The responses of the Vietnamese students made it clear they frequently experienced whole-class instruction and whole-class discussion as well as personalised guidance (OECD 2016b: 284). The PISA survey strengthens the conclusion that Vietnamese teachers combine 'student-centred' approaches with more traditional 'teacher-centred' techniques. This underscores the professional nature of teachers' approach to their responsibilties and supports the proposition that the quality of teaching has improved in the last twenty years through better support services, greater professional autonomy and better initial and in-service education.

In overall terms, Vietnamese teachers are impressive in many ways. Although our research did not involve direct observation of classroom practice, we developed a strong sense of the mature and self-confident way in which Vietnamese teachers view their professional practice. Vietnamese teachers discuss pedagogy in a way that goes beyond the sterile binary juxtaposition of 'teacher-centred' and 'student-centred' practice. They under-stand the importance of good quality feedback to students and they are proud to be government school teachers.

7.2.4 School Leadership That Focuses on the Classroom

7.2.4.1 *Principals Have a Clearly Defined Role As Leaders of Teaching and Learning* When we asked principals about their responsibilities, they often replied that their duties were clearly described in school governance 'charters' published by the ministry. These charters unambiguously state that the principal is personally responsible for internal management and educational quality. The primary school charter defines the school principal as 'the person responsible for organising and managing the school's activities and quality of education'.[5]

Significantly, the ministry school charters require principals to maintain their status as practising teachers, with a minimum commitment of two teaching periods a week. The principal is seen as a teacher and a leader of teachers. Principals attributed particular significance to the monitoring of educational quality and monitor teaching quality closely. We asked school principals to tell us about a typical day in their professional life. There were many similarities between their accounts and the monitoring of teacher classroom performance featured prominently in all narratives. Principals spend time directly observing practice and receiving reports on observations that have been undertaken through the subject group peer review system. The partnership between the principal and the heads of the school subject groups is at the heart of the monitoring regime.

Monitoring teaching quality is an essential responsibility which goes beyond checking for quality and compliance. Principals and teachers see the monitoring role as a developmental one, based on the diagnostic feedback that the principals provide.

The following comments from one teacher focus group give a sense of how teachers see the work of principals:

- The principal and vice principals supervise us very thoroughly.

- The principal visits classes with or without warning to check how we prepare for classes. Assessments are conducted very carefully.

- In addition, traditional assessment methods are still in use, such as reviewing notebooks, student profiles, etc.

- The principals discuss with us how the classes went, very clearly.

(Ha Giang secondary school teachers)

---

[5] Circular No. 41/2010/TT-BGDDT, Article 20.1.

7.2.4.2 *Principals Confidently Described Their Views on the Characteristics of High-Quality Teaching* We asked school principals about the qualities they believed excellent school principals needed to possess. All talked of a combination of a strong moral or ethical standing and leadership skills. They also emphasised the importance of strong teaching and pedagogical skills. A key component of being an excellent school principal lies in understanding what is required to be an excellent teacher. Principals must be able to lead by example and need to understand what pedagogical excellence looks like.

The principals we interviewed spoke confidently about both ideal teaching styles and the characteristics of highly effective teachers. We asked principals about the model of pedagogy promoted at their school. The following response is typical.

> A variety of teaching methods should be used such as whole-class teaching, group teaching and individualised teaching in a flexible and mutually supportive fashion. Each teaching method and approach has its own merits and demerits. (Ha Giang secondary school principal)

We asked principals about the model of pedagogy that was promoted at their school. They often stressed the need for a repertoire of teaching skills. We also asked principals how they might recognise an excellent teacher. Again, the responses were multi-faceted and included moral/ethical traits, commitment to professional learning and technical pedagogical skills.

7.2.4.3 *The Vietnamese Model of School Leadership Is Very Different from Some Aspects of 'Western' Practice* While principals have substantial in-school power there are distinct limits to their autonomy and decision-making. Notably, they must report on a regular basis to higher authorities outside the school and have limited powers in staff appointment and financial planning. The PISA 2015 survey of principals confirmed our view that the Vietnamese model of school leadership is quite different from 'western' models of highly decentralised school-based decision-making. Survey questions explored how far principals were permitted to make important decisions related to resources, such as on selecting teachers for hire; firing teachers for underperformance; establishing teachers' starting salaries; determining teachers' salary increases; and formulating the school budget. Vietnamese principals have much less authority in these areas than their peers in most OECD countries.[6]

[6] See PISA 2015 'Index of Autonomy': OECD (2016b: 337).

The actions of principals in Vietnam are subject to tight external control. There are two major forms of oversight – via the 'middle-tier' agencies for technical educational matters and via the local agencies of the Communist Party on general matters. In addition, the Parent Board has, at least in theory, powers that circumscribe the work of the principal (see Section 7.2.2.3).

There are minimal financial incentives for school principals. We asked principals in Ha Giang and Hanoi about their salaries. They described their monthly pay in late 2017 as ranging between eight million and eleven million VND (approximately 470 USD). This is no more than that of many experienced teachers. They told us they were paid less than some of their most experienced teachers.

School principals are usually highly experienced teachers. Those we interviewed had between ten and thirty-five years of teaching experience. Becoming a school principal is not a planned career move. Principals had not applied for their posts. Instead they had been approached by the authorities and invited to undertake the role. Regulations limit post-holders to a five-year period of tenure, although it is possible to be given a second five-year term. The principals we interviewed considered school leadership an honourable responsibility that they were surprised to be given.

To conclude these reflections on leadership, school principals play a central role in the functioning of Vietnamese government schools. They embody the concept of the instructional leader and are expected to be champions at school level of excellence in pedagogy. The leadership model does not align precisely with western models of school leadership; they are expected to concentrate on educational quality and not financial decision-making.

7.2.5 Partnership between Schools and Parents

7.2.5.1 Parents Expressed High Levels of Satisfaction with the Government School System In our parents survey results there was an overall positive response about their children's school and the extent to which schools were responsive to their concerns. They respected the skills and professionalism of the teacher workforce. Virtually no parents had serious concerns about the aptitude or attitudes of Vietnamese schoolteachers. Over 90 per cent considered the current teacher workforce to be 'good' or 'excellent' in terms of how far teachers cared about student progress and 90 per cent rated government schoolteachers as 'good' or 'excellent' in terms of professional ability.

The parents were also happy, overall, with teacher quality and believed that schools had improved since they were children. The most marked agreement about improvement was on school facilities and the majority of parents also saw improvements in curriculum, teacher attitudes and teacher experience.

7.2.5.2 *Some Vietnamese Government Schools Have Good Systems to Foster Parental Partnership* Parents also reported that their local school listened and responded to them, with nearly 80 per cent feeling that they were listened to 'always' or 'most of the time'. Not a single parent agreed with the statement 'I never feel listened to'.

These findings are in keeping with other evidence. According to reports by school principals in the PISA 2012 survey, Vietnamese parents had, in international comparative terms, an extremely high level of interaction with schools (OECD 2013). This included both informal discussion about individual children and their progress and formal 'governance' arrangements for the management of the school.

The 2012 PISA data appears to suggest that *parent-initiated* conversations about either the behaviour or the academic progress of students are markedly more common in Vietnam than in OECD country averages. Vietnamese parents appear to feel comfortable taking the lead in ensuring dialogue with teaching professionals about their children's behaviour and progress at school.

Vietnamese parents also appear, according to the 2012 PISA Survey, to be highly visible as volunteers in school. Vietnamese principals reported that about 40 per cent of parents assisted a teacher in the school in the past academic year. This was the highest level of reported in-school volunteering of any country that participated in the 2012 PISA survey, and was far above the OECD average of 5 per cent (OECD 2013: 143).

Parental partnership is mandated by the government of Vietnam as a formal school responsibility. Ministry regulations require that teachers work closely with individual parents to ensure children do well. While teachers are obliged to work with parents regarding the progress of individual students, schools are also required to consult parents collectively. Unusually in international terms, every single class in a government school should have a Parent Committee that reviews educational activities and the partnership between parents and teachers. Some of our expert witnesses suggested that there was considerable variation in the way these Parent Boards and Committees functioned.

7.2.5.3 *Through the Policy of 'Socialisation' Parents Are Expected to Make Additional Contributions to Their Local School* For over twenty years the government of Vietnam has pursued a policy known as *xa hoi hoa*, or 'socialisation', in education and health, which involves an invitation to service users, local community members and community organisations to make financial or in-kind contributions to the cost of running services. At school level, parents, unless they are particularly disadvantaged, are expected to make such contributions. This is both a means of securing additional resources and an expression of the view that service users and local communities, as well as the Vietnamese state, must shoulder the burden involved in ensuring good services.

Some experts have been critical of socialisation, seeing it either as a form of 'privatisation' or as an undesirable crisis measure that should not be necessary in more settled times when tax revenues are sufficient to fund services. Such critics highlight the risk that socialisation may provide opportunities for corruption or favour economically more privileged communities over disadvantaged communities or the possibility that the children of parents who fail to contribute will be stigmatised.

Socialisation appears to be an important part of the current financial model for many schools in Vietnam. According to the PISA survey of principals in 2012, over 60 per cent of Vietnamese parents contributed to fundraising for their local school in the previous academic year. This was by far the highest figure of all countries participating in PISA 2012 and compared with an average for OECD countries of 10 per cent (OECD 2013: 143).

Our school-based participants were largely positive about socialisation. Many principals described how additional facilities had been made possible through socialisation. Perhaps conscious of suggestions of corruption, teachers and principals were keen to emphasise that socialisation revenue was managed by the Parent Board. They were also eager to describe the careful scrutiny that parents applied to all decisions about socialisation revenues and the way socialisation-funded projects were monitored by the Parent Board.

> Many parents contribute. This air conditioner for example is from parents' contributions. (Binh Dinh lower secondary school principal)

> Last year, the parents saw the canteen was in a really hot condition. They decided to install fans for their children. (Hanoi lower secondary school principal)

In our parental survey over 80 pe cent of parents stated that they made contributions to the school via the policy of socialisation. There was considerable variation in the amounts paid. Many of the parents in our sample said they were content to make socialisation payments as a way of improving school facilities but 10 per cent thought the payments were compulsory, even though the law stipulates they are voluntary. While our sample is not comprehensive it seems that parental attitudes towards family or community contributions are broadly positive. But there are some dissenting thoughts, notably concerns that the children of significant contributors will get favoured treatment.

In summary, the Vietnamese government school system benefits from an unusual level of parental involvement. Parents are highly visible in Vietnamese schools. They tend to have high expectations and apply accountability pressure on teachers. At the same time, parents are held to account by schools and expected both to support the learning of their children and to provide resources via the distinctive policy of 'socialisation'.

7.3 CONCLUSION

We have sought to describe five distinctive features of how government schools operate in Vietnam. We have presented them sequentially, but they are interconnected and to some degree mutually reinforcing; as one feature underpins another.

The story we tell here is consistent with much previous commentary about improving and high performing education systems:

1. Policymakers have a key responsibility to adopt evidence-informed policies and to be consistent and persistent about implementation over the long-term, not sapping energy from the system through frequent changes of direction.

2. Implementation in a large school system will benefit from the existence of an effective 'middle tier' which can mediate policy and provide feedback so that, while policies are consistent, detailed implementation can be adaptive in response to the realities of the 'frontline'.

3. Education professionals benefit from a judicious balance of accountability, support and incentives. While there is a role for external accountability, internal accountability systems are also important, including peer review. Parents have a part to play in applying pressure for beneficial change.

4. The quality of the teacher workforce is a key determinant of student outcomes. There is a need to recruit and retain talented people into the teaching workforce. Teachers should be encouraged to use a repertoire of pedagogical techniques.

5. School leadership is another powerful factor and the best school principals are 'instructional leaders' who are directly concerned with quality at the level of the classroom. Instructional leaders simultaneously provide challenge and support to teachers.

6. If schools can harness the power of parental partnership they can greatly enhance the chances of success as measured by learning outcomes. Parental partnership ideally operates on two levels: parents work together with the teachers of their own children and parents are involved in the governance of the school.

We have described aspects of the internal workings of the Vietnamese school system that seem to contribute to marked improvements in learning outcomes and the overall quality of children's school experience. Of course, we recognise that these apparent successes also depend upon powerful social factors outside the schools and the prevalent view in Vietnam that educational success could help an individual avoid a life of poverty:

> In Vietnam everyone believes that we should learn to have a new life and learning is important, especially for the poor. Parents always teach their children when they are small that learning will make their life better in the future. (Hanoi upper secondary teacher)

> In Vietnam we believe that studying is the only way to overcome poverty, so children from poorer families are more willing and determined to study, and the elderly in the families also invest more and encourage their children to study hard. (Binh Dinh primary school teacher)

When we asked teachers to explain the success of Vietnamese students in the PISA tests, they rarely attempted to take the credit as education professionals. Instead, they identified cultural issues, in particular the strong pro-education culture in Vietnamese society, as major causal factors. They repeatedly talked about 'the learning tradition' at the heart of the Vietnamese view of life. The consequences of this 'learning tradition' include high parental aspirations and an expectation that children will respect teachers and work very hard at school. The achievement of Vietnamese students in academic tests is, of course, influenced by such factors.

It is impossible for other countries to replicate the Vietnamese 'learning tradition'. Every place has its own unique history and culture. However, our investigation suggested that, in addition to cultural factors, there are distinctive and promising features to the internal working of the school system in Vietnam. Here, there is scope for an important Vietnamese contribution to a global dialogue about school effectiveness.

References

Boyden, J. (2013). What can Vietnam's excellent schools teach us about education quality and equality? Available at: https://oxfamblogs.org/fp2p/what-can-vietnams-excellent-schools-teachus-about-education-quality-and-equality/ (accessed April 2018).

Dang, H. A. H. and Glewwe, P. (2017). Well begun, but aiming higher: A review of Vietnam's education trends in the past 20 years and emerging challenges. RISE Working Paper 17/017, December. London: DFID.

Elwick, A. and McAleavy, T. (2015). *Interesting Cities: Five Approaches to Urban School Reform*. Education Development Trust. www.educationdevelopmenttrust.com/our-research-and-insights/research/interesting-cities-five-approaches-to-urban-school

General Statistics Office of Viet Nam. (2016). *Viet Nam Statistical Handbook 2016*. Hanoi: GSO.

OECD. (2013). *PISA 2012 Results: What Makes Schools Successful? Resources, Policies and Practices*, Vol. IV. Paris: PISA, OECD.

OECD. (2016a). *PISA 2015 Results: Excellence and Equity in Education*, Vol. I. Paris: PISA, OECD.

OECD. (2016b). *PISA 2015 Results: Policies and Practices for Successful Schools*, Vol. II. Paris: PISA, OECD.

Sarason, S. (1990). *The Predictable Failure of Educational Reform: Can We Change Course Before It's Too Late* San Francisco, CA: Wiley.

VUFO (Vietnam Union of Friendship Organisations). (2015). *Vietnam Maintains 20% of State Budget Spending for Education in 2015*. Available at: www.ngocentre.org.vn/news/vietnam-maintains-20-state-budget-spending-education-2015 (accessed November 2017).

World Bank. (2003). *World Development Report 2004: Making Services Work for Poor People*. Washington, DC: World Bank.

8 Reform Implementation Lessons

A Case Study of High-Performing Singapore

Saravanan S. Gopinathan and Edmund Lim

8.1 INTRODUCTION

Singapore is today regarded to have a high performing education system. Over the last two decades, in global assessments like PISA, TIMSS, PIRLS and University rankings, it has ranked amongst the very top. This consistent performance, coupled with Singapore's transformative economic growth over the last half century, provides credence to the OECD's claim that the quality of human capital, achieved through education, is related to a country's potential for economic growth. In this chapter, we examine the achievements of Singapore's education system, the principles underpinning policy and practice, the challenges that were met and are to be met in the new century and the prospects for successfully meeting these challenges.

8.2 DEVELOPING THE SYSTEM (1965–1997)

To appreciate why Singapore's education and skills development merited such significant attention it is essential to understand its political history, social demographics and limitations. The core political argument in the 1950s, as the British Empire was fading, was that Singapore was too small and resource starved to be a viable nation state. Singapore became part of the Malaysian Federation in 1963. This was an ill-fated experiment and Singapore became an independent nation on 9 August 1965. The new nation state had no natural resources, unlike its larger and resource-rich neighbours. The entrepôt economy developed during colonial times could not provide jobs and wealth to build a modern society and the school system was segregated by language of instruction, reflecting Singapore's ethnic diversity and colonial history. Education policy in the early years of independence, termed the era of 'survival', had to and did respond to these challenges.

A major policy challenge was unifying a segregated education system and sorting out the medium of instruction issues: English–Mother Tongue bilingualism, via a high standard public system of education. Perhaps the most important education policy decision in the first decade of independence was adoption of the English–Mother Tongue model of bilingualism. The choice of English as the main medium of instruction was strongly opposed by a significant number of the Chinese educated. Founding Prime Minister Lee Kuan Yew noted 'For political and economic reasons, English had to be our working language' (Lee 2012: 59). He justified the compulsory learning of mother tongue thus: 'if we were to become monolingual in our mother tongue, we would not make a living. Becoming monolingual in English would have been a setback. We would have lost our cultural identity, that quiet confidence in ourselves and our place in the world'.

The leadership was also able to use Singapore's small size to attend simultaneously to different parts of the system. Efforts to raise K–12 standards went hand in hand with strengthening vocational and technical education. The National Industrial Training Council was established in 1968, followed by the Vocational and Industrial Training Board in 1979. An Adult Education Board was established much earlier, in 1960. to promote adult literacy and numeracy. However, policy development with regard to early childhood education did not merit much attention, until the recent decade.

While a political solution to linguistic diversity has been found in the formula of one national language (Malay), four official languages (English, Chinese, Mandarin, Tamil), inadequate attention was paid to the complexities of implementing school level bilingualism. A principal problem, especially for many ethnic Chinese students, was that English and Mandarin were not the languages of the home. Educational quality suffered as a consequence, leading to semi-lingualism and increased attrition rates. This in turn led to the adoption of a policy of tracking, which has remained a key feature of the system.

Notwithstanding the above and given the poor state of the education system in the mid-1960s, it is remarkable how much progress was made in three decades. A segregated system was unified, a common curriculum and rigorous assessment framework established and, given the importance of English proficiency to industrialisation, its use as a medium of instruction was removed from political contestation. Close and consistent attention was focused on curriculum development, textbook development and teacher preparation. One of the key elements responsible for the transformation was the attention paid to teacher and school leadership preparation to ensure that there were enough well-qualified and motivated teachers to teach a rigorous English, Mathematics and Science curriculum. An Institute of Education was established in 1973 to strengthen initial teacher preparation and professional development (PD). The Curriculum Development Institute of Singapore (CDIS) was established in 1980 to spearhead curriculum change to ensure educational relevance. Further steps were taken to further upgrade teacher preparation with the establishment of a National Institute of Education in 1991, as part of Nanyang Technological University. This 'universitisation' of teacher education was enormously significant in improving teacher quality, enabling Singapore to rapidly move towards an all graduate teaching force. Teaching attracted more able and better qualified students and the Institute developed postgraduate programmes and undertook high quality education research with generous government funding.

Another feature of Singapore's education system that merits attention is its multi-tracked structure. While many developing country systems sought, at least in principle, to implement policies on inclusion, Singapore sought early on to identify the best and most talented students. Outstanding colonial era schools like Raffles Institution, Chinese High and Anglo Chinese School were allowed to retain their rigorous admissions criteria. The Gifted Education programme was introduced in 1984, initially designed to identify the top .25 per cent of the primary cohort. This effort to identify the highly intelligent was later followed up by the establishment of independent schools which principally catered to the cognitive elite. In Singapore, the inclusivity challenge was aggravated by the insistence that all pupils had to attain bilingual proficiency. It could be argued that some of the effects of tracking were mitigated by the fact that Singapore has a strong public system of schooling, a common curriculum and assessment system.

However, it is in educational quality terms that the tracking policy can be best justified. Data shows that attrition was consistently reduced substantially; more students stayed in school longer and, over time, the performance level of students rose. In 2018, 89.7 per cent completed grade 10. In a speech in 2011, then Minister Ng Eng Hen noted that in 1980 only a quarter of those aged twenty-five to thirty-nine years had completed secondary education and above. This jumped to 90 per cent in 2010 (Ng 2015). In the 1995 TIMSS assessment, Singapore's thirteen year olds topped mathematics and science; while the international average was 500, Singapore students achieved 643 marks. In the latest PISA assessments in 2019, Singapore students were second to three Chinese cities.

8.3 POST-INDUSTRIAL INNOVATION ECONOMY (1997–2020)

The government, as the state's economic guardian, was alert to the changes in the global economy that began in the 1980s: it recognised the rising tide of globalisation and foresaw the consequences for Singapore's high-wage work-force relative to populous countries like Indonesia and China. To grow economically, Singapore had to move up the value chain into higher value-added production, expand its services sector and to be more productive, innovative and entrepreneurial.

These strategic shifts posed a challenge to a successful education system built upon standardisation and mastery of academic content that was becoming too assessment-driven. There was and is a strong need to develop twenty-first century competencies. Education quality had to be reconceptualised, to go past knowledge recall to application; indeed, to not just find solutions but even to find problems! Students' active involvement in their learning, experiential learning, learning using technology and other twenty-first century competencies had to be part of education quality.

Drawing from the neoliberal perspectives ascendant in the United States in the 1980s, the government in 1987 encouraged twelve high-performing schools to go 'independent'. These schools were given greater autonomy to modify and enrich the curriculum and, independent of the Ministry of Education (MOE), recruit a proportion of staff. Principals were responsible to a Board of Governors rather than directly to the MOE. Even while the state-control model was dominant, the new education narrative was about choice, autonomy, client driven and market share. But the most significant system-wide initiatives were to be found in the *Thinking Schools, Learning Nation* (1997), *Teach Less, Learn More* (2004) and *ICT Master Plans* policies. The shared aim of these initiatives was to move Singapore schooling into a more open, questioning, instructional mode with student learning not teach-ing as the prime focus of classroom instruction. In 1997 former Prime Minister Goh Chok Tong, launching the *Thinking Schools, Learning Nation* (TSLN) initiative, said:

What is critical however is that we fire in our students a passion for learning, instead of studying for the sake of getting good grades in their examinations ... It is the capacity to learn that will define excellence in future, not simply what our young achieve in school. THINKING SCHOOLS must be the crucibles for questioning and searching, within and outside the classroom, to forge this passion for learning among our young.

Schools must be centres for questioning and searching within and outside the classroom ... Children must continually be pressed to raise questions and accept challenges, to find solutions that are not immediately apparent, to explain concepts, justify their reasoning ...[1]

In making this shift, the Singapore education system faced a number of challenges. Why did a system that did well on international assessments need to change? Could a system which pursued student academic performance in high-stakes examinations shift to one that valued both academic and non-academic talents? Could curriculum, assessment and, most importantly, teachers, move from being content experts to facilitators of student learning? Could there, within a national school system and a culture of standardisation, be greater variety, a wider range of knowledge generation pedagogies; could learning be fun, student-owned and serve multiple purposes? A short answer to these questions is that education policies and practices needed to evolve to meet changing circumstances, for example, globalisation, the need for an innovation and enterprise driven economy.

8.4 BUILDING A SYSTEM OF 'BRIDGES AND LADDERS'

Two key reforms, the Integrated Programme (IP) and the Direct School Admission (DSA) Scheme, were introduced in 2004. The IP enabled academically bright students to engage in a seamless six-year education after their Primary School Leaving Examinations (PSLE) in selected schools. These students enter in Secondary 1 (Grade 7) and complete their studies in the final year of junior college (Grade 12). They do not need to take the GCE 'O' levels national examinations at the end of Secondary 4 (Grade 10). This initiative was to address the concern that too much time was spent on revision in grade 10; the 'freed up' time would enable IP students to engage

[1] www.nas.gov.sg/archivesonline/data/pdfdoc/19970602_0001.pdf, p. 5, last accessed March 2021.

in a wider variety of educational and co-curricular programmes. This was welcomed by the academically strong students and their families. It provided for greater variety in education, as well as more customisation of learning. However, even the capable implementation of good reforms can have unintended consequences and side-effects. The initial implementation of IP resulted in greater competition between schools for talented and academically strong students. Even leading schools that did not offer IP initially joined the competition. Streaming at grade 6 also limited opportunities for those students whose talents emerged during secondary schools as they were not able to join these IP schools, though there were other options for them.

The Direct School Admission (DSA) scheme sought to address another key 'problem' in Singapore's education system, a high stakes assessment regime that funnelled bright students into top schools. DSA enabled grade 6 students to be admitted to specific secondary schools based on their distinctive strengths, instead of sole reliance on the Primary School Leaving Examination (Grade 6) results. This opened multiple opportunities to students of various capabilities in sports, dance, music and other spheres. This also led to a boom in private coaching and tutoring in these other non-academic spheres. Schools were also encouraged to develop distinctive niches and strengths. This led to the creation of specialised schools like the Singapore Sports School (2004), the NUS High School of Mathematics and Science (2005), the School of the Arts (2008) and the School of Science and Technology (2010).

The term 'bridges and ladders' was first used by then Education Minister, Heng Swee Kiat in 2011. Its rationale was best expressed by Wong S. H., the Director General of Education. The innovations of the previous decade provided a foundation to make the system even more responsive to student needs amid economic change. Wong (2019: 3) stated that 'all our policies have been formulated to cater to changing needs, interests and abilities of our students. With multiple pathways, the student has the advantage of making the best choices according to his talents, capabilities and inclinations'.

The Singapore education system provides bridges and ladders that enable every student to learn well and be able to take advantage of multiple pathways. This recognises that students may be late bloomers and need opportunities to further their education. It also recognises that ten years of schooling ought to be considered a minimum. For instance, the system allows students who have done well in the technical track at high school to move on to the Institute of Technical Education and, depending on performance, to go on to earn a polytechnic diploma. A small number of students have gone on to study engineering at the university. As a consequence of this system, some 95 per cent have some form of post-secondary education; some 40 per cent of polytechnic graduates have access to university education.

8.5 REFORM IMPLEMENTATION IN SINGAPORE (1997–2019): CHANGES TO CURRICULUM AND PEDAGOGY

Now (2020) is as good a time as any to assess the success of the policy initiatives. Overall, it is clear that, while high-stakes examinations remain and the system continues to be competitive, learning environments in Singapore's classrooms have changed considerably. This is principally because the Ministry implemented a cluster of policies, incrementally changing key variables. The main message, consistently emphasised, was that parents, employers and students should embrace twenty-first century competencies as a key outcome of schooling. In practice this meant that a public, standardised system of education had to provide for diversity and choice. As noted in Section 8.4, the school system was further diversified with the creation of specialist schools. Learning from the experience of independent schools, the MOE adopted a looser governance model via the creation of school clusters helmed by cluster superintendents, who were experienced principals that could guide and mentor principals and facilitate sharing of good practice with the aim of raising standards in weaker schools. Curriculum and textbooks were progressively changed, augmenting established content with ways for students to critique the content and to apply knowledge to real life problems. Teachers and students worked together to co-create knowledge. The lower secondary social studies textbooks, for example, used an explicitly source-based learning approach. Assessment structures were also changed to test students' deep understanding of core concepts that underpin disciplines and their ability to apply their knowledge.

Education was and remains a vital component of Singapore's impressive economic growth and nation-building efforts. Building on the emphasis on loyalty to nation, social cohesion and multi-culturalism that pervaded the education system in the first decades as an independent state, Goh (1997) laid out a vision of 'Thinking Schools, Learning Nation' (TSLN), to guide the education system towards preparing citizens for a post-industrial society. TSLN provides a cogent and compelling vision that has contributed significantly in building a high performing system. In 1997 also, the Desired Outcomes of Education (DOE) frameworks were introduced for schools in

Singapore, ranging from primary to post-secondary. These shared DOE provided clear guidelines about the intended growth and outcomes for the Singapore students. This lucid set of guidelines and outcomes proved to be a useful guide for schools throughout Singapore's schools and over the decades.

The 1997 TSLN initiative can be considered as a policy to prepare 'future ready' students. For example, it led to the MOE's First Masterplan for ICT, issued in 1997, to provide schools with the curriculum, software, hardware and network to enable staff and students to access a wider range of education resources and technology. It was clear to planners that members of a technology driven post-industrial society needed to be familiar and comfortable with technology. Technology was also seen as a vital enabler of 'anytime, anywhere' learning, in addition to making personalised learning feasible.

The Second Masterplan for ICT in Education was introduced in 2003. Building on the First Masterplan,[2] it promoted the active, effective and widespread use of ICT by establishing baseline ICT standards and integrating ICT into the curriculum. These methodical and responsive masterplans facilitated the sustained implementation of ICT in a structured and systematic way in schools. Policymakers were aware that responses to these reforms varied. Some schools and educators respond faster than others. Some schools required stronger leadership, more time, additional resources and effort. The seeding of the innovative use of ICT and the conscious plans to support and expand effective ICT use helped schools with various capacities to significantly improve via the greater utilisation of ICT in teaching and learning. The successful implementation of the ICT initiative in Singapore's schools amply demonstrates the need to take into account variable capacities of schools, timely teacher upgrading and alignment between policy and practice needs.

To strengthen the reforms initiated by TSLN in 2005, Prime Minister Lee Hsien Loong introduced the *Teach Less, Learn More* (TLLM) initiative. The aim was to boost students' inquiry-based learning and critical thinking skills. The implementation of this reform took years and involved support from the Ministry of Education, school leaders, teachers and the education fraternity. The combined effort and teamwork yielded positive results as students improved in their learning, thinking and performance, as seen in the international assessments. Reforms which aim to change deeply embedded pedagogical practices like 'teaching to the text' require close collaboration and ongoing two-way support from the top and ground.

---

[2] www.unesco.org/new/fileadmin/MULTIMEDIA/HQ/ED/images/singapore.pdf, last accessed March 2021.

To remain relevant and successful, education systems require ongoing review and refinement. In order to assess the fidelity of evolving pedagogical practices to the visions outlined in TSLN and TLLM, MOE in 2010 undertook significant reviews of these initiatives via the *Primary Education Review and Implementation (PERI)* reports, as well as the *Secondary Education Review and Implementation (SERI)* reports.[3] The broad aim of the reviews was to ensure the effectiveness of reform implementation. The areas identified for improvement included social-emotional development, non-academic curriculum and life-long learning. Following the reviews, key reform initiatives such as the *Programme for Active Learning* (PAL) for lower primary students; *Holistic Assessment*, which sought to move learning assessment beyond marks and grades; *Engaging Pedagogies* that sought to enhance the quality of teaching and learning, and infrastructure development to further enhance the learning environment in schools were introduced in phases. Initiated by PERI and SERI committees, these multi-faceted reforms were implemented system-wide.

In 2013, MOE introduced the *Applied Learning Programme* (ALP) initiative to develop interdisciplinary knowledge and apply their skills to problem solve in real-world contexts. The ALP was started in all schools in 2017. Schools were allowed to adapt and customise the programme to meet cohort needs. In this way, schools had the flexibility and ownership of these school-based initiatives arising from well-intentioned reforms from the Ministry. Policymakers understood that complex reforms require considerable support to schools and more time to be fully implemented. Careful planning, preparation and relevant implementation strategies, as well as time and resources, are all required for the reforms to be effective.

In addition to these initiatives to nurture academically successful students, MOE invested in holistic education and the development of values and character. A major initiative, entitled *Values-In-Action* (VIA), was launched in 2012 to provide value-rich learning experiences that enabled students to be involved in the community to build empathy and nurture them to be caring and socially responsible citizens. This initiative was strengthened by the *Learning for Life* programme (2015), which cultivates interpersonal skills and values and enhances positive character development.

---

[3] https://planipolis.iiep.unesco.org/sites/planipolis/files/ressources/singapore_peri_2009.pdf; https://planipolis.iiep.unesco.org/sites/planipolis/files/ressources/singapore_seri_2010.pdf, last accessed March 2021.

These reforms, which substantially changed the instructional climate in schools, offer ample evidence of the success of TSLN and TLLM implementation. Substantial planning, intelligent policy development, investment, preparation and effort are required in implementation. These carefully conceptualised reforms were introduced gradually and systematically to win the support of the education community and society. Implementation invariably started with pilot projects in selected schools and eventually expanded to include all schools. Also conducted were ongoing micro reviews. For instance, the initiatives for ALP went through a cycle of conceptualisation, piloting, implementation, review and refinement, which can take more than a year. As a result, of careful planning, engagement and resourcing, these reforms were successfully implemented and changes to established pedagogical practices achieved.

For large scale reforms to be effective, they need multiple iterations for initial successes to be sustained. The third and fourth ICT Masterplans built upon careful reviews of earlier plans. Reforms are often relevant for that particular phase of time, even though the expectations for outcomes may move over time. Hence, there is a need for subsequent variations and strong follow-up effort that stay true to the core goals and aligned to the others, while being updated for the evolving or new context.

8.6 DEVELOPING TEACHER AND SCHOOL LEADERSHIP CAPACITY

The quality of all education systems is dependent on the quality of its teachers. Throughout the decades, there have been regular reforms to boost the education quality and the professional development of teachers. There was a commitment in the 1990s to making teaching an all graduate profession when resources and conditions permitted. Improved preparation for elementary teachers has significantly strengthened teaching and learning at the elementary level. A major reason for Singapore's educational success and the capabilities of its students is the attention that Singapore pays to teacher selection, preparation, deployment, incentivisation and retention. Both initial teacher training and professional development and career development are considered very important, as is the performance management of teachers.

Teachers and school leaders are obviously a key element in the creation of a high performing education system. Singapore's colonial educational inheritance of a four medium of instruction system required preparation of teachers to teach in language segregated schools; an additional complication was, as noted earlier, resistance from Chinese medium teachers to use English as the main medium of instruction across all schools. Further, the rapid evolution of Singapore's economy, an industrial component supplementing a port-based trading economy, required an expansion of the education system, requiring more teachers to be trained.

Formal preparation to build a national teaching cadre began with the establishment of the Teachers' Training College (TTC) in 1950. It initially trained only primary school teachers for English medium schools; secondary school teachers were trained at the University of Singapore's School of Education. In 1955, a Certificate in Education for Chinese and Malay medium teachers was launched. The two streams were unified in 1969 when the TTC took over responsibility for preparing secondary school teachers as well.

The TTC was upgraded in 1970 and established as the Institute of Education (IE). The IE comprised schools of professional studies and curriculum studies and included preparation for vernacular medium teachers. The key certification programmes included a full-time, two-year Certificate in Education programme for non-graduates for teaching in primary schools and a full-time, one-year Diploma in Education programme for secondary school teachers.

A further enhancement of Singapore's educators' capacity came with the upgrading of the Institute of Education into the National Institute of Education, which was established in 1991. Twenty-five years after Singapore's establishment as an independent nation, a well-developed and resourced public education system had been established. Singapore's industrial economy had taken off, and policymakers recognised new opportunities in globalisation. They also recognised that a more skilled and capable workforce was needed. A major review of the university sector by Lord Dainton in 1989 recommended that a National Institute for teacher training be established as an integral part of Nanyang Technological University (NTU). Lord Dainton noted several significant shortcomings. He was concerned that little emphasis was being paid to the creative arts, that the College of Physical Education was not a part of IE and that there was a 'lack of esteem' between primary school teacher qualifications, a Certificate of Education was obtained after two years of study and the secondary school teachers with degrees pursued a Post Graduate Diploma in Education.

As Lord Dainton noted, 'it is in everyone's interest and indeed of vital importance that Singapore should have the best possible teacher training system'. This 'universitisation' of teacher education enabled NIE to set university appropriate standards of entry and graduation, and to introduce degree programmes – BA (Arts) and BSc (Science) with Diploma in Education. The subsequent integration of NTU and NIE on a single campus was also beneficial in that it enabled NIE students to access a wider range of electives offered by NTU schools and a steady build-up of post-graduate programmes.

One recommendation seldom remarked upon is his recommendation that the NIE begin as 'an associated institute or college, with an independent governing board and financial support provided directly by the Ministry of Education . . .'. This enabled NIE to be strongly aligned to the mission and policies of the MOE and ensured adequate levels of funding. Thirty years on, the enactment of this recommendation has enabled NIE to develop a high performing institute of teacher education, able to be both a national asset and an exemplar international institute. Singapore's model of teacher preparation has been adopted in countries as diverse as Indonesia (Sampoerna School of Education), the United Arab Emirates (Emirates College for Advanced Education) and Bahrain (Bahrain Teachers College). Joint postgraduate pro-grammes were launched with Teachers College, US and with the Institute of Education, London.

In 1995, a unique innovation in leadership preparation was the develop-ment and implementation of a teacher assessment tool, the Current Estimated Potential (CEP). Beyond annual performance reviews, which were required for all teachers and provided a fair basis for promotion and add-itional financial incentives, the CEP was a tool to assess and provide for further development and act as a teacher talent pipeline (see Chew et al. 2003). Here the assessment focus was on capacity and attributes to hold specialist positions in counselling, assessment, subject specialisations and departmental and school leadership positions.

To further develop the capabilities of teachers, in 2012, MOE introduced the Teacher Growth Model, which is a professional development model to promote an educator's lifelong learning, development and well-being. Such a framework enabled educators to see and value development pathways and encouraged long-term commitments. This complemented the introduction of the Teacher Careers Framework in 2001. The Framework has three pathways, Teaching, Leadership and Specialist, enabling the MOE to systematically build up human capital and provide a structure for teachers' choice with regard to future professional and career development.

In addition to investing in lifting the quality of teachers, the government made the capable leadership of schools a key priority. It was inevitable that key leadership qualities and skills would be highly valued by a political leadership which had thought deeply about policies and processes and was very performance-oriented.

Formal training for school leadership began in 1984 with the Diploma in Educational Administration (DEA). Policymakers had determined that the almost two-decade effort in developing a national system and implementing the bilingual model was reaching maturity and the focus now had to be on setting standards for and sustaining individual school and system level excellence. A one-year full-time Diploma in Educational Administration was the system's answer to the need for capable school leadership. However, the Thinking Schools, Learning Nation (TSLN) initiative challenged the existing model. While curriculum and assessment would still be centrally mandated, school leaders would now have to be innovative and entrepreneurial, to give schools a distinctive character and to lead, model and enhance teacher professionalism. To foster these leadership capacities in 2001, the Leadership in Education Programme (LEP) was launched. It was positioned not as a conventional school leadership diploma but as a six-month executive programme designed to equip individuals with the skills to lead in conceptualising programmes, designing effective instructional environments and building teacher capacity. Participants had opportunities for two-week-long study visits to overseas schools and systems to learn about best practices and for a Singapore school internship where they had to plan an innovative project. The programme also included interactions with senior education and government officials, as well as visits to NGOs (Ho and Koh 2018).

School principals have special responsibility to undertake rigorous reviews of teacher performance and all teachers are entitled to 100 hours of professional development annually. In line with previous policies to incrementally enlarge school and teacher autonomy, and to more firmly establish teaching as a profession, MOE encouraged the formation of the Academy of Singapore Principals in 2002 and the Academy of Singapore Teachers in 2010. These were significant initiatives that enabled school leaders and teachers to be involved in educator-led professional development. These were supplemented by initiatives to encourage Lesson Study, Action Research and Communities of Practice, all of which can be considered school-based professional development activities.[4]

---

[4] https://academyofsingaporeteachers.moe.edu.sg/professional-excellence/professional-learning-communities, last accessed March 2021.

8.7 CAPACITY BUILDING IN EDUCATION RESEARCH

We noted earlier that the launch of Thinking Schools, Learning Nation, and ICT Master Plans were responses to changing economic environments nationally and globally. The integration of NIE with NTU prepared the ground for an increased emphasis of relevant and timely education research. This was in part necessitated by the need to develop postgraduate programmes but also to place both education polic making and teacher preparation on a rich, contextualised research base. The Teach Less, Learn More initiative launched in 2004 signalled a need to move towards a more student-centred applied learning mode. A small start to produce research to underpin this move had been made in 1994 with the establishment of the NIE Centre for Educational Research but considerably strengthened by the establishment of the Centre for Research in Pedagogy and Practice (CRPP) in 2003. The Ministry provided an initial grant of S$48 million and in 2008 provided another grant of S$100 million to undertake education research over a five-year period. Ms Grace Fu, Senior Minister of State, Ministry of National Development and Ministry of Education, speaking at the Opening Ceremony of the Second Asia Pacific Educational Research Association Conference stated 'this concerted effort among practitioners, researchers the teachers training institute is laudable. This will help create a culture of evidence-based practice which will be critical to sustain and help scale up important education reforms'.

According to the Office of Education Research, CRPP has identified five priority research areas 'to provide a future ready learner's research agenda around purposeful learning'.

- Schools, Leadership and System Studies

- Cognitive, Emotional and Social Development

- Teacher Professionalism and Learning

- Learning Sciences and Innovation

- Lifelong Learning, Cognition and well being

It will be clear from the above that the state and especially the MOE anticipated the enormous capacity building initiatives that would be required to successfully implement system-wide reform, attending to the needs of individual schools. As the design of the LEP shows, MOE had the confidence and the ability to create and innovate task-specific programmes. It had also, as the establishment of NIE indicates, the vision and resources to build the institutional capacity to upgrade the whole of the teaching force.

8.8 EXPLAINING SUCCESSFUL REFORM IMPLEMENTATION IN SINGAPORE

There is now a considerable literature on high performing school systems, due in part to national and international policy focus on the contribution education makes to strong, resilient societies and economic growth. It is reasonable to assume that intelligent policy, adequate resources and effective implementation are essential. It is also clear that rising expenditures on education have not always led to improvements. Finally, international assessments of student performance have focused attention on strengths and weaknesses of systems and generated various prescriptions for how outcomes can be enhanced. For example, the report 'How the World's Best Performing School Systems Come Out on Top' by Barber and Mourshed (2007) placed a huge emphasis on teacher quality; it did not think that smaller class size was a good remedy for underperformance.

Andreas Schleicher (2011), writing after a visit of Singapore, summed up the Singapore model in these words:

> This is a story about political coherence and leadership as well as alignment between policy and practice; about setting ambitious standards in everything you do; about focussing on building teacher and leadership capacity to deliver vision and strategy at the school level; and about a culture of continuous improvement and future orientation that benchmarks educational practices against the best in the world.

Two further points he made are pertinent to our analysis:

- *Coherence.* In Singapore, whenever a policy is developed or changed, there seems enormous attention to the details of implementation – from the Ministry of Education, to the National Institute of Education, cluster superintendents, principals and teachers. The result is a remarkable fidelity of implementation.

- *Clear goals, rigorous standards and high-stakes gateways.* The academic standards set by Singapore's Primary School Leaving Examination and O- and A-levels are as high as anywhere in the world ... Rigour, coherence and focus are the watchwords ...

With regard to both of these points, it is clear that Singapore has turned its small size into an advantage. Strong alignment, consultation and co-operation between actors like the MOE, post-secondary institutions, the National Institute of Education and the schools are easier to achieve in a small system with a notable continuity of political leadership. Both have fostered implementation fidelity.

The successful implementation of reforms in Singapore, since 1997, are due to multiple factors that we summarise as the '3C model'.

1. The first C is context. Singapore was in an unenviable situation post-World War II. In addition to material damage to schools, houses and industrial entities, there was the psychological trauma of the Japanese occupation of Singapore, especially for ethnic Chinese Singaporeans. British power and authority were markedly diminished. As noted earlier, small size, lack of natural resources, a plural society dominated by a Chinese majority and a segregated school system raised questions about Singapore's future viability as a sovereign nation state. The failure of merger with Malaysia was a further set back.

   Fortunately, Singapore had a political and administrative elite, both English and Chinese educated, who were up to the task of rebuilding. Their ability to mobilise the population, to turn crisis into opportunity, to set out a compelling vision for the future, advocate values of co-operation and co-existence, of performance, merit and effort were vital to Singapore's success. The education system was a key instrument in realising vision and goals for national development.

   Fundamental to the vision of state, nation and society of the founding leadership was the concept of meritocracy. This was a radical departure from prevailing norms in Asian societies where family connections, and personal relationships underpinned the distribution of opportunity; for example, in neighbouring Malaysia public resources and educational opportunities were often allocated explicitly as a matter of policy, on the basis of ethnicity. The sustained attention paid to meritocracy in Singapore has paid dividends. Overall, since Independence, governance has been of high standard, efficiency and performance highly valued and rewarded. Fifty plus years on, though, there is now a vigorous debate about the merits of Singapore-style meritocracy.

   The meritocracy policy coupled with the commitment to identify, develop and incentivise Singapore's limited human capital has had hugely beneficial effects on the evolution of Singapore education. Though there is a degree of elitism, represented by the high performing schools, access to these schools is by merit. MOE developed a system of high stakes examinations at grades 6, 10 and 12 as objective measures of student performance; an existing policy of automatic promotion was discarded. Rigorous high stakes examinations with their focus on merit and performance are a visible sign of the importance of meritocracy. It resulted in strong social mobility, enhanced human capital development and the linking of reward with performance. Initiatives like the Gifted Education Programme nurtured talent and ability and there was public recognition of high performing students who could compete for prestigious President's Scholarships. In parallel, the MOE emphasised the importance of talent and ability and a culture of lifelong learning for entrance to and progression within the teaching profession. Recruitment standards were progressively raised, a commitment made to an all graduate teaching force, with carefully structured career pathways and access to higher/specialist qualifications. All these initiatives, diligently implemented, were reviewed and modified as circumstances changed.

2. Culture is the second C underpinning the role and significance of education. In Singapore, though a large percentage of citizens are local born, the older generation continues to value tradition and to maintain links with ancestral homelands. There has been a clever drawing upon, especially in education policy, the best of these traditions. Moral and ethical values of the various ethno-religious groups are codified in texts like the Confucian Analects, the Koran, the Bhagavad Gita and Thirukkural. These ethnicities were the traditional 'cultures of the book'. In the Chinese classical tradition, there was a blending of diligent scholarship with merit and effort; thus, the Imperial Examinations could be considered a forerunner of Singapore's present preoccupation with performance, assessment and reward.

3. The third C is capacity. Singapore is an exception among newly-independent countries in having, from the very beginning, a well-educated and capable political leadership with a commitment to meritocracy and exacting performance standards in administration. They replaced a colonial-era bureaucracy with one strong on technocratic expertise. Political leaders like Lee Kuan Yew, Singapore's first and longest serving prime minister, and Dr Goh Keng Swee, at various times deputy prime minister, finance minister, defence minister and education minister, took the lead in advocating, developing and overseeing implementation of

pragmatic policies. Lee, educated at Cambridge, was a strong advocate of Singapore-style (English–Mother Tongue) bilingualism and a unified school system. Goh Keng Swee argued for an education system that was relevant and responsive to human capital needs and addressed critical issues of quality and attrition through a policy of tracking students. Goh Chok Tong, an economist by training, who served as prime minister (1990–2004), initiated the reorientation of the education system towards a knowledge-based economy, by advocating and overseeing implementation of TSLN, while Lee Hsien Loong, the current prime minster since 2005, has led and supported many initiatives to reform pedagogy, such as the 'Teach Less, Learn More' initiative.

8.9 EMERGENT CHALLENGES

An earlier developmental state model, privileging economic growth, led to the development of a strong administrative state and a public school system that was well-led, well-resourced and committed to continual improvement and relevance. But fifty plus years on, will these previous strengths be future weaknesses? Success in TIMSS and PISA, though well-deserved, are not the whole story of a complex and ever-evolving system. All policies have consequences, some unintended. We highlight here two critical features of the present system.

8.9.1 The Bilingual Model

Policy development and early implementation of the bilingual model were marked by errors, especially by a failure to appreciate the gap between home language and dialect use and the requirements of school system level bilingualism in conventional languages. Over time, with strategic policy interventions, especially the building of teacher capacity and establishing more realistic proficiency requirements, delivery problems were effectively tackled. Today, Singapore's school leavers at grade 10 are effectively bilingual. Student proficiency in English at grade 10 is the highest in Asia. The politicisation of language issues so prevalent in the 1950s and 1960s no longer troubles policymakers.

One problem that has arisen is that English is now a dominant language, surpassing the usefulness of other languages. Home use of Chinese and Tamil is declining. Students master the languages required as it is compulsory, but the patterns of usage are not what policy intended. Some commentators even claim that English is now the de-facto National Language!

The policy was also based on an assumption that language equals ethnicity and culture. But Singapore today is a much more diverse society due to the rising incidence of inter-racial marriages and the increased numbers of immigrants. English use is pervasive across all domains, even in culturally significant locations like temples. A major consequence is that students seek to reach specified language performance levels largely in order to gain selection to prestigious academic tracks and schools rather than for communication or deeper cultural understanding.

Given the state's continued insistence on the significance of mother tongues as a valued marker of tradition, identity and culture, in the face of Singapore's evolution as a more diverse society and the clear utility of English proficiency in Singapore's globalised economy, it is hard to see how the present bilingualism model can be sustained. The state's power to dictate which mother tongue a student should study is now weakened. One potential solution is to give families and students greater choice in the mother tongues they study in school.

8.9.2 Meritocracy

Meritocracy has been a cardinal principle in Singapore's nation building efforts. In the first two decades of independence, meritocracy enabled the state to build up and effectively allocate its only resource – its human capital. It kept elite English and Chinese medium intact, but actively enlarged access. Its pro-capital economic policies led to successful industrialisation, which in turn created new and enlarged job opportunities. The utility of higher academic and skills credentials was clear to all school goers and their parents. The government pointed to evidence of social mobility as proof that meritocracy worked.

As Singapore evolved into a high income economy and society from the 1980s onwards, it also had to keep its economy competitive by leveraging its location, to become a major financial centre and transportation hub in the midst of an emerging Asia. As a consequence, Singapore now requires highly skilled talent, a need which is being met in part with increased immigration. One consequence of these shifts is increased inequality.

The neo-liberal turn in the economy is also represented in education policy and practice. Policies promoting choice, flexibility, differentiation and privatisation, within a unified national system, led to considerable differentiation in curriculum and pedagogy and large between-school differences. While differentiation catered well to individual differences, aspirations and talents, it also increased competition for access to high prestige schools. Today, Singapore has a S$1.4 billion tuition industry to meet parental anxiety about their children's educational chances. Obviously, those with greater resources are capable of investing greater amounts. Gee (2002) notes that at the extreme end of the income divide, households with monthly incomes of S$10,000 and above spent twenty-seven-times more on tuition than those with less than S$1,000. So competitive is the education environment today that, though high performing, Singapore students are also afraid of failure. The pressure to succeed is drowning out efforts to promote 'the joy of learning'; teaching to the test is a real hindrance to the more progressive pedagogies that the government is promoting.

Finally, despite the state's commitment to treat all citizens equally, to provide equality of educational opportunity and promote social mobility, it has not been possible to achieve equity. In 2010 – Chinese, Malay and Indian students constituted 74.9 per cent, 16.3 per cent and 7.2 per cent of enrolment in educational institutions. For university enrolment, the figures were 86 per cent, 2.7 per cent and 11.8 per cent, respectively. The Malay community has not yet been able to catch up. Lee Kuan Yew observed in 2011 after visiting a number of high performing schools that the percentage of fathers with degrees did not dip below 50 per cent. By contrast, in four neighbourhood schools serving a wider community the highest percentage was only 13.1 per cent (Chang 2011: 3).

8.10 CONCLUSION

Notwithstanding the emerging challenges, it is clear that Singapore's policymakers, since the early 1960s, were aware of the challenges they faced in developing education policy. These included the need for consistency and sustainability of policies, for significant resourcing levels and developing and retaining public acceptance. They optimised Singapore's small size to build a 'bridges and ladders' model that created multiple pathways within levels and between sub-systems, the stages and forms of education. This has resulted in a very large percentage of grade 1 students completing grade 12, and a large percentage going on to post-secondary education and training. In addition to this, almost universal access, completion and high standards have been maintained as evidenced by results in TIMSS, PIRLS and PISA.

The Singapore model also demonstrates that a public system can both raise the floor and ceiling in student achievement, even though a gap will inevitably remain. A national system need not mean uniformity. The Singapore model accommodates high performing autonomous schools (in Singapore terminology, 'independent schools'), special purpose schools like the School of the Arts and schools which offers a mixed academic cum-vocational curriculum. It is no longer the case that bright students automatically opt for the year 11 and 12 academic track. Indeed, increasing numbers opt for the polytechnics, given their high quality and relevance to employment.

There is no gainsaying the fact that its educational successes were only possible because Singapore is a successful developmental state. It optimised on its small size, policy continuity through decades of one party dominance, a well-educated and capable political leadership and a performance oriented bureaucracy. It successfully transformed the economy, creating employment opportunities for those with education and skills credentials. With meritocracy as a core value, it built acceptance of a system of rewards for effort, merit and excellence, all of which benefitted the education system as a key institution. There is every reason to believe that Singapore is well equipped to meet future state development and education challenges.

References

Barber, M. and Mourshed, M. (2007). *How the World's Best Performing Schools' System Come Out on Top*. McKinsey & Company.

Chang, R. (2011). Parents backgrounds the edge for students: MM. *The Straits Times*, 25 January, 3.

Chew, J., Stott, K. and Boon, Z (2003). On Singapore: The making of secondary school principals. *International Studies in Education Administration*, 31:2, 54–75.

Gee, C. (2002). The education 'arms race': All for one, loss for all. Institute of Policy Studies Working Paper.

Goh, C. T. (1997). Speech delivered at the opening of *The Seventh International Conference on Thinking*. Suntec City Convention Centre Ballroom, Singapore, 2 June. Available at: www.moe.gov.sg/media/speeches/1997/020697.htm (accessed 25 August 2017).

Ho, J. M. and Koh, T. S. (2018). Historical development of educational leadership in Singapore. In Koh, T. S. and Hung, D. (eds.) *Leadership for Change*. Singapore: World Scientific Publishing Co., pp. 49–51.

Lee, K. Y. (2012). *My Lifelong Challenge: Singapore's Bilingual Journey*. Singapore: Straits Times Press.

Ng, I. (2015). Education and social mobility. In Yahya, F. B. (ed.) *Inequality in Singapore*. Singapore: Institute of Policy Studies; World Scientific, pp. 25–50.

Schleicher, A. (2011). Singapore: Five days in thinking schools and a learning nation. *Education Today* (blog post 8 November 2011). https://community.oecd.org/community/educationto day/blog/2011/11/08/singapore-five-days-in-thinking-schools-and-a-learning-nation.

Wong, S. H. (2019). Bridges and ladders: The new and the old. *Principia*, 11:1, 3–5.

9 Qatar's Road to Education Reform

The Need for Teacher Autonomy

Asmaa Alfadala, Stavros N. Yiannouka and Omar Zaki

9.1 INTRODUCTION

The government of Qatar embarked on the *Education for a New Era* (EFNE) reforms with the objective of improving the quality of education and equipping young people with the skills needed to participate in a knowledge-based economy. In 2001 the government invited the RAND Corporation to examine the nation's K–12 education system and to recommend how best to build a world-class system that addresses the country's needs. RAND's assessment identified four drivers of reform: autonomy, accountability, variety and choice.

Pursuing these themes led to the creation of a system of Independent Schools modelled on US Charter schools. Alongside new curriculum standards, professional development for school leaders and teachers were enhanced to better link curricula to both international standards and national assessments. However, in the post-reform evaluation, the reforms were found not to have fully achieved their targets. Evaluators, as well as school leaders and teachers, attributed the unsatisfactory outcome to structural impediments and implementation challenges, including 'continuous and sudden changes' in policies (Romanowski et al. 2013). Supporters of the changes contend that the reforms were not given enough time to work and that there were signs of progress evident by students from Independent schools outperforming their Ministry peers (Zellman et al. 2011).

In this chapter we examine the EFNE reforms in Qatar with an emphasis on school autonomy. We provide background to Qatar's education system prior to the reforms and explain how this led to the need for change. This is followed by an overview of EFNE and an analysis of challenges faced during and prior to the implementation of the reforms, as well as a look at what was achieved. Secondly, we explore Qatar's objective to become a knowledge-based society, as envisioned in the Qatar National Vision 2030 and argue the case for greater teacher autonomy as a condition for impactful education in support of this goal. Finally, we look at the Empowering Leaders of Learning programme devised by the World Innovation Summit for Education (WISE), as an example of a local professional leadership development programme to enhance teacher autonomy and to pick up where the EFNE reforms left off.

9.2 THE FIRST STAGE OF FORMAL EDUCATION IN QATAR

Prior to the discovery of oil in 1936 there was no formal educational system in Qatar. Teaching was primarily conducted by *Khattabs*, known as 'travelling educators' (Nasser 2017: 1), who would travel between villages teaching language and Qur'anic studies. The system insisted on the primacy of learning the Arabic language, so students could effectively study the Quran both in verbal and written forms. Young males were taught in the *kuttab*, schools located in Mosques. The same system applied to young females, but they were taught within the home. Learned men or women would come and teach girls inside their houses, with family supervision. Eventually, a total of twelve *katatib* (plural for place of learning) would be created, which both boys and girls attended.

Following the creation of the State of Qatar, the government established the Ministry of Education (*Wizarat Al Maarif*) in 1956 as one of the first ministries in the country. The increased income from oil enabled the State to provide its citizens with social-welfare benefits. The first of these were free education and healthcare. It was around this time that Qatar established comprehensive and formalised education (Nasser 2017: 1). Education was made free to boys and girls and a monthly stipend was provided (Brewer et al. 2007: 2) and the government encouraged schooling for girls, establishing the first girls' school in 1956.

Throughout the 1950s and 1960s the Ministry essentially copied the Egyptian system of education, importing both books and teachers from Egypt and other Arab countries. With the Egyptian system came a broader curriculum adding disciplines and subjects; yet effective communication, problem-solving and critical thinking were not prioritised. In the absence of these key components, any notion of further innovation within the educational system was stifled (Alfadala 2019). Despite its longevity, the Egyptian system was perceived as lacking in many key areas in comparison to western education models. This perception, coupled with an increased drive to embrace modern international business practices, became the catalyst for Qatari leaders to concede that the old system was failing to deliver (Alfadala 2019).

While Qatar succeeded in eradicating illiteracy with the expansion of its school system, there were no aspirations other than delivering basic education (Nasser 2017: 2). By the late 1990s and onwards the quality of education became a subject of government concern and public discussion. The school system was struggling to produce quality student outcomes in terms of academic achievement, college enrolments and entry into the labour market (Nasser 2017: 2). Few graduates entered prestigious universities abroad or selective programmes in Qatar University. College officials and employers complained that graduates struggled to write and converse well in English, perform basic Mathematics and accounting tasks or use computers (Brewer et al. 2007: 37). With increased revenue from the oil and gas sector helping to propel economic growth, Qatar's leadership began to prioritise improvement of the education system so that young people could gain the skills needed to diversify its economy and enhance knowledge creation. An initial step was commissioning the RAND Corporation to conduct a national assessment of the educational system.

9.3 EDUCATION FOR A NEW ERA (EFNE)

9.3.1 Background

The RAND Corporation was asked in 2001 to examine the nation's K–12 education system and to recommend how best to build a world-class system. In May of that year the RAND research team proposed a study to describe and understand the Qatari school system, identify problems with that system and recommend approaches for improving the performance of schools and students within the system (Brewer et al. 2007: 33).

A scoping study conducted between September 2001 and May 2002 confirmed dissatisfaction with the state of education. The study noted that problems persisted, 'because the attempts to alleviate them were fragmented, rather than systemic, and were not part of an integrated vision for the education system' (Brewer et al. 2007: 33). Despite the Ministry of

Education (MoE) achieving its primary goal of providing free, standardised education for all Qatari children, it had not reached the goals set by the country's leadership. RAND identified several weaknesses across the education system. The main challenges identified were the lack of vision or mission in the development of the education system and the highly centralised and rigid organisational model which stifled innovation and precluded consideration of other school models or thinking about how to create better value to meet the needs of education stakeholders.

Another issue with the MoE as the RAND team noted, was 'piecemeal growth without a view of the whole system'. As it grew, it added departments, procedures and rules in a piecemeal fashion without factoring for the whole system. Also, it expanded to meet problems as they emerged, failing to evaluate the system and take opportunities to develop coherent strategies. Furthermore, the MoE lacked purposeful organising principles, it expanded to meet problems as they emerged but failed to develop coherent strategies and goals (Brewer et al. 2007: 38).

The MoE's hierarchical organisation structure made it antithetical to innovation or change. Employees worked in isolation within their respective departments and waited until they received orders from above. Questions and concerns raised by teachers were sent up the chain and it could take some time until answers were provided. In addition, there were no clear lines of authority between the schools and the MoE, with limited communication both within the MoE and with stakeholders (Brewer et al. 2007: 39). The RAND study identified several issues regarding teachers, notably low pay and poor incentives. Teachers' salaries were comparatively low in Qatar compared to other countries in the region and contracts were renewed annually, causing teachers to be apprehensive. There was a lack of training and professional development for teachers (Brewer et al. 2007: 41) and teacher allocation policies were also poor. Teachers were transferred to schools with no consultation or notice and teachers were sometimes assigned to teach subjects they had little or no training for.

Lastly, the outmoded curriculum outlined by the MoE was incrementally adopted, grade by grade, without consistent guidance, largely at the teacher's own time, effort and expense (Nasser 2017: 2). The curriculum was based on a rote learning model and therefore not conducive to student-centred classrooms or student-to-teacher interactions (Zellman et al. 2011).

9.3.2 The Reform Model

RAND's initial assessment of the Qatari school system showed that a system-change reform was needed. Given the weaknesses identified it also became evident that 'reforming the Ministry of Education would be a Herculean task for even the most dedicated internal change agents' (Brewer et al. 2007: 44). The 'overly centralized and hierarchical Ministry had constructed a complex, inefficient set of processes, rules and regulations to exert control over the schools and the education agenda' (Brewer et al. 2007: 44). This web of control was designed to ensure compliance but lacked mechanisms for monitoring or assessing performance or for implementing change.

Given these findings from RAND, the strong will of Qatar's leadership to turn a new chapter for the education system and that existing institutions were not producing desired results, it was clear there needed to be structural and systemic change. The solution was to develop new institutions in the system and alter the distribution of authority and responsibility (Brewer et al. 2007: 44). The RAND team offered three models for the future development of the national school system: first, a modified centralised system; second, a charter school system; and; third, a student voucher model. Qatar's leadership opted for the charter school model (Brewer et al. 2007: 56). The RAND team then refined the charter model, customising it to the national context.

The Independent School model was deemed ambitious and unusual for the Middle East by some observers, as for the first time there would be a role for the private sector in school education. Nevertheless, the leadership saw this model as ambitious and efficient, because it would mean some control over publicly funded schools through the charter school mechanism but with no large central bureaucracy (Brewer et al. 2007: 54).

Accordingly, the Independent School model served as the blueprint for the design of the reforms and was guided by four driving themes (Brewer et al. 2007: 2):

1. Autonomy: schools would 'operate autonomously, subject to the conditions specified in a time-limited contract';

2. Accountability: providers would be 'accountable to the government through regular audits and reporting mechanisms, as well as student assessments, parental feedback, and other measures';

3. Variety: each school would be 'free to specify its educational; philosophy and operational plan'; and

4. Choice: 'parents could select the school that best fits their child's needs'.

This model was a marked shift from the existing centralised system to a decentralised and accountable system with more school choice, more monitoring and evaluation of students, teachers and school administrators and with less direct government control (Brewer et al. 2007: 58). Qatari parents would be able to choose from a variety of schools with different missions, curriculum and pedagogy, all developed with the involvement of teachers. Significantly, the model vested decision-making authority in those closest to the work, school leaders and teachers (Brewer et al. 2007: 58). Along with enhanced flexibility for educators, EFNE reforms called for a restructuring of the relationship between the MoE and the Independent Schools, allowing the latter to operate autonomously with time-limited contracts subject to a set of regulations common to all schools (Brewer et al. 2007: 59). To ensure accountability, RAND recommended a standards-based system in which curriculum standards would be applied at every level of the school with a set of matching national assessments at each grade level (Nasser 2017: 4). The curriculum standards covered four mandatory subjects (Arabic, English, Mathematics and Science) and other elective subjects. Performance standards and associated assessments were developed in parallel to the curriculum standards. The curricula were linked to international standards and national assessments (Nasser 2017: 4).

As mentioned in Section 9.3.1, the RAND team identified several structural problems in Qatar's education system which included lack of vision in setting educational goals, piecemeal growth without an overall consideration of the whole system and an inflexible hierarchical organisation structure with unclear lines of authority and top-down control of curriculum and teaching (Brewer et al. 2007: 38). Therefore, new infrastructure would be needed to support the Independent School Model. The RAND team proposed new permanent institutions to operate separately from but in tandem with the MoE. A new governing body, the Supreme Education Council (SEC), established by Emiri Decree No. 37 in 2002, would oversee and implement the education reforms. Under the SEC three further institutions were established: (a) the *Education Institute*, which was tasked with developing national curriculum standards, and providing professional development programmes to teachers and administrators; (b) the *Evaluation Institute*, which was responsible for monitoring the performance of schools, developing national assessments, preparing annual reports and operating the national education data system (Zellman et al. 2009); and (c) the *Higher Education Institute*, which was in charge of the development of higher, technical and vocational education, as well as providing career counselling and academic scholarship programmes.

9.3.3 Implementation of the Reforms

The roll out of the new Independent school system had three phases, as shown in Figure 9.1. To minimise disruption, existing Ministry schools would remain unchanged in Phase I which started in the Autumn of 2002, with the implementation team setting up the organisational and policy infrastructure of the SEC, the Education Institute and the Evaluation Institute and recruiting staff. This phase included the development of curriculum standards and standardised national tests, which would later be used to determine if the Independent school model was working (Brewer et al. 2007: 81). In this phase, the SEC asked RAND to work with the Education Institute to create an initial teacher-training programme to train teachers for the opening of the Independent Schools. The contract for designing the Teacher Preparation and Certification Programme (TPCP) was awarded to the Centre for British Teachers (CfBT), an organisation with strong experience in designing curriculum standards in the United Kingdom. The CfBT trained teachers in teaching strategies, planning and assessment and ways to incorporate learning technologies (Brewer et al. 2007: 107).

Phase II saw the rolling out of the new schools and testing students. This started in early 2004 with the first nationwide administration of student tests and school evaluation surveys, which were intended to provide a baseline of

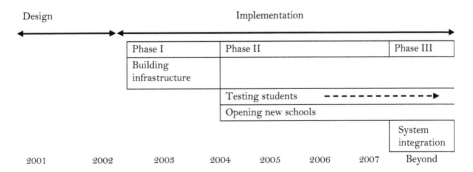

Figure 9.1 Timeline of reform phases (Brewer et al. 2007: 81)

the education system and to generate data which would inform the Qatari leadership on whether to proceed with Independent school model. In September 2004, the first cohort of Independent schools opened. Each subsequent year would allow for additional cohorts of Independent schools, with the number dependent on identifying suitable school operators. It was expected that this second phase would take three to seven years to implement (Brewer et al. 2007: 82).

Finally, phase III was the system integration part of the reform. This focused on the Qatari leadership's decision on whether to continue with the new model and decide whether to retain the parallel structure of the SEC managing the Independent schools and MoE managing Ministry schools or whether to integrate the MoE into the SEC. The leadership decided to proceed with the reform plan and the parallel system was kept until 2010, at which point all the Ministry schools were turned into Independent Schools and the MoE was restructured into the SEC (Brewer et al. 2007: 88).

9.3.4 Achievements and Challenges in the Reform

Any type of public sector reform is complicated as it involves several interdependent processes and different stakeholders, each with differing perspectives and interests. Currently in Qatar, all public schools have been transformed into Independent Schools and made substantial progress in adopting a standards-based system that guides schools, curriculum assessment and professional development and budgeting (Nasser 2017: 13). At the governmental level, the reforms succeeded in altering the division and patterns of authority thanks to new institutions (the Education and Evaluation Institutes) that are still operational.[1] At the system level, the reforms succeeded in establishing education standards for grades K–12 benchmarked against international renowned standards. The current system also captures education data from the schools and descriptive information from students, teachers and parents on overall performance (Brewer et al. 2007: 158). Furthermore, accountability and transparency increased, as evident by the SEC sharing information online and holding engagement events with the public. The reforms caused a significant increase in communication with parents, and parents were more involved in their child's education (Romanowski et al. 2013). At the school level, Independent Schools have

---

[1] The SEC was renamed the Ministry of Education and Higher Education in 2014.

provided better quality education with longer instructional times, 180 school days per year, smaller class sizes of 25 students as opposed to 35 to 40 in Ministry schools, and teachers being more involved in the pedagogy. Furthermore, access to professional development for teachers improved (Brewer et al. 2007: 1).

A review of reform progress conducted by RAND in twelve Independent schools and four Ministry schools over two years from 2005 to 2007 found that students in Independent schools generally outperformed their Ministry peers (but overall achievement remained low), that classroom practices in independent schools were more student-centred than in Ministry schools and that students and parents demonstrated a higher level of satisfaction with Independent schools (Zellman et al. 2011: 57). Also, students in the Independent schools benefitted from improved facilities and teachers were better prepared and trained in accordance with internationally benchmarked standards (Nasser et al. 2014: 13). Teachers in these schools also emphasised testing their students' cognitive skills and expected students to demonstrate what they learnt.

Despite some of these achievements, challenges did emerge during and after the implementation phase of the EFNE reforms. The RAND team did expect some challenges to arise, noting in their report that the Independent School model was, 'completely new to the education system in Qatar and that successful adoption would require behavioral changes on the part of school leaders and administrative staff, teachers, and parents' (Brewer et al. 2007: 83). The reforms also required building up human resource capacity, given that most education professionals only had experience in the Ministry system and would need substantial support to deliver the new curriculum (Brewer et al. 2007: 143).

Judging by the short time frame from the initial assessment of the Qatar education system in 2001 to the opening of the new Independent schools in September 2004, it was clear that the Qatari leadership was anxious to start the reform of the school system and show results to the public (Brewer et al. 2007: 88). This left little time to fully develop a reform plan and even less for implementation. The frame raised some challenges. For instance, with the speed of implementation the Teacher Preparation and Certification Programme could not recruit enough teachers with English language skills to benefit from the classes and keep the course aligned with the design (Brewer et al. 2007: 108). The pressure to show results was felt by principals, who spoke of 'sudden changes from the SEC' and high demands imposed on schools and teachers and a 'rush to get results' (Romanowski et al. 2013: 119).

The transition to a standards-based curriculum produced both benefits and difficulties. The transition from relying on a centrally mandated, predetermined course of study to developing an instructional programme at the school level aligned with new standards was a significant shift in practice, with some challenges. The SEC and Education Institute provided programmes to teachers which included training on curriculum standards, preparing students for assessments and student-centred approaches. These programmes were designed to improve teacher's knowledge and skills of experienced teachers, with the aim for them to lead their own training, develop coursework, mentor teachers and potentially become head teachers (Nasser 2017: 7). The more engaged type of teaching in Independent school meant an extra workload, particularly for curriculum development (Romanowski et al. 2013: 120). However, for many teachers, collaboration around the curriculum and materials was a positive feature of their work (Zellman et al. 2011: 57).

Early in the reform, one significant challenge faced by teachers was the change in instructional language from Arabic to English for Mathematics and Science subjects. Many of the teachers in Qatar who worked in the Ministry schools were used to teaching in Arabic and were not proficient in English or qualitied to teach in the Independent schools (Nasser 2017: 12). This lack of fluency in English had knock-on effects, for instance parents and principals became concerned with teacher's ability to use the standards and to teach Mathematics and Science in English because a lot of time was spent on translating the curriculum to English (Nasser 2017: 12). The change in language was problematic considering that cohorts one to six had already had their classes in English and curriculum, resources and textbooks were in English.

The RAND post-reform study noted concern from parents and the public about the Independent Schools. Parents were worried that school operators would cut costs on the purchase of school materials to increase their profits. The other concern from parents was that English was taking precedence over Arabic and their children might lose their facility with Arabic and their cultural identity (Zellman et al. 2011: 59). Another problem was the difficulty in attracting enough teachers, as some saw work at Independent schools as unattractive due to the longer school days and the need to write lesson plans and choose curriculum and materials (Zellman et al. 2011: 59). In response to these public concerns, policymakers at the SEC increased its regulatory activities which meant reduced operator autonomy.

In the post-reform evaluation, RAND researchers concluded that the K–12 education system did not adequately prepare Qataris for work or postsecondary study and that more time would be needed to determine whether the system would meet the needs of students (Stasz et al. 2007). Despite these challenges, principals, teachers and some parents felt the reforms were not given enough time to work. This can be put down, at least in part, to the many policy changes and reversals made at the SEC. One principal complained, saying there were 'lots of changes in roles and policies' and 'continuous adaptation and change of policies at the level of the SEC' (Romanowski et al. 2013: 119). Despite the negative attention raised about the unsatisfactory 2009 and 2011 PISA results for Qatar and growing complaints from parents and students, there was support from principals and teachers in Independent Schools for the reforms. Teachers reported that the reform impacted their teaching, causing them to adapt and develop their teaching style and strategies and over half of them cited use of modern instructional strategies as an advantage of the reform (Romanowski et al. 2013: 120).

The ambitious reforms were implemented in the space of a few years, with clear, defined goals. Over the past two decades standards have improved considerably and Qatar's PISA scores have improved over time. Progress towards the four goals (accountability, variety, choice and autonomy) is mixed. The reforms succeeded in laying the foundation of a new schooling system and including sets of standards that now guide schools (Nasser 2017: 13). The reforms also helped bring to attention the importance of education as a national priority. Accountability to a large extent was achieved by creating curriculum standards and presenting more information about the range of available education options. On autonomy, choice and variety, there has been a change of direction. Independent Schools were brought under government-led authority in response to public concern about the perceived low-quality and the lack of operators establishing new Independent schools after the first cohort. More work is needed to make Qatar's education system reach the potential sought by the nation's leaders. This will need the recruitment of the high-quality personnel necessary both in the central governing bodies and within schools and renewed diversification of streams of schooling, as illustrated by the Academyati and Qatar Academy of Science and Technology (which are part of Qatar Foundation). One particularly strategic investment needed to improve the quality of education is enhancing teacher autonomy.

9.3.5 Autonomy in the EFNE Reforms

Autonomy was a crucial peg in the reforms, as it connected to many of these weaknesses identified by RAND's assessment of the education pre-reform. In

2002, RAND noted that 'school administrators had little authority' and that principals 'were only able to evaluate teachers in conjunction with Ministry inspections' (Brewer et al. 2007: 40). The report also noted that school leaders wanted more autonomy and more authority over their school and that some school leaders had 'ideas for developing special programmes to increase student motivation and participation' but no freedom to pursue them (Brewer et al. 2007: 43). Teachers also had little professional autonomy and were constrained by annual contracts, low pay and the risk of transfer to another post without consultation. There was a lack of training and professional development (Brewer et al. 2007: 41–42).

With increased autonomy, Independent Schools could overcome the hierarchical structure, have clearer lines of authority and develop new and student-centred curriculums based on the school's mission. Moreover, schools and teachers could make decisions on professional development and pedagogy; the intention being that schools would develop their own identity and independence on how best to educate their students, without the constraints of top-down policies and rules enforced from the Ministerial level. The absence of school autonomy was one reason why school leaders and teachers lacked the flexibility to innovate with the curricula. This fed into other issues such as poor motivation among teachers who wanted their professional judgement to be trusted.

With greater decision-making authority built into the Independent School model, reformers expected that educators would be empowered and motivated (Brewer et al. 2007: 58). By enhancing autonomy, the reform model sought to provide more 'freedom in the classroom', giving teachers the ability to 'adapt their teaching strategies and techniques to the standards and to meet individual student's needs' (Brewer et al. 2007: 67). The expanded autonomy of schools would encourage teachers and leaders to be innovative in developing curricula and creative in delivering content, increasing motivation and job satisfaction. Furthermore, the additional flexibility for the Independent Schools would enable them to determine how to select, recruit, train and reward teachers, which could help retain high-quality teachers in the system. Schools would be able to compete for the best teachers (Brewer et al. 2007: 67).

Following the establishment of the Independent Schools, one of the important changes that the reforms brought was the introduction of curriculum standards in four compulsory subjects: Arabic, English, Mathematics and Science. In keeping with the autonomy and choice reform themes, Independent Schools were expected to develop their own curriculums that aligned to the standards, with teachers developing their own academic programmes (Nasser 2017: 5). Many teachers were overwhelmed by this task as they were coming from the Ministry system where content was pre-determined and provided to teachers.

Despite some of improvements, greater autonomy in teaching did not fully materialise. It was expected that the autonomy of schools would encourage teachers to be innovative in developing the curricula and in delivering content instruction. Teachers recruited for the Independent schools were trained to adopt a student-centred pedagogy, promote small group instructions and assess students using the Bloom's Taxonomy of Educational Objectives (Zellman et al. 2009). However, a review by RAND noted that some teachers remained in a teacher-centred mindset; teachers were not interacting with students, instead remaining behind desks and mostly engaged in whole-group activities as opposed to small team activities. Those teachers that did try different approaches were hampered by administrative paperwork and writing weekly reports. Teachers were more likely to use the lower tier of Bloom's taxonomy, focusing on understanding and application (Zellman et al. 2009). This shows that further training and recruitment of better-quality teachers was needed. The Education Institute did advertise teaching positions abroad, but there were few applicants due to the short duration of the teaching contracts (Brewer et al. 2007: 85).

The autonomy envisaged in the design of EFNE was not fully achieved in implementation. All the Independent Schools were brought under government-led authority and their autonomy was confined to hiring staff, making decisions regarding teaching methods, teacher incentives, professional development plans and budgeting (Nasser 2017: 13). The objective of making schools autonomous entities which could determine their own educational missions and philosophies did not materialise.

In the final analysis, there was little for the EFNE reforms to build on. School leaders and teachers had very little experience in exercising professional control before the reforms were enacted. This was a major weakness. It meant staff lacked motivation and were used to following orders through convoluted lines of authority from a central bureaucracy, even if this did not provide a high-quality education. Part of the goal of the EFNE reforms was to enhance school autonomy and give teachers – along with professional training – the ability to be more involved in the formation and exercise of a pedagogical approach and in expressing their teaching styles. But while the schools have not become autonomous entities as envisioned, the increased autonomy that the schools now possess in the areas of development teaching methods forms a base for the pursuit of reforms which can strengthen Qatar's education system. It is our view that the next wave of reform should extend the autonomy and professional development of school leaders and teachers as they play a significant role in leading class and school improvement and, in turn, raising the expectations, hope and achievement of learners.

9.4 THE NEED FOR TEACHER AUTONOMY

In October 2008 the General Secretariat for Development Planning launched the Qatar National Vision 2030 (QNA 2030). The plan provides a roadmap for Qatar to become an 'advanced society capable of sustainable development for all citizens' by the year 2030. The national vision was developed to address challenges facing Qatar including balancing modernisation and preserving traditions, managing growth and maintaining an equilibrium between Qataris and expatriates (whom comprise 90 per cent of the population). The national vision is built around the four interconnected pillars of human, social, economic and environment development. It is in the human development pillar where the importance of education to the vision is highlighted, stating that education is central to the country's 'future economic success' which 'will increasingly depend on the ability of the Qatari people to deal with a new international order that is knowledge-based and extremely competitive' (QNA 2008: 13). To prepare for that future, Qatar aims to build a 'modern world-class educational system' and provide citizens 'with excellent training and opportunities' (QNA 2008: 13). This will need educational institutions which are 'well-developed, independent, self-managing and accountable ... under centrally-determined guidelines' (QNA 2008: 16).

The QNA 2030 and Qatar National Development Strategy plans acknowledge the eventual end of hydrocarbon as the primary source of economic growth and the need to adjust Qatar's overreliance on skilled labour from abroad. As was highlighted in RAND's initial assessment in 2002, the 'Ministry achieved its initial purpose of providing free education to all Qatari children' and serving its 'societal purpose in providing abundant civil service jobs within both the Ministry and the schools'. However, these goals, despite being achieved, were clearly not enough in supporting the 'far-reaching societal changes that the Qatari leadership aims to bring about' (Brewer et al. 2007: 37).

At present most of Qatar's secondary school graduates go on to be absorbed into the public sector after completing higher education. The Gulf Cooperative Countries (GCC), which includes Qatar, have heavily invested in infrastructure and construction in recent decades and the private sector remains dominated by capital from hydrocarbon revenues spent from government budgets (Alaref et al. 2018: ix). To reduce dependence on public sector employment, reforms are needed in the areas of social protection, labour law, corporate governance and education to encourage more GCC citizens to accept private sector jobs (Alaref et al. 2018: ix). In its 2018 report, *The Jobs Agenda for the Gulf Cooperation Council Countries*, the World Bank states that 'education reforms are needed to ensure that GCC citizens are not just willing, but also able to compete for jobs with the right set of skills. Reforms require a combination of education and skills development activities ... that produce stronger systems with clear learning standards and good teachers', in order 'to strengthen pre-employment skills to ensure a smooth transition into the labour market' (Alaref et al. 2018: xi). For Qatar to adapt to the new 'knowledge-order' it is essential that schools help foster an entrepreneurial and innovative mindset so that current and future generations of Qataris can engage in business, research and development and the sciences. The same World Bank report encourages the Gulf States to enhance institutional and professional autonomy, to provide greater flexibility and empowerment to teachers and in turn improve teacher morale (Alaref et al. 2018: 59).

This transition to a knowledge-base requires effective teachers who are the central figures in any education system as they can make a significant difference to student attainment. For Qatar this means continuously improving teaching quality through training, professional development and enhancing their autonomy. As Harris and Muijs (2007) point out, schools that see improved performance tend to have invested in their teacher's leadership skills. These systems build the capacity of teachers to motivate them and ensure they are given leadership responsibilities for improved services. In the past two decades, as McLaughlin (2016) notes, 'many countries that have implemented major reforms of their education systems have focused on creating high-quality teachers' and a learning educational system. Evidence from the highest performing school systems indicates a positive correlation between professional development of teachers and student outcomes; in the countries that invest in teacher development, teachers have more involvement in curriculum and assessment development and decision-making (Darling-Hammond et al. 2010). In other words, the highest performing countries in education are those that invest in professional development for teachers and grant them greater autonomy in their roles.

The EFNE reforms highlighted the need for leadership in Qatar's education system be devolved to the school level, which would allow school leaders and teachers to take centre stage and promote effective learning. However, for teachers to truly be given centre stage and be effective educators, they need autonomy (Pont et al. 2008: 3) and the right guidance, support and access to professional development. Teacher autonomy is important for four main reasons, as Cribb and Gewirtz (2007: 206–7) argue. First, autonomy is a precondition for the exercise of teacher's professional expertise. Teaching students requires an understanding of their contexts and individual strengths and weaknesses and the ability to tailor to each unique learning situation. Teachers also make normative judgements about attributes, ideals and values they want to instil in their students and the pedagogies and forms of assessment that are worthwhile. Second, autonomy is a source of job satisfaction, health and wellbeing for teachers. For individual teachers the freedom to decide what to teach and how to teach forms an active part in decision-making and is a source of job satisfaction and mental wellbeing. When teacher autonomy is curtailed and their workload increases to meet accountability and reporting measures, stress increases, morale declines and individuals tend to leave the profession. Third, autonomy is a source of creativity, experimentation and variety. It is essential for ensuring a learning environment that addresses children's diverse needs. Just as learners require the flexibility and space to learn, so do teachers. A system that encourages variety of provision allows teachers to deploy their personal resources and to innovate and experiment, which in turn can open new conceptions of good practice. Lastly, autonomy is a source of effectiveness; if it makes teachers happier in their jobs and allows them to be creative and experiment, they tend to get better student outcomes and are most likely to stay in their jobs, ensuring greater continuity.

In sum a culture of educator autonomy must be encouraged, starting from a place of trust and confidence in teachers. With the right guidance, teachers can innovate, experiment and find impactful and sustainable ways to teach the subject matter to students. This is guiding the current cycle of education reform and development in Qatar's school system which WISE is playing a role in, by concentrating on leadership empowerment as a strategy to foster professional autonomy at the school and classroom levels.

9.5 EMPOWERING LEADERS OF LEARNING: SUPPORTING TEACHER AUTONOMY THROUGH SCHOOL LEADERS

WISE was established by the Qatar Foundation in 2009 under the leadership of Her Highness, Sheikha Moza bint Nasser. WISE began as an annual summit in Qatar to elevate the discussion on education to a global level and serving as a multi-sectoral platform for creative, evidence-based thinking, debate and purposeful action on addressing problems within education and devising creative solutions.

Currently, WISE serves as an incubator for innovative approaches within Qatar Foundation's Education City. One of those initiatives is the Empowering Leaders of Learning programme (ELL) which aims to foster a sense of independence and pedagogical change and trial and error in the classrooms. The ELL programme is administered in collaboration with Learn Labs, an Australian based learning and design agency focused on building collective capacity to drive innovation for better student learning. The purpose of the ELL programme is to equip school leaders with instructional leadership capabilities to improve student learning by ensuring that teachers are continuing to improve their classroom practice. The programme's purpose it to:

- Provide quality, blended professional learning and opportunities for Qatari school leaders to share expertise and learn together;

- Provide ongoing professional coaching for school leaders to hone and deepen their leadership for practice;

- Deepen collective capacity for system-wide school improvement in Qatar;

- Create opportunities for purposeful school leader development and collaboration in productive cycles of design, action, and feedback; and

- Create a community of practice where school leaders can continue to learn, create impact and disseminate best practices.

The programme is undertaken by school leadership teams from a network of other schools working to improve learning outcomes. These teams work in three phases:

- Phase 1: teams narrow their focus for improvement and collect baseline evidence of student learning;

- Phase 2: teams lead at least two short improvement sprints and collect evidence of student learning progress to support teacher teams to adapt their teaching approaches based on evidence of progress; and

- Phase 3: teams deliver professional learning to support a growing number of teachers to understand and utilise high-impact approaches to teaching.

This process helps teachers to focus on small but incremental areas for improvement and improve with evidence-based strategies by working in small sprints.

The thinking behind ELL came from the view that systemic change cannot be achieved in Qatar without stronger leadership development as it enables teacher learning and development (Hallinger 2010: Leithwood and Seashore-Louis 2011; Robinson 2011). ELL is grounded on the proposition that more impactful change can be brought to Qatar's school through the school leaders and in turn the teachers (Breakspear et al. 2017: 9), because leaders achieve their greatest impact by developing the capabilities of teachers (Dinham 2016; Wiliam 2016). This includes respecting teachers' autonomy by allowing for focused, continuous improvement of teacher practice. This means maintaining professional conversations about student learning and supporting teachers as they work on their practice. Part of the programme's overarching philosophy is that solutions to further improvement within Qatari schools will be found and constructed within their professional communities. They will not come from central mandates and requirements. As Breakspear et al. (2017) articulate in their work on Agile Leadership:

> Developing leadership must go beyond a series of small-scale sporadic 'programs and courses' and move toward a career-long growth of individual and collective leadership practices, much of which will be embedded within the daily work of schools. (p. 2)

It is about less and better reform in schools. Educators do not need another 'what' but a better 'how' approach to address the issues in their schools. ELL organised its workshops along two tracks, one for school leaders from the Ministry of Education schools and the other for Qatar Foundation schools. In collaborating with the Ministry of Education, ELL worked with an initiative of the Ministry called Maharty, which was able to recommend the most suitable leaders from the Independent schools. In working with the Qatar Foundation, ELL collaborated with the Education Development Institute (EDI) to identify educators from its six academy schools.

The structure works on a selective basis, to ensure that teachers with the motivation and desire to make a change are impacted. The format of the sessions follows the three phases mentioned. In the first session of each cohort, school leaders/teachers are informed on pursuing an evidence-based focus and to apply research on effective teaching. Then the teachers are given a set of tasks to carry out in their respective schools before the next workshop. These tasks involve harnessing collaboration among committed teachers to define and understand specific learning difficulties students face and to design creative ways to help them find solutions. Based on this collaboration, the participants will launch two 'sprints' in their schools; these experimental activities could include teaching team building, using student work samples and exercises to collect evidence and recognise concerns, identifying improved new practices that can be emulated. In the second session of each cohort, the participants will report and build on their experiences and efforts to engage teachers and students. This process takes a targeted approach as opposed to an open approach. School leaders who attend the workshops become a community of school leaders who can then inform other school leaders and teachers, thereby encouraging others to take and apply approaches learned from ELL.

ELL has succeeded in giving more confidence to over 150 school leaders about their ability to generate improvement from within themselves and their schools as opposed to relying on external direction. While initial response has been very positive, more time is needed to measure the impact and scale before an overall assessment of its success can be made. In addition, the programme is still at a small scale. There are 845 schools in Qatar and over 16,000 teachers, led by around 1,600 principals and academic vice principals. WISE is currently in the process of shifting from the two-a-year cohort meetings into a fully embedded learning and coaching programme to support the Qatar's Ministry of Education and Higher Education in achieving its goals for school and system improvement through building the capacity of K–12 school leaders.

At present, the ELL operates at a small scale primarily in the capital of Doha. However, there is the potential for the programme to be scaled across the country, but this will require the support of the Ministry of Education, which has the resources to bring this programme to all schools.

9.6 CONCLUSION

This chapter began with exploring the *Education for a New Era* reforms in Qatar and how these reforms were developed in response to several weaknesses in Qatar's education system. An analysis was given of some of the achievements and challenges of an initial series of reforms, particularly the creation of the new school system of Independent Schools and efforts to enhance school autonomy. The aim was to enable Independent Schools to have more administrative control and for teachers to apply their own teaching methods and be innovative in developing the school's curricula.

Despite some notable achievements, the reforms failed to reach all their targets, particularly on the objective of school autonomy. This was in large part due to increased regulatory actions taken by the SEC in response to public concerns about the quality of the Independent Schools and low demand. At present all the Independent Schools are under the guidance of a government-led authority but retain some independence in budgeting, hiring of staff, making decisions on teaching methods and professional development plans. Overall, the reforms did manage to create a new schooling system with more flexibility and autonomy than the prior school system.

We make a case for building on these achievements by enhancing teacher autonomy – in conjunction with greater investment in professional and teacher training. These steps are essential for the development of teachers' professional expertise and to strengthen their motivation and wellbeing. These are important investments in Qatar's school leaders and teachers, who will play a vital role in leading improvement and raising the achievement of learners. This is particularly significant considering the Qatar National Vision 2030 and how it emphasises the importance of education in the country's aim to be a knowledge-based society. The need for teachers to be innovative and experiment in their teaching has greater meaning now due to the need for Qatar's schools to adopt an entrepreneurial and innovative mindset, so that current and future generations of Qataris can engage in business, research and development and the sciences. The reforms have presented an opportunity to look deeper into the classrooms and see how greater teacher autonomy can make more impactful teachers.

Drawing from the evaluations and critiques of the initial waves of reform the ELL programme has been designed and is being tested as an example of a local programme that seeks to promote teacher autonomy. The ELL was established with the belief that systemic change cannot be achieved in Qatar without stronger leadership development as school leaders achieve their greatest impact by developing teachers' capacities. ELL sought to provide school leaders in Qatar with a better 'how' not 'what' approach. With some early successes the challenge now is to take the ELL programme to scale.

References

Alfadala, A. (2019). *Qatari School Leadership Portraits: Lessons Learned from Education for a New Era reform*. Doha: HBKU Press.

Alaref, J. J. S., Koettl Brodmann, J., Onder, H., Rahman, A., Speakman, J. F., Beschel, R. P., Malik, I. A., Vodopyanov, A. and Quota, M. B. N. (2018). *The Jobs Agenda for the Gulf Cooperation Council Countries (English)*. Washington, DC: World Bank Group.

Breakspear, S., Alfadala, A., Peterson, A. and Khair, M. (2017). *Developing Agile Leaders of Learning: School Leadership Policy for Dynamic Times*. Doha: WISE – Qatar Foundation.

Brewer, D. J., Augustine, C. H., Zellman, G. L., Ryan, G. W., Goldman, C. A., Stasz, C. and Constant, L. (2007). *Education for a New Era, Executive Summary: Design and Implementation of K–12 Education Reform in Qatar*. Santa Monica, CA: RAND Corporation. www.rand.org/pubs/monographs/MG548z1.html.

Cribb, A. and Gewirtz, S. (2007). Unpacking autonomy and control in education: Some conceptual and normative groundwork for a comparative analysis. *European Educational Research Journal*, 6:3, 203–13.

Darling-Hammond, L., Chung Wei, R. and Andree, A. (2010) *How High Achieving Countries Develop Great Teachers*. Stanford Center for Opportunity Policy in Education – Research Brief.

Dinham, S. (2016). *Leading Learning and Teaching*. Camberwell, Vic: Australian Council Educational Research.

Hallinger, P. (2010). Leadership for learning: What we have learned from 30 years of empirical research. Available at: http://repository.lib.eduhk.hk/jspui/handle/2260.2/10503 (accessed March 2021).

Harris, A. and Muijs, D. (2007). *Improving Schools through Teacher Leadership*. Maidenhead: McGraw-Hill International (UK) Ltd.

Leithwood, K. and Seashore-Louis, K. (2011). *Linking Leadership to Student Learning*, 1st ed. San Francisco: Jossey Bass.

McLaughlin, C. (2016). Teachers matter: the role of teachers in reform and scaling it up. In *Education Insights from Cambridge, from Pupil to Teacher: Why Do Teachers Matter?* Cambridge: Cambridge University Press, pp. 12–14). Available at: www.cambridge.org/files/7315/4780/8457/why-do-teachers-matter.pdf (accessed April 2020).

Nasser, R. (2017). Qatar's educational reform past and future: Challenges in teacher development. *Open Review of Educational Research*, 4:1, 1–19.

Nasser, R., Eman Zaki, E., Allen, N., Al Mula, B., Al Mutawaha, F., Al Bin Ali, H., & Kerr, T. (2014). Alignment of teacher-developed curricula and national standards in Qatar's national education reform. *International Education Standards*, 7:10, 14–24.

Pont, B., Nusche, D., Moorman, H. and Hopkins, D. (2008). *Improving School Leadership*. Paris: OECD.

Qatar National Vision 2030 (QNA). (2008). General Secretariat for Development Planning. Available at: www.psa.gov.qa/en/qnv1/Documents/QNV2030_English_v2.pdf (accessed March 2021).

Robinson, V. (2011). *Student-Centered Leadership*, 1st ed. San Francisco, CA: Jossey Bass.

Romanowski, M., Ellili-Cherif, M., Badria, A., Ammari, A. and Attiyah, A. (2013). Qatar's educational reform: The experiences and perceptions of principals, teachers and parents. *International Journal of Education*, 5:3, 108–35.

Stasz, C., Eide, E. and Martorell, P. (2007). *Post-Secondary Education in Qatar, Employer Demand, Student Choice, and Options for Policy*. Santa Monica, CA: RAND.

Wiliam, D. (2016). *Leadership for Teacher Learning: Creating a Culture Where All Teachers Improve So That All Students Succeed*. West Palm Beach, FL: Learning Sciences International.

Zellman, G. L., Constant, L. and Goldman, C. A. (2011). *K–12 Education Reform in Qatar*. Santa Monica, CA: The RAND Corporation.

Zellman, G. L., Ryan, G. W., Karam, R. T., Constant, L., Salem, H., Gonzalez, G. C., Orr, N., Goldman, C. A., Al-Thani, H. and Al-Obaidli, K. (2009). *Qatar's K–12 Education Reform Has Achieved Success in Its Early Years*. Santa Monica, CA: The RAND Corporation.

10 Implementing Educational Reform

Some Reality Checkpoints

Colleen McLaughlin and Alan Ruby

10.1 INTRODUCTION

These case studies have been prepared by people who have been around and close to the action. In some cases, they were designers, in others, evaluators or action researchers and sometimes they acted as advisers. In all cases the authors sustained an enduring engagement with one or more aspects of the reform in question. They are not innocent bystanders, nor are they unquestioning champions of the programmes. They do offer rich accounts; situating policies and actions in national and historical contexts and identifying choices and constraints faced by policymakers and practitioners. Our overarching instruction to the authors was to illuminate a much under-researched and underdeveloped area, the implementation of educational reform.

In selecting the cases we opted for a mix of nationally and locally mandated reforms with five examples from nations where the state initiated and guided reforms, which is the norm for most countries. But because of the impact United States and United Kingdom examples have had on the field of education reform in the last fifty years we offer two cases where the choice and pursuit of better learning strategies has been the decision of a school or a school district. We did not emphasise or suggest that authors look closely at student outcome data or graduate destinations or international benchmarking exercises, rather our interest is in implementation, on how ideas were

This is written on a lamp post in the middle of Parker's piece in Cambridge, see http://cambridgehistorian.blogspot.com/2013/06/reality-checkpoint.html, last accessed March 2021.

enacted. This has also meant that we have relatively short time horizons which, as Hargreaves and Goodson (2006) point out, is a shortcoming in much of the educational change literature. But in some instances the reforms we examine here stretch over many years so we can see changes in emphasis, shifts in direction and in some cases reversion to the norm as implementation unfolds and we find that time is an important factor in execution.

Our task in this concluding chapter is to look back across the cases for patterns, the commonalities and differences, for disparate responses to shared concerns and for similar policies with distinct motivations. In one sense we are picking up a suggestion of forty years ago and doing some 'backward mapping' by looking for the intersection of administrative action and individuals' choices (Elmore 1979–80: 604), where the individuals can be parents, teachers and students, as well as government officials, policy advisers and politicians. Perhaps this is why our first set of observations about the cases are primarily about context.

10.2 CONTEXT COUNTS

Context can refer to a nation's history, or more expansively to the enabling environment;

> the whole panoply of national and international policies, measures and institutions in the economic, social, legal and political domains that influence or affect the growth and development prospects of a country. (UN 1997: 2)

Context can also focus more specifically on issues of risks and resources or be shaped by the political and economic aspirations of a community. All these different formulations of 'context' are displayed in the cases. For example, 'history' can be as straightforward as the legacy of former rulers or colonisers, as we see in the cases of Kazakhstan and Hong Kong. The Soviet legacy of a strong focus on mastering physics and mathematics came coupled with a lot of memorisation and rote learning. It also left a strong tradition of compliance and conformity that constrained professional autonomy. Indeed, in all cases we see different levels of professional autonomy. While the Vietnam and the UK Challenge cases refer to instances where school level actors provided critical feedback about policies and priorities, overall there are few references to teachers' voices, to professional associations like a national mathematics teachers' forum or to teacher unions and the role they can play in facilitating and constraining educational reform. This is not a product of deliberate omission by the authors but reflects the limited roles afforded to classroom-level practitioners.

The leadership continuity that we see in Singapore, Kazakhstan and Vietnam provided a certainty of direction and made the pursuit of particular reforms a constant in the professional life of teachers and school leaders. Yet in other instances, like the case in Qatar, the legal framework that governs the daily life of citizens and institutions was not attuned to or able to accommodate a concept like charter schools that emerge from a completely different legal tradition. In the cases that we present here resources were not a constraining factor: able to draw on revenues from oil and gas, Qatar and Kazakhstan underwrote the costs of quite substantial reforms. The notable exception among the cases is that described by Rowan, in Chapter 6, where lack of resources led schools and school districts to limit the purchase of support services that, coupled with materials and new technology, might have had greater effect at the classroom level and on student performance.

Historical contexts and traditions are important in their intersection with a reform, for beliefs and values shape and are embedded in practices. There are other aspects to context: there are the political, social and educational contexts and they too intersect with the values and understandings of a proposed change. These values and beliefs are interpreted and celebrated and hence have different meanings for the various groups or constituencies involved in or impacted by a change in policy and practice. Consequently, there will be tensions between competing interests as change is proposed, enacted and resisted. There are lessons to be drawn from the instances of context interacting with possible reforms described in these cases. We are trying to draw attention to the importance of knowing and understanding the context and using that knowledge to shape the design and implementation of reforms, as well as to how and when those reforms are evaluated and assessed.

In the five postcolonial nations we examine here, Hong Kong, Singapore, Kazakhstan, Qatar and Vietnam, the state has been, and continues to be, a clear and present actor in educational policy and practice. It is engaged in setting directions, marshalling and delivering resources, communicating priorities and preferences and judging success. The state's role can be enabling or constraining, regulations can be empowering or confining, and both types of regulations can be enacted simultaneously in one state. Too often the state's role is conceived and analysed in linear terms, which overlooks the higher interactive nature of public policy and the communal nature of social institutions like schools and universities. The power to act in a particular way is diffused throughout institutions which makes changing how individuals act difficult. But the fact that power is diffuse does not negate the importance of the state's role, nor lessen the need to study and understand the extent and nature of the state's authority in designing and implementing education reforms.

Developing, codifying and applying that understanding takes time and histories of school reform written in the last fifty years have all pointed to the relatively short time spans that political leaders and educational practitioners have, or are willing to invest, in particular strategies or programmes before looking for results or observable differences. It is noticeable that five of the cases that we present here have benefited from the gift of time. We are presenting instances where reform programmes have run largely in the same direction for ten to twenty years. In contrast the UK and US cases have been more constrained for time, particularly in the examples of new technologies described by Rowan, in Chapter 6, where the time from adoption to abandonment is relatively short. The United Kingdom case also shows the disadvantages of political shifts in priority. Sarason (1990) argued for the urgency of those involved in change and reform to become more politically critical and historically aware. Among researchers, change needs to be viewed in the mirror of reflection and not just placed in the service of policymakers' driving ambition for political success.

10.3 TIMESCALES TAKEN

The most striking examples of sustained commitment to a policy direction are Singapore and Hong Kong, where the reforms played out over an extended period which was as planned. The policies evolved, adapted and were adjusted but overall there was a sense of movement in one direction. There was notable political continuity, not just in terms of the same majority party ruling for the whole period, but also a continuity of 'personality', with national leadership being held by the same people for long periods and key individuals leading the reform activity, in both elected and appointed office.

At the agency level in Singapore there seems to have been a continuity of purpose – captured in part by five-year plans and the persistence of key policy documents which were public and shared widely. As Gopinathan and Lim point out in Chapter 8, the implementation of these reforms took years. In Hong Kong the framework that guided policy development and implementation provided stability and continuity by keeping a focus on four key areas: people and development; planning and support; coherence and structure; and learning and teaching (Chen, 2019). Similarly, the Vietnam case documents a long standing policy framework – the idea of 'socialisation', moving part of the cost of services to the local community, has been operating for over twenty years, as has the push to include more active pedagogy in the repertoire of teaching.

It is hard to generalise about the 'life' of the US cases. One of the programmes, *Success for All* (SFA), is still operating after more than thirty years and was active in over 1,000 schools in the United States in 2018 and had a presence in schools in Canada, China and the United Kingdom. Schools have joined and left the programme at different times. *America's Choice* operated for about twenty years but never reached as many schools as SFA. It was acquired in 2010 by Pearson's, the educational materials and services conglomerate, which eventually took it off the market. The commercial nature of these products and services makes them vulnerable to market forces while many of the other cases are shaped principally by government policy and funding decisions and by changes in political leadership. We see the importance of political leadership clearly in the Hong Kong and the UK Challenge cases where changes in leadership disrupted and impeded implementation. Conversely the Singapore and Vietnam cases show the benefits of political continuity.

Yet we are led to the conclusion that time spent in understanding the context and shaping initiatives and testing ideas and practices from other realms and environments is time well spent and more likely to lead to more effective and more sustained implementation. Time also allows for the flow of ideas and information throughout the community or the system; it is companion to good communication.

10.4 COMMUNICATION

Communication is one of the linchpins in effective implementation. It is not just the matter of how the policy intent is communicated throughout the system of schooling or within a school site or across the profession. Nor is it simply a matter of telling students, parents and teachers that this is what needs to be done or how something must be done. In several cases here there is an underlying message about the power and persuasiveness of expressing the essential purpose of a reform initiative in terms that are connected to key values like national identity, economic survival or individual opportunity. This is striking in the case of Singapore, where survival of the nation and the quality of life for its citizens is a pervasive and recurring theme shaping the messages about the nature and purpose of schools and education. Both the Hong Kong and Singapore cases also highlight how important communication is to effective implementation. In Singapore it was the emphasis on communicating about the nature and direction of reforms that built a remarkable degree of consensus or support for the various waves of reform. Apart from some initial opposition on the question of the language of instruction, the Singapore reform seemed to gain and keep a lot of support from stakeholders, from parents, from employers and from practitioners. It is not just that the communication was persistent and pervasive, it also permeated the different parts of the education system. The messages were also accessible and appealed to the economic and personal interests of the actors.

In contrast, the cases dealing with Kazakhstan's educational reforms suggests that there was some under-communication and that, while the overall imperative for the reforms echoed the economic and cultural identity issues expressed in the Singapore example, the messages were not as effectively crafted and did not immediately appeal to or evoke an interest in the nation's future and in the formation of a national identity. The messages needed to get to the stakeholders, such as parents, and they needed to be in a form that was accessible or mis-interpretation could occur. For example, it is difficult to explain the benefits of formative assessment to parents and grandparents who are used to the Soviet model of daily summative scores on a five-point scale if there is not some immediate connection to them and to a wider powerful goal. The policy implementers soon realised the need to increase communication by undertaking a national communication exercise addressing town hall meetings in regions.

The commercially-based programmes discussed by Rowan, in Chapter 6, relied on communication about the effectiveness of the service to recruit schools and drive sales. *Success for All* (SFA) was successful in its communication efforts, as evidenced by its growth. But, overall, its communication strategies did not extend to channelling the voice of practitioners about what works, about what support they needed and how much time they had, back to SFA's designers and advocates. This produced a disjunction between the expressed policy, the intended courses of action and what was implemented, how often and at what intensity. The UK Challenge programme was very practitioner-focused and driven, so communication was less problematic; it was the political continuity that mattered for programme continuity.

In this set of cases we have instances where communication was central to implementation and where we can see the commitment to communication and particularly the mode and intensity of communication, influencing the enabling environment and being shaped by the central values of the environment. In short, context and communication interact and influence implementation in a process Supovitz (2008) calls an 'iterative refraction'; reform ideas adjusting to the environment and being adjusted by practitioners and designers as they are put into use.

10.5 MODELS OF IMPLEMENTATION

There are distinctly different models playing out in the described cases. The United Kingdom and United States examples reflect the decentralised nature of the school systems in those nations. Cohen et al. (2017: 206) note that, while the US public school systems are mature, having developed and operated for over 100 years, 'only a few seem to have developed the infrastructure that would have enabled them to tightly guide instruction'. The United States and United Kingdom reform programmes described are not the expressions of national or central governments as they are in the other cases: the decision to take up one of these reform packages is a matter for individual schools or districts. In addition, the discourses about why improvement is needed varied. In the Asian examples the discourses emphasised economic gains and focused on the need to update the education system in line with other global systems. International comparisons often played a part. The United Kingdom example emphasised equality of outcome to an extent not matched in other cases.

The United States programmes are at heart commercial transactions, with materials and services being bought and sold. In contrast, the Kazakhstan cases are championed by central authorities and use demonstration and diffusion models with a university (NU) and a network of schools (NIS) as experimentation sites to test and adapt practices. They were to serve as a 'demonstration and innovation site, a beacon of change and reform' (Ruby and McLaughlin 2014). This is in the tradition of industrial innovation and trade liberalisation pioneered by free-ports and continued as Special Economic Zones and Education cities, places free from regulatory constraints and the strictures and socialising norms of an existing organisational culture.

Similarly, the Qatar reforms, influenced by the charter models in the United States, opted to create new schools and to emphasise school autonomy. The new schools adopted common curriculum standards, used national assessments and, despite training programmes encouraging a shift in pedagogy, the result was 'autonomy deferred'. Teachers grappled with reporting requirements and school leaders had to navigate a governing environment that had no prior experience with independent entities and had not established an enabling legal framework for the new schools.

It seems as if the Qatar reforms were heavily influenced by recent reform practices elsewhere, by a desire to adopt the 'right' reforms and emulate others rather than create reform strategies that were likely to be effective in the local environment and build on existing successful or culturally mandated practices. This echoes the findings of Harris and Jones (2018), in a cross-national study of education reforms in seven nations, that context mattered. This reinforces our observations in Sections 10.2 and 10.4 about the significance of the enabling environment.

The Qatar case contrasts with the two Kazakhstani cases, where there was a degree of customisation and adjustment in the design and implementation of reforms which took time to create and enact. For example, formal and explicit recognition of the largely autonomous nature of NU and NIS was embedded in legislation within five years of the university's formal opening, while the legal system in Qatar still seems to be underprepared for independent schools.

The pursuit of new practices and behaviours through the creation of new sites, which hopefully would develop new cultures and norms, contrasts with the reforms in Vietnam, Hong Kong and Singapore and with the UK Challenge programmes and all the United States examples, which worked with existing schools which have prevailing institutional cultures. Recognising the power of inertia, of established repertoires of practice, the UK Challenge schools were encouraged to focus on service improvement. The aim was to adopt practitioner-focused, highly collaborative, evidence-based approaches to finding more effective ways of working. In this the Challenge programme is different from the other cases, with an explicit role for classroom practitioners in the crafting of new methods of practice. The other programmes tacitly omit a role for teachers, especially those who will be implementing the initiative, in constructing better approaches to pedagogy and learning. As Ainscow points out, in Chapter 2, this is a different viewpoint on who creates the knowledge around reform. Is the knowledge on how to improve practice and learning outcomes brought in by those who have created it outside or some distance from the school? Or is the knowledge developed, tried and adjusted by those in the system, and if so at what level and how is it used and shared with other practitioners?

10.6 INTERNAL AND EXTERNAL ACTORS

In the US case all programmes and products were designed by actors external to the systems responsible for delivering education opportunities. As a result, adoption and take up begins with a purchasing decision rather than a decision to design a solution or innovation to solve a problem or improve an outcome. It is a little like the difference between buying clothes that are 'ready to wear' and not 'bespoke', discussed beforehand, to establish the preferences and unique features of the client so the garment can be tailored to suit. Rowan refers to this as the 'discretion that schools have to work on instructional improvement' which comes in part from the diffuse and weak governance structure for school education in the United States.

At a more granular level the US cases illustrate different models of implementation, which Rowan discusses in some detail in Chapter 6. For example, two of them sought to standardise instruction by specifying routines for teachers and students. For teachers there are 'scripts' to be used in classes in a pre-determined sequence. For students there are pre-determined reading materials and assessment tools. This is a 'high fidelity' model which can also be characterised as a 'low trust' model, where there is limited room for professional judgement which might see teachers adapting materials or techniques to respond to the needs of individual students. The interest in fidelity has been influenced by the literature on highly reliable organisations that serve significant regulatory functions, especially in the transportation sector. While it is an appealing idea that schools would always operate 'without critically cascading errors' from the first day (Stringfield et al. 2012: 45) our cases show that the image does not really capture behaviours in complex social institutions with multiple missions. The cases show that work practices change as ideas are disseminated, interpreted, applied and adapted. The result is not a waterfall of mistakes but an iterative process of action, reflection and adjustment that forms and validates practice knowledge.

Lessons from similar fields like drug use prevention programmes in schools (Dusenbury et al. 2003) suggest that 'highly detailed protocols have low success rates' in institutionalising changes (p. 253) while teachers who were able to modify the 'curriculum were more motivated, and creative in general and thus better teachers' (p. 252). Carroll et al. (2007) develop these observations into a framework which distinguishes between elements which contribute to 'adherence' to a design and those which moderate fidelity including the complexity of design, how responsive or motivated participants are and the nature and quality of training and other support strategies. This framework underscores the weakness of simple implementation attempts which expect early and complete adoption of new work practices or materials.

Similarly, the externally designed US models were distinguished by the pursuit of structural changes to augment or strengthen pedagogical leadership. For example, *Success for All* expected schools to have a full-time literacy coordinator overseeing the reading programme. These approaches are essentially cautious or incremental, bolting or grafting something onto the existing organisation and hoping that it would not be too disruptive or rejected. The weakness is that it is not an integral part of the school and can be ignored by participants. Anderson (2017) looks closely at the issue of fidelity of implementation of *Success for All* and *America's Choice* and concludes that the conventional view that fidelity is less likely when the proposed reform is larger or more fundamental may not be true. Rather, she suggests that 'the salience of very large changes may actually help teachers shift their thinking in ways that promote high-fidelity' (p. 1309). The importance of a large motivating message seems to be part of the apparent success of the educational reform programmes in Singapore, Hong Kong and Vietnam reported here.

In the cases of Hong Kong, Qatar and Singapore, the reform process tended to be iterative; ideas were tried and tested, evaluated and modified, even if the process was occasionally reactive rather than intentional. This was not necessarily a linear process, nor was it a process that only involved officials and experts. In the Qatar case, parental choice not to send their child to a charter school led to a reappraisal of the change strategy, as did other factors. In Singapore, we see twenty years of implementation, reaction, adjustment, further implementation and evaluation and another adjustment. There is a whole process of policy learning and policy adaptation that is being led by the state, but which involves a range of actors: parents as well as school leaders and employers. One thing to note about the Singapore case is that the process was purposeful. There was a clear assumption that policies would and should change and improve over time.

The recalibrating of reforms is a distinctive element in the Singapore case and to a more limited extent in Hong Kong. We see references to feedback, iterative loops in design and implementation processes and beta testing in different literatures but the key point is that the design process seldom, if ever, produces something perfect. But it does produce something that can be improved as implementation (trialling, testing, de-bugging) takes place. Elmore (1979–80) calls this 'fixing'. This can be a structured process with external evaluators or a collegial process where practitioners share experiences and describe adjustments and refinements.

The Vietnam case shows how there is a feedback loop from practitioners to the middle level and from them back to the MOES. The presence of these processes in a small system like Singapore and in a nation twenty-times larger in population and with vastly greater distances between school and central MOES suggest it is not simply scale and dispersion that fosters these formal structures. The 'effective middle layer' of actors, often drawn from the profession rather than from a purely political or administrative cadre, makes a difference.

The learning we take from this is that educational policies are not conceived as if they were fully formed ideas or models. They adapt and evolve over time shaped by circumstances and the actors themselves. The importance of adapting a programme or policy to the environment or to maximise the capabilities of current practitioners as implementation proceeds evokes Supovitz's (2008) iterative refraction notion we referenced in Section 10.4. The practice knowledge and the realities of infrastructure and resource constraints can shape the design and implementation. It is not a simple linear one-directional process of conception, proclamation and execution. Ideas get tried, evaluated, modified and improved and tried again to get a better or more appropriate way of acting. We have described elsewhere (Ruby and McLaughlin 2014) the process of beta testing which characterises the Kazakhstani school reforms. This parallels the views of commentators ranging from scholars (for example, Hargreaves 2012) and development agencies (World Bank 2018) that educational reform or change is more dynamic and multi-pathed because of the presence, participation and impact of different actors which shape educational systems at all levels.

10.7 STAKEHOLDERS AND THEIR ROLES

Once we acknowledge the presence and legitimacy of multiple actors in educational change processes we need to pay more attention to their interests, concerns and responsibilities. One avenue for deepening our understanding of stakeholders and their roles is to pursue what Elmore (1979–80) described as the importance of 'backward' and 'forward mapping' distinct ways of analysing implementation approaches and policies, identifying who is involved in doing what and the power and knowledge they have. He calls the process forward, mapping the 'noble lie' of policy analysis for it is built on 'the notion that policymakers exercise – or ought to exercise – some kind of direct and determinant control over policy implementation' (p. 603). Forward mapping relies on logical, linear, objective-driven policy formation, is driven from the top and usually outside of schools. Backward mapping takes the policymaker's perspective on the implementation process, it does not assume that policy is the only – or even the major – influence on the behaviour of people engaged in the process. It takes more account of reciprocity in relationships between authority hierarchies and looks closely at the role of key behaviours and points in the process close to the goal of the change.

These differences have concomitant implications for the roles adopted by and power given to various stakeholders. As Ainscow said in Chapter 2, within different models are views of who creates and holds the knowledge and where power, authority, control and responsibility for problem-solving lie. We have already discussed the position of teachers in the reform process and the importance of context, here we are pointing to the need for real and legitimate engagement of practitioners in design, execution, evaluation and adaptation. This is what Datnow et al. (2002, 2006) and Datnow (2020) argue is an understanding of educational reform implementation as a co-constructed process; where the relationship between structure, culture and agency is dynamic. The causal arrow of change can move in more than one direction. It can move in an upward direction as well as a downward one, not just 'from the statehouse to the schoolhouse, so to speak' (Datnow 2020: 435). However, the role of teachers and their actions at the site level are central and we see different levels and forms of stakeholder engagement in our cases.

A common view of Singapore's reform culture is that it is centrally driven and 'top down'. While wider national priorities shaped and drove reform priorities, as captured in centrally planned and promulgated documents and five-year plans, there is evidence that stakeholders were involved at different points of implementation and in re-calibrating reforms. See this from the Chapter 8:

The implementation of this reform took years and involved the support from the ministry headquarters, school leaders, teachers and the education fraternity. The combined effort and teamwork yielded positive results as students improved in their learning, thinking and performance. Reforms which aim to change deeply embedded pedagogical practices like 'teaching to the text' require close collaboration and ongoing two-way support from the top and ground.

Similarly, authorities in Hong Kong viewed engagement with stakeholders as central to real change. The process began with a vision established by the most important stakeholders represented on the Education Commission. There was a map of the key stakeholders and real attempts to engage with them systematically.

The Vietnam case study illustrates the way formal structures of school boards and committees offered channels for the involvement of parents and local community members in school governance, including exercising some decision-making power over how local financial contributions are applied.

Kazakhstan is a good example of forward mapping in two senses. First, it was the decision of parents to opt out of national schooling due to unhappiness with the quality of education that prompted the change in the first place and then, the realisation that there was under-communication with parents led to much more engagement with parents. When there was unrest about the use of formative assessment and other aspects of the new curriculum, a communication exercise was undertaken and it involved going to local areas and engaging with parents and community members. This was an example of listening to the local actors and responding. In the Qatar case there appeared to be a lack of real stakeholder involvement exacerbated by attempts to fit borrowed strategies and approaches to the local environment and a lack of local knowledge.

The UK Challenge approach placed stakeholders in schools centre stage. Networks of schools were established. The engagement and leadership from teachers, headteachers and advisers drove the approach. Teacher voices were largely absent from most of the other cases.

Elmore's words are an appropriate summary, 'the implementation literature provides strong support for an analytic framework that takes account of reciprocity in the relationship between superiors and subordinates in organizations; the connection between hierarchical control and increased complexity; discretion as an adaptive device; and bargaining as a precondition for local effects' (Elmore 1979–80: 612). Or more simply, things work better when people talk and listen to each other.

10.8 REALITY CHECKS

Looking across the cases there are some observations or lessons for designers, advocates and deliverers of educational changes and reforms. There are practicalities and truisms that are often overlooked in the rush to govern or manage a system to respond to a political imperative. We like to think of them as reality checks, reminders that educational changes involve real people with direct and indirect interests in what they do in their working and learning lives, people with a deep understanding of their environment and thousands of hours engaged in learning, years of professional experience and stores of practice knowledge. Yet these obvious and readily observable lessons are often overlooked.

For example, it is obvious that the first attempt at reform is not always successful. The three model universities that preceded the establishment of Nazarbayev University are a ready illustration. It was not that these three institutions did not work, and indeed all three still operate, it was that they did not fully respond to the central concern of government. The challenges and constraints each faced shaped their successors and deepened understanding of the legal and legislative changes that were necessary for greater impact. The design and implementation of reform is a learning process where ideas are tried, tested and adapted.

The second truism is that ideas change as they are implemented. This can be as simple as something that children learn from party games like 'pass the message', and 'rumours' – a game that has many names in different cultures. But it is more than understanding that long chains of communication can distort messages. Ideas change as they transfer across national and cultural borders and as they move from 'centre to periphery' or become 'official gossip' where the meaning of the policy statement, while changed, is still legitimate (Lima de Sousa 2014: 197). One of the reasons that message varies and adapts is that the scale of the process varies and the composition of those participating differs. Anderson (1972), writing about theoretical physics, observed that as scale increases things become more complex: 'more is different' (p. 393). This reminds us that as the number of sites increases – be it individual learners, numerous groups of learners or aggregations of those groups – new constraints and opportunities emerge. Or we can look at this in terms of 'de-coupling', the term that Meyer and Rowan (1977) use to refer to instances where what policymakers intend or promote is not what happens in practice. Decoupling is more likely to occur when the intended outcome is perceived to be largely symbolic or when there is little capacity or motivation to adopt the new practices. It is tempting to see our Qatar and Vietnam cases as instances of de-coupling, but we suspect that they are more accurately described in terms of adaptation, acculturation or vernacularisation; a policy is adjusted by practitioners to meet local needs and constraints and to build on existing successful methods of work. This is consistent with Coburn's (2004) proposition that reform proposals or mandates are (most effectively) enacted through a process where teachers' beliefs, experiences and existing modes of work shape what is implemented. Teachers' knowledge and values also shape their responses to intended reforms. Choi (2017) argues that as teachers become 'comfortable' (p. 597) in searching for and applying new solutions and materials they adjust their practice. Training, repetition and support can provide 'scaffolding' to help teachers adopt reforms. Opportunities for teacher training and the design and delivery of materials to argument new practices increase when there is more time set aside for implementation. More time for design, delivery, use, testing and adaptation and more time before evaluation are recurring themes in these cases.

The third piece of common wisdom is that change requires a detailed analysis of the context into which the practice is being implemented, this includes examining the potential barriers and supports, as Lewin's (1943) forcefield analysis taught us. He also talked of balance and dissonance. 'To bring about any change, the balance between the forces which maintain the social self-regulation at a given level has to be upset' (Lewin 1943: 558) and then a new balance established with the competing cultures weakened. If the analysis is undertaken then there can be clarity about what is required – what needs lessening, removing and strengthening. It is grounded in the opportunity to learn, like Carroll's (1963) theory of learning, and time on task models of schooling: What needs to happen and how much time needs to be invested in a particular behaviour or practice to realise an effect? Sometimes this is discussed in terms of frequency, be it an additional class a week devoted to our topic or a theme or the opportunities for training and scaffolding available and accessed to support an initiative. Or it can be intensity, duration and length of implementation. And, as we have seen from Rowan's observations, in Chapter 6, recommended time allocations are not always followed because there were competing priorities or established routines which left little place for 'new' practices. In other cases, the frequency fades because of teacher turnover and reassignment, as in the Qatar case, where all the trained teachers had left the school site after a few years. Yet teacher attrition is a well-known feature of US public schools (Boruch et al.

2016) and can be factored into the design and implementation strategies of a reform programme.

Finding and allocating the time and resources and ensuring that they are well used is one of the fundamentals of planning for change that gets overlooked or dismissed, with a blithe aside, that it can and will take care of itself. It does not. To accommodate a new or different practice, something has to be displaced, slimmed down or the learning day extended. If instead the change demands additional effort or more intense effort by teachers and learners the consequences are likely to be teacher burnout, overloaded academic calendars and learner fatigue. And soon the impetus for improvement is dissipated and lost.

A highly related point is that supporting change in learning practices often requires a bundle of changes; more time, more teacher professional development, more materials or resources, a change in legislation or reallocation of time and resources. What is highly counterproductive is to imagine that these elements can be unbundled and stripped away without consequence. Unbundling often happens when there is not enough money to initiate and support a change or there are too many priorities or there is a need to seek a quick win. Our case studies show the consequence of altering the bundle as the reform progresses so that it is set up to fail.

Our final reality check is to make sure the objectives of the change are well articulated and aligned with enabling environment. Rowan's survey of various US initiatives reminded us of Lawrence Stenhouse's essay on the limitations of specifying objectives when designing curriculum reforms. While they can be helpful and appeal to a desire for logic and rationality, behavioural objectives tend to encourage over-simplification and to undervalue or to even ignore the 'complexity of schools and classrooms'. In many of the cases here implementation was impeded by a lack of understanding of 'the presence of many variables and uncertainties' (Stenhouse 1970–71).

Objective setting is always challenging when there are multiple stakeholders and priorities. Sometimes objectives are underspecified and ambiguous, fostering uncertainty and a search for clearer direction, or it can encourage inaction and 'non-compliance'. Poorly-specified objectives lead to poor communication, which limits support for change. Objectives can also be overspecified, ignoring professional judgement which is often a criticism of behaviourist approaches to learning. This problem of specification is sometimes embedded in notions of how much the teachers and school leaders can be 'trusted' to implement appropriately or with fidelity. It also ignores the well-established value and importance of 'involving individuals in the design of their own jobs'. Engaging practitioners in the task of finding better ways to do something, like new structures and patterns of work 'creates stronger skill matches and smoother transitions' (Hancock et al. 2020: 68). It is also more likely to be effective.

10.9 FINAL WORDS

We have borrowed from a Cambridge lamp-post the idea of 'reality check-point' – the words which are carved into a lamp post in the middle of a green near to the city centre. The Cambridge historian[1] puts forward three common stories to explain this. One was that when lost and you cannot see where you are due to fog or stormy weather, the lamp-post was a marker as to where you were. Two was that the lamp-post is found in the middle of two paths that intersect, so anyone who is in a daydream could walk into the lamp-post, hence 'reality checkpoint'. The third is that the lamp-post marks the end of the University and the beginning of the town, so you were either entering or leaving reality, and possibly gives you an opportunity to change direction.

We see strong analogies with the work herein. First is that we need to have a simple accessible way or means to find out, or know, where we are in implementing something as the process occurs. Not to wait to find out at the end when it is too late. We need markers in the fog. This connects to the second fact; we often stray onto another path and walk inadvertently into an abyss or a wall – usually a painful experience. We need forward and backward mapping. Finally, the implementation of change in practice through a change in 'policy' involves actors from very different worlds, each with their own perceptions and realities and each with a distinct set of expectations and understandings. None of the constellation of actors, teachers, learners, parents, policymakers and community members knows which is the prevailing reality and so there is a need for all to engage with and understand the lived realities and their impact on others in the world of education. There is a need to check, understand and respect the realities of others and to have markers, milestones and lodestars, so we know where we are in the journey and where we want to go, for all our paths intersect.

---

[1] http://cambridgehistorian.blogspot.com/2013/06/reality-checkpoint.html, last accessed March 2021.

The cases here are rich and varied, testimony to hard work and authentic efforts to improve education for young people. There are of course other motivations too – building a country, building an identity or strengthening an economy. There are many lessons we have learned from these stories and from the messages on the Cambridge lamp-post.

References

Anderson, E. R. (2017). Accommodating change: Relating fidelity of implementation to program fit in education reform. *American Educational Research Journal*, 54:6, 1288–315.

Anderson, P. W. (1972). More is different, *Science*, 177:4047, 393–96.

Boruch, R., Merlino, F., Bowdon, J., Baker, J., Chao, J., Park, J., Frisone, M., Ye, T., Hooks, T. and Porter, A. C. (2016). *In Search of Terra Firma: Administrative Records on Teachers' Positional Instability across Subjects, Grades, and Schools and the Implications for Deploying Randomized Controlled Trials*. Available at: http://repository.upenn.edu/gse_pubs/393 (accessed 14 March 2021).

Carroll, C., Patterson, M., Wood, S., Booth, A., Rick, J. and Balain, S. (2007). A conceptual framework for implementation fidelity. *Implementation Science*, 2, Article 40.

Carroll, J. B. (1963). A model of school learning. *Teachers College Record*, 64, 723–33.

Chen, K. K. (2019). Implementing large scale curriculum reform – Twelve lessons. *Keynote Address at the XI NIS Conference*, Astana, Kazakhstan, 24–25 October 2019.

Choi, J. (2017). Understanding elementary teachers' different responses to reform: The case of implementation of an assessment reform in South Korea. *International Journal of Elementary Education*, 9:3, 581–98.

Coburn, C. (2004). Beyond decoupling: Rethinking the relationship between the institutional environment and the classroom. *Sociology of Education*, 77:3, 211–44.

Cohen, D. K., Spillane. J. S. and Peurach, D. J. (2017). The dilemmas of educational reform. *Educational Researcher*, 47:3, 204–12.

Datnow, A. (2020). The role of teachers in educational reform: A 20-year perspective. *Journal of Educational Change*, 21, 431–41.

Datnow, A., Hubbard, L. and Mehan, H. (2002). *Extending Educational Reform: From One School to Many*. London: RoutledgeFalmer.

Datnow, A., Lasky, S., Stringfield, S., & Teddies, C., (2006). *Integrating Education Systems for Successful Reform in Diverse Contexts*. Cambridge University Press, Cambridge.

Dusenbury, L., Brannigan, R., Falco, M. and Hansen, W. B. (2003). A review of research on fidelity of implementation: Implications for drug abuse prevention in school settings. *Health Education Research*, 18:2, 237–56.

Elmore, R. E. (1979–80). Backward mapping: Implementation research and policy decisions. *Political Science Quarterly*, 94:4, 601–16.

Hancock, B., Lazalroff-Puck, K. and Rutherford, S. (2020). Getting practical about the future of work. *McKinsey Quarterly*, 1, 65–73.

Hargreaves, A. and Goodson, I. (2006). Educational change over time? The sustainability and nonsustainability of three decades of secondary school change and continuity. *Educational Administration Quarterly*, 42:1, 3–41.

Hargreaves, D. (2012). *A Self-Improving School System in International Context*. Nottingham: National College for School Leadership.

Harris, A. and Jones, M. (2018). Why context matters: A comparative perspective on education reform and policy implementation. *Educational Research for Policy and Practice*, 17, 195–207.

Lewin, K. (1943). The special case of Germany. *The Public Opinion Quarterly*, 7:4, 555–66.

Lima de Sousa, H. (2014). Playing Chinese whispers: The official 'gossip' of racial whitening' in Jorge Amado's *Tenda dos milagres*, *Forum for Modern Language Studies*, 50:2, 196–211.

Meyer, J. W. and Rowan, B. (1977). Institutionalized organizations: Formal structure as myth and ceremony. *American Journal of Sociology*, 83:2, 340–63.

Ruby, A. and McLaughlin, C. (2014). Transferability and the Nazarbayev Intellectual Schools: Exploring models of practice transfer. In Bridges, D. (ed.) *Educational Reform and Internationalisation: The Case of School Reform in Kazakhstan*. Cambridge: Cambridge University Press, pp. 263–87.

Sarason, S. B. (1990). *The Predictable Failure of Educational Reform: Can We Change Course before it's Too Late?* San Francisco, CA: Jossey-Bass.

Stenhouse, L. (1970–71). Some limitations of the uses of objectives in curriculum research and planning. *Paedagogica Europaea*, 6. The Changing School Curriculum in Europe / Le changement des programmes d'études en Europe/Die Curriculumreform in Europa, 73–83.

Stringfield, S., Reynolds, D. and Schaffer, E. (2012). Making best practice standard and lasting. *The Phi Delta Kappan*, 94:1, 45–50.

Supovitz, J. A. (2008). Implementation as iterative refraction. In Supovitz, J. A. and Weinbaum, E. H. (eds.) *The Implementation Gap: Understanding Reform in High Schools*. New York: Teachers College Press, pp. 151–72.

United Nations, Economic and Social Council. (1997). *Fostering an Enabling Environment for Development: Financial Flows, Including Capital Flows, Investment and Trade*. Report of the Secretary-General. E/1997/100. Geneva: UN.

World Bank. (2018). *Learning to Realize Education's Promise. World Development Report 2018*. Washington, DC: International Bank of Reconstruction and Development.

INDEX

For EU product safety concerns, contact us at Calle de José Abascal, 56–1°,
28003 Madrid, Spain or eugpsr@cambridge.org.

www.ingramcontent.com/pod-product-compliance
Ingram Content Group UK Ltd.
Pitfield, Milton Keynes, MK11 3LW, UK
UKHW030904150625
459647UK00022B/2821